SOME SORT OF A LIFE

Ⓑ

SOME SORT
OF A LIFE

My Autobiography

by Miriam Karlin

As told to Jan Sargent

OBERON BOOKS

LONDON

First published in 2007 by Oberon Books Ltd
521 Caledonian Road, London N7 9RH
Tel: 020 7607 3637 / Fax: 020 7607 3629
e-mail: info@oberonbooks.com
www.oberonbooks.com

A catalogue record for this book is available
from the British Library.

ISBN: 1 84002 780 0 / 978 1 84002 780 8

Cover photographers: unknown (front); Nobby Clark (back top right); unknown (back left)

Printed in Great Britain by Antony Rowe Ltd, Chippenham

Every effort has been made to trace the photographers of all pictures reprinted in this book. Acknowledgement is made in all cases where photographer and/ or source is known.

CONTENTS

v

PREFACE

HAVING BEEN A LIFE MEMBER of the voluntary euthanasia society for over 30 years – originally called EXIT when I joined and now re-christened Dignity in Dying (in itself a contradiction in terms) – I thought I might write a book before invoking their assistance. I came to be with them in the first place because of what happened to my mother. She had always been a brilliant woman, speaking five languages, a great reader – and not an archetypal Jewish mother at all – but when my father died after a marriage of over 58 years she lost it, and I had to get her into a home. That was a pretty bloody painful thing to do, and not something that one wants to do to a parent, but there was no way to carry on with my life, going away on tour, being in the theatre and so on, and I found I just couldn't cope. So I had to get her into Nightingale House, the best Jewish old age home in the country. Oh, but the guilt.

After that I began to believe that if my mother had gone this way there was a strong possibility that the daughter would follow. So I joined. In those days it was £30 for life. I think nowadays it is £50 for a year. So I've had my money's worth, because I am still here.

I have never, ever wanted to write an autobiography. The number of times I have been approached and every time I said, 'No, no, it's a wank'. This effort has evolved purely from therapy: I talked to my splendid friend Jan Sargent, who is not only a brilliant director – and has directed me in, I think, three or four plays – but also happens to be a trained therapist. Once she heard that I was going to have six and a half weeks of radiotherapy every day, and chemo, she suggested, as a friend, that it may be a good idea if she came around with a tape recorder and we just talked about things that had interested me throughout my life. We didn't actually talk about anything to do with the theatre, television and film: we talked about politics, trade unionism, religion, education – issue-based things. This exercise proved to be a wonderful focal point for me, and after my medical therapy was over, Jan continued to come round once a week and we realised that we may have something approaching a book, which was never the intention.

Although I have acted for over 60 years, this is certainly not going to be a glorified CV. If the reader finds me straying into that, I give them full permission to chuck this into a car boot sale.

MIRIAM KARLIN

INTRODUCTION

OVER THE LAST YEAR, since her diagnosis and successful treatment for cancer, Miriam has been talking about her life, which includes over 60 inspirational years in theatre, film, radio and television, working with some of our best known stars and directors. She talks about her early life during wartime London, the origins of her politics and her absolute commitment to justice. Her passionate views are reflected in her feelings about people, and there are many revelations and intimate reflections on her relationships with friends, lovers, and the addictions that have shaped her health. A natural mimic since the age of five when she used to do impressions of Hitler, her voice is distinctive, from the time we heard her bawl 'Everybody out' in *The Rag Trade*, to the present when she has learned to train her tongue to compensate for the loss of part of it to cancer.

Miriam is a spectacularly transforming actor, a fiercely independent campaigning force, and a loyal and perceptive colleague and friend. She came from a middle-class family, with a father that believed in education for his daughter and encouraged her socialism, and a mother who made her giggle.

The normal 'struggle' for fame and fortune was apparently easy for her, her confidence and ability to feel equal to anyone – including the Queen – never in doubt, but the fight against addictions and ill-health continues to undermine her well-being. Nevertheless, in her eighties she is still working, passionate, up-to-date, sophisticated, wise-cracking, and appallingly outspoken!

Miriam's life was indelibly marked by an early incident on Hampstead Heath when her beloved father was called a 'dirty Jew'. She became fiercely involved in politics, battling against racism and inequality, and for better conditions for actors; she has never flinched from taking on causes near to her heart.

She is unlikely to become a 'treasure' like some others of her generation: she has been too difficult to pin down, too outspoken to fall into a safe category, and her work too varied to compartmentalise.

Her career stretches from the early days of television and film to cabaret and stage, and she says she has done a bit of everything except ballet and the circus! Her most noted productions include *A Clockwork Orange*, *The Rag Trade*, *Torch Song Trilogy*, *The Diary of Anne Frank*, *Fings Ain't Wot They Used T'Be* and *Fiddler on the Roof*. As well as working with Kubrick and Littlewood, she has performed with Sybil Thorndike, Laurence Olivier, Peter Sellers and Bing Crosby. But underlying this glamorous life she has had a secret. In 2004 she admitted to a friend that she had had an eating disorder for nearly 50 years, dieting drastically in order to play a certain part in the theatre. Once she started on prescribed pills and laxatives she became addicted: she believes that over the years her health was wrecked, resulting in the debilitating peripheral neuropathy she suffers from now.

Her enthusiasm has carried her through decades of fighting for socialism and a fairer world: she has worked for Harold Wilson, James Callaghan and Neil Kinnock, receiving her OBE when she was fifty. Her fury at the Blair government and the actions of Israel knows no bounds, and she recently renounced Judaism, God and the Labour Party, preferring to become a Humanist.

When I first directed Miriam in the theatre in the late 1970s, I was surprised by her versatility and dedication. Her receptivity in rehearsals was extraordinary, and her vulnerability and openness to her colleagues genuine. She has an easy intimacy, as have many actors, but her brutal honesty and childlike capacity for trust extended to areas I hadn't encountered before. She arrived late from the dentist one morning and presented me with her blackened and bloodied molar newly removed for my reluctant inspection. Bodily functions were not a thing to be hidden in Miriam's book.

Later, when I had newly given birth, we went to Hong Kong to open a play, and I was struck by her unspoken regret over her childlessness. Although neither of us believed in a God, she became 'godmother' to my daughter Lucy. What I wasn't prepared for were the taxis that drove up every year on her birthday containing toy pianos, books and huge parcels wrapped in lovely paper. What I did expect was an inspirational 'fairy' godmother for my daughter, which I got in spades.

After forty hours of tape, a selection had to be made, but I hope the choice presents a fair summation of the noisy presence and passionate contribution her life has made to all of us.

JAN SARGENT

Acknowledgements

MIRIAM would like to thank: Antony Sher, for letting us use his wonderfully apt quotation on the cover; Neil Kinnock, for allowing us to quote him at length; Barry Humphries, for permission to include his letter; Ugly Duckling Films, for generously providing production stills from their forthcoming film *Flashbacks of a Fool*; Sylvie Webb, for helping me find relevant material amongst the messiest mounds of papers ever seen; the book's editor Stephen Watson, for his incredible patience in dealing with my multitudinous neuroses; James Hogan, for his warmth, generosity and faith; and Philip Hedley, Ann Mitchell and Syrrel Lehman, without whose love, friendship and care I could not have survived cancer. Of course, the greatest thanks go to Jan Sargent, whose amazing friendship and initiative saw me through the whole period of recovery, and who has put untold time and care into shaping this book.

JAN would like to thank the following people who worked hard to bring this book to fruition: Leigh Wood, Emily Marcuson, Lucy Irving, Kate O'Brien, Sarah White and Magnus Vaughan for their transcription and copy work; George Irving; Brie Burkeman; and the staff of Oberon Books for their unfailing support.

1

LATE TALKER

In which I turned blue and nearly died, developed a sense of humour, became aware of the family I was growing up in, enjoyed being Jewish, and learned to impersonate Hitler and Jesus.

I DIDN'T TALK UNTIL I was quite old in the normal scheme of things. I wonder if I was listening intently, waiting until I could form fluent and coherent sentences in order to stun my public.

Apparently I said nothing until I was about two and a half, by which time my parents were very worried. Then one day, when I was sitting on my father's knee, I pointed to a button on his waistcoat and said, 'Dis is a buckon?' My brother Michael, who is five years older than me, started running round and round saying, 'She's spoken, she's spoken!' After that, I became unstoppable and conversation became the most important thing in my life: even now, the sound of the human voice is so reassuring I sleep at night with Radio Five Live chatting away in my ear.

When I was a tiny baby, only about a couple of weeks old, I turned blue. As a little girl I was very proud of this fact, and would go around telling everyone, 'I went blue.' While it was happening, of course, my mother was in a blind panic, because she didn't know what to do; this time, my brother was running up and down the corridor shrieking that his little sister was dying. We lived in a flat then, and the neighbour who lived above us, who had been a nurse, told Ma to shake me upside down quite vigorously, whereupon my complexion came back to normal.

I didn't grow up with the notion that I had nearly died – well, maybe subconsciously, who knows what goes on in a baby's head? – but this early brush with death always makes me think about my mother marrying in this country and not in Holland or Belgium, because I know that if she had stayed there, I may not have survived at all.

My very earliest memory is peeing on the sands. I don't even remember which beach: it might have been Broadstairs, or a beach in Belgium where we went regularly for summer holidays. We had a hut, and I remember crawling behind it, and peeing, and I can still remember the warm feel of it in the sand. I covered it up rather as a cat does when it goes in the garden.

Everything that happens when you're a child, you retain with such clarity. My mother took me to Regent's Park Open Air Theatre to see *A Midsummer Night's Dream* when I was five, and I remember that experience better than I do some plays that I saw three or four months ago. It was an amazing June. The sun was shining and the park was looking glorious. I remember saying, 'Oh mummy, I am so happy.' It is extraordinary to be aware of being happy at a particular time, when one is normally only aware of happiness in retrospect. I was so conscious of it, and I knew then that theatre was what I wanted to do.

Later, I remember seeing Michael at school in another production of the *Dream*, playing a fairy or Titania (I'm not sure which), and I became used to the idea that performing was something one could do. I had already been to pantomimes, and when they asked children to sing, first the boys and then the girls, I would sing louder than anybody else.

I was also brought up with the idea that 'famous' and 'powerful' people were not out of reach. For example, my parents were invited to 10 Downing Street when Stanley Baldwin was the Conservative

Prime Minister. (I found out many decades later that some members of the opposition were always invited on these occasions.) In those days you really got dressed up for something like that – men would almost always wear tails. Apparently, whenever they were going out to some 'do', Dad would take his evening clothes to his chambers to change there, and he and my mother would meet nearby. So off they went to Number 10, and it was only when they were home and getting undressed that my father, who used to take his trousers off and leave them on the floor for my mother to pick up, left the navy blue turn-up trousers from his daytime suit that he had worn with a stiff white wing-collar shirt and tails. When my mother picked them up, she was furious and said, 'Thank God I didn't see them when you were there, otherwise we would have gone straight home!'

My father had stood as a Labour candidate. The issues he campaigned on were health, education and housing – and what has changed? He was passionate about education because he came from a large family who were not very well off and, though he had an outstanding intellect, he had to fight to have a real education. He had been born and raised in Liverpool, which was full of slums, and because of this he cared hugely about housing.

Dad had had a difficult time being Jewish when he was young and one day, when he and Emanuel Snowman were walking out of the synagogue, they discussed where to send their five-year-old sons to school, because they wanted them to have a basic education in Judaism. Emanuel Snowman was a well-respected man in the community who afterwards became Mayor of Hampstead. They founded this school, the West Hampstead Day School for Jewish Children, which at the beginning consisted of just two pupils: Michael Samuels (that's my brother – Samuels is my family name) and Kenneth Snowman. Interestingly, they would both go on to become world authorities in their respective careers: Kenneth on Fabergé, and Michael on linguistics. I went to the school too when I was five. My mother was the school's Honorary Secretary, and because of this

I behaved appallingly and used to say to the other pupils, 'I'll tell my mother, I'll tell Mummy about you.' I can't remember if she ever took any notice.

I was really taken with religion then, learning to read Hebrew and becoming obsessive about my Jewishness. I have always gone over the top, right from being very small: my father recognised it in me early on because I remember him saying 'Oh Min' – his name for me, from the way I used to say my name when I was tiny ('Minnum') – 'you are so compulsive', and that is what I have been all my life, compulsive and extreme.

The school was moved to Willesden Lane – my mother found the building for it – and it is still there. It's now called the North West London Jewish Day School and has become the best-known primary day school for Jewish kids in north-west London. What is so ludicrous is that I only have to hear politicians talk about faith schools and I start shaking with rage because I think that, living as we are today, we are creating ghettoes. Then another part of me questions this assumption and thinks that as long as separate schools are only for the very young to understand their roots it's fine. But it is a dilemma.

A couple of times we went on holiday to Westgate. My father once took me to see Will Hay at the Pavilion in Margate. He was playing a comic schoolmaster and I laughed so much I banged my nose on the seat in front of me. It started bleeding profusely, but Dad simply dabbed it and put a plaster on it. He should really have taken me to a doctor to have stitches put in because I have grown up with a bump in my nose which had been perfectly straight. But God, Will Hay was funny and we didn't want to miss a minute. This was my earliest experience of a real live comic on stage.

Within my family I developed a scatological sense of humour: everything to do with farting, shitting, peeing, still makes me laugh, and this was one of our shared sources of humour. My brother used to run out politely into the garden to fart, and we all found that funny, even though others thought it rude.

My father was a wit, with an ironic and self-deprecating turn of phrase, who had a capacity for being able to come up with extraordinarily clever remarks. I discovered that he kept a joke book in which he had written down funny stories under headings. I once caught him having a look under the table just before he came out with something that was hugely apposite to what was being said at the time. Of course he was knowledgeable and a brilliant public speaker, so it wasn't exactly cheating.

I learned very early that impersonation would make my parents laugh. I began doing them from the moment that I could talk. I suppose I had been watching and listening all that time and would imitate everyone who came to our house. There were some incredibly 'Jewish' characters, archetypal Jewish women, amongst our visitors and relations. My parents would even get me to mimic people who were sitting in front of us. I impersonated my Auntie Nora to her face, but she took it well because she had a good sense of humour and managed to see herself in my rather pathetic attempts. My mother would bribe me with a chocolate to do an impression, so I suppose I was trained from an early age to get up and do my tricks, like a performing dog. A few years ago, when I got cancer and started having bits of my tongue cut out, part of me thought I must have brought this on myself because I used to make fun of people with impaired speech: there was the deaf dressmaker who had something wrong with her tongue, and an old cleaning lady with a cleft palate when we were in Westgate on holiday one year.

I soon began to expand my repertoire. I had long, very dark hair which I wore in plaits in the week and curls at the weekend. I would pull my hair down against my face, trying to look like the Jesus that I had seen in pictures. I would lean against the wall with my feet crossed and Michael would come along shouting, 'I'm a Roman soldier, I'm a Roman soldier', miming the hammering of nails into my hands and feet. Then I would run into the kitchen shouting, 'Mummy, Mummy, Michael is crucifying me.' The last time I was in Glasgow, about seven years ago for Michael's eightieth birthday, we did it again and fell about laughing. It's crazy really. (I suppose one could justify it as a historical reconstruction, as Michael knew about Roman soldiers.)

Hitler came much later. I heard him on the radio and had seen pictures of him so I knew about the moustache and I would stick some hair over my lip and stand there doing the Nazi salute. I used to say *'Hitler ist ein fürchterlicher Schwein'* – in other words, 'Hitler is a terrible pig', which is the sort of thing he would say about the Jews. There was a little gallery looking down on the hall above a flight of stairs and when my parents invited people in they would say, 'Do your Hitler.' So this was my first 'stage'…

By now we had moved into a larger house in Brondesbury with a garden, and we played games of all sorts (no television, you see). We used to play a really complicated game called 'British Empire'. I remember I used to say to Michael, 'Let's play 'shempire.' On this great board all of the places marked in red were British. When you think about it, we had the world; it was disgusting. I remember when Monopoly first came out we went Monopoly crazy too. I never wanted Mayfair – too bloody expensive. I liked Vine Street a lot. (Where is Vine Street?)

I was quite convinced that my mother preferred my brother, because he never made a fuss. He was very quiet, and I used to upset and annoy him when he was trying to do homework. I was so noisy after I learned to talk. We had a box room in our house and he turned it into a railway room. He used to go to the Caledonian Market and buy railway stock and stuff for his railway. He had a great friend and the two of them used to race their engines. I wanted to join them and play with trains but they wouldn't have me in there. I was upset because I didn't think of a railway as being a boy's game.

6

I had dolls, of course. I had a beautiful doll's house and used to go to a shop called 'The Doll's Hospital' in West End Lane with a few pence to buy furniture, lovely little chairs and all sorts of things. I was quite practical in that I had things like a lavatory – a piss pot – and a little cooker and pots and pans in there. But I had no people in it at all.

I was quite good with my hands, and we had a big bag of different coloured beads. Once, when I was ill with chicken pox and possibly a little delirious, I found some bits of silk which I cut up into shapes. Although I can only have been about five, I managed to thread the needle and sewed some beads on to the silk. When my mother asked what I was making, I said, 'I'm making boots for poor children.' Perhaps I had been told, 'Now you eat that up, or poor children would be glad to have it', but I certainly had a latent social conscience.

I seemed to enjoy Jewish rituals and once asked my maternal grandfather why we had to do such and such a thing – why we had to have separate china for Passover, for instance. He said then that all of these customs and rituals have kept the Jews together as a people for two thousand years, otherwise they would have disappeared. 'When we have a country of our own you will find that all of these trappings will go and we won't need to stick to them.' He said that to me 75 years ago, and the first thing many Israelis do when they come over to the UK now is to eat the 'forbidden' foods.

My grandfather was passionate about Zionism. He went to the very first conference in Vienna in the early 1900s where Theodore Herzl spoke. Herzl was the founding father of the concept of the state of Israel. Grandpa went back to Amsterdam, where his family were then living, completely imbued with the idea that the only answer to the 'Jewish Question' was to have our own country. He became the President of the Jewish National Fund in Holland and Belgium, and then in England when they came over in the First World War as refugees. We children had to buy trees in Palestine, and on my tenth birthday ten trees were planted in my name. We kept little blue boxes and any small change went into them. Every Jewish family who cared at all about the concept of the state would put in money. Grandpa spent his whole life thereafter preaching to people on Zionism, and he lived long enough to see the state created. He knew Israel's first president Chaim Weizmann very well, and they died within a few months of each other. Grandpa was a great, great man and I often wonder what he would be saying about Israel now.

My father was absent during the day because, being a barrister, he went to his chambers in the Temple. If he was going on a lecture tour – he used to give lectures on trade union law – he would be away, but only for a couple of nights, not for any length of time.

Our parents were always there for us, and the only time we were apart was when my father had a nervous breakdown. This was when I was about six. In those days people didn't know how to deal with things like that, so my mother sent Michael and me off to Liverpool to stay with Dad's father who was still alive, living with one of Dad's sisters and her daughter.

They had a very different lifestyle. They used to kick us out of the house very early because they didn't want us hanging about. Now I come to think about it, we were treated pretty casually, because Michael and I would be walking the streets by ourselves. They probably thought that it was good for us to go out and get some fresh air. Michael, being older, would tease me to make me scared. When we were walking on the Boulevard in Liverpool, he said: 'There's a policeman. I am going to send him after you', and that made me terrified of policemen.

In Liverpool my Aunt Carrie thought it would be nice to take me to a grotto to see Father Christmas in one of those big stores. I was quite unimpressed by the man himself and concentrated completely on the present. I was going to be given something awful which I didn't want and I cried that I wanted a particular box I could see.

You could lift the lid and inside it was filled with different coloured pencils and crayons. I really wanted it badly, and found I could turn on the tears for others, because I got it.

We were away all during the Christmas holiday. I'll never forget coming home and being so happy to see my mother as she came running along the platform wearing a pony-skin coat and a pretty hat.

As a boy, my father had won a scholarship to Liverpool College and then a scholarship in Classics to Wadham College, Oxford. I still have a copy of the play he wrote in Greek in 1914, when he was 21 – what an amazing thing to have done! He then took up law. His family regarded him with huge admiration, and always turned to him for advice on various matters.

Dad had taken Michael away from his school, Haberdashers', because it wasn't academic enough, and he put him in a cramming school called Warwick House. He won his scholarship to St Paul's from there, so I was sent there too.

There were only two other girls there. However, both of them also had brothers who had been at the school, so it didn't seem strange at the time. I enjoyed studying Ovid and Virgil, which were taught to us by Mr Dallas the headmaster, a brilliant classicist. Even though I was only ten, I realised he was also an alcoholic and slightly crazed. We were just getting American movies over here and Mr Dallas couldn't bear to hear anybody speak in American slang. If anybody said 'Okay' or 'Sez you', they had to write out 100 lines – 'I must not indulge in vulgar transatlanticisms' – and if any of the boys were wearing Brylcreme on their hair he would pull it with great force, muttering 'Filthy bugjuice.'

Dad would have loved me to go to a more academic school like Michael, but I just wasn't that way inclined. I sat the exams for St Paul's School but didn't get in, so I was sent to South Hampstead High School for Girls. This happened to be a smashing school – very arts-orientated. Although I have regretted all my life that I didn't get a degree and use my brain fully, it was a stroke of luck that I went to this school where my leanings towards the arts would be nourished.

It was a religiously mixed school, which was new for me: I had never been to an assembly first thing in the morning. Because there were a lot of Jewish girls there, once or twice a week there was Jewish assembly. There was an RE teacher called Miss Moose, who was a Liberal Jew. I used to argue with her like mad because I was so Orthodox. I discovered that I was pretty good at arguing: I'm not sure why, but I think it was a combination of feeling clever, having an audience and being able to show I was 'right' where she was 'wrong'. Of course, it's much harder to be Liberal and see ambivalence, but I didn't know that then.

I remember Miss Moose had been on a skiing holiday and our Headmistress Miss Potter came into Assembly on the first day back after the Christmas holidays and announced with a long face that she was very sad to say that Miss Moose had broken both her legs in a skiing accident. I became hysterical with laughter and made the others laugh at the thought of it. It felt like the biggest joke of the century, simply because I used to argue with her on religious matters. But she encouraged my capacity for enjoying argument, so I'm grateful to her. In fact, a few years ago I went to her centenary birthday 'do' at the school. Quite a reunion for those of us still alive.

Dad's sister in Liverpool had found us a strange girl called Kitty to help out in the house, and she loved to frighten me with her stories. I did impersonations of her – people were always asking me to 'do Kitty'. She was paid about £1 a week, had one afternoon a week off and would go shopping a lot. One night when my parents were out, she said to me in her thick Scouse accent:

> I was working with a family in Liverpool and they had a little girl just your age a burglar came in and he bound her up and

tied her to the floor and there she was this little girl all gagged they gagged her up and stole all the stuff and do you know when her parents came back there she was all gagged and they had to untie her she was just your age.

I was petrified. After a day out she always had a story.

There was a Jewish family in Liverpool and the man he set fire to the shop and I had to go to court as a witness and swear that he didn't want to do no such thing and there was a judge there cross examining you on this that and the other and do you know I told a pack of lies I swore red in the face that he didn't want to do no such thing and the man gave me a half crown for myself for saving their lives.

I'm not sure how much help Kitty was to my mother, but Ma never seemed to be tied to domestics. I certainly didn't get any housewifery or cooking skills from her. I learned to read recipe books to make up for her inadequacy in that department, becoming a better cook than she was. I remember coming home from school for lunch to find her sitting in front of the coal fire reading *The Times* from cover to cover toasting her legs with the paper open. She'd look up and say, 'Oh, are you home already? I was just going to go out and get some fish.' I'd whine, 'Mummeeey, I've got to be back in an hour', and go and make my own. At school they noticed that I arrived early in the morning, because I'd got my own breakfast, and then was late in the afternoon as she hadn't cooked my lunch.

I learned precisely one domestic hint from my mother, about tulips: she used to wrap them up in newspaper, stick them in water up to their necks for an hour or two and then remove the paper so they remained upright. (The fact that she was born in Amsterdam may explain how she knew about tulips…)

Above all when I think back, I remember her consumed with laughter. Because she spoke five languages, there were days when she and I only spoke German, French or Dutch. This was another thing we enjoyed together. She had a really good ear, and I must have got mine from her.

My father had started a boycott of German goods long before the war. I had been encouraged to go to school with a little blue badge, which said 'Boycott German Goods', just as we all used to boycott South African foods later on during Apartheid. I did this happily, without really understanding the implications of what it meant, but then an event happened that changed my perception completely.

I used to go up to Hampstead Heath with Dad every Sunday: it was a routine, a ritual. Just Dad and me. Ma would be cooking Sunday lunch at home or reading the Sunday paper. Michael would be doing homework: if he went for a walk, he went for a walk on his own. He was very solitary person actually, with just a couple of really good friends.

Well, on these walks I used to get Dad to ask me to spell long words because I was very proud of my spelling. So I would say, 'Ask me how to spell *peculiar*', then it would be, 'Ask me how to spell *particular*'. Anyway, we were just passing the white stone pond where Oswald Mosley's Black Shirts used to stand on their orange boxes and spout, rather like a mini Speaker's Corner. This particular Sunday we stopped and listened to this lout on his orange box. Dad asked a question in his articulate fashion which the man obviously couldn't answer, and he simply said, 'Oh shut up you dirty Jew.' That was a like a dagger going into my heart. I couldn't believe that anybody could say that to my Dad: having been very, very talkative all the way up to the heath, I didn't speak again until I got home.

2

EVACUATION DOGGED MY LIFE

In which I enjoyed school, visited aunties up North, heard Myra Hess at the outbreak of war, was evacuated to Berkhamsted, went to RADA with June Whitfield, became aware of the true nature of war and changed my name.

EVACUATION AS A WORD has become increasingly associated with bodily functions the older I have got, but my real evacuation was to be a mild affair, moving *en famille* at the outbreak of war to spend the time in the relative safety of a country town at a girl's school with other chums. Up until then our school was still on the South Hampstead premises, but then we were all moved to the equivalent school in Berkhamsted.

At this time I was physically active and enjoyed school and holidays, and I think I was fairly popular with friends. I suppose that my education amongst boys had given me a certain expectation, as I was never led to believe that girls couldn't do the same as boys. Even though my parents were very protective, I took it for granted that I could play cricket, ride a bicycle and have the freedom to go where I wanted.

I still largely got my way, and sometimes if my mother denied me anything I would say, 'I'm going to get on to the Society for the Prevention of Cruelty to Children.' Other times I would announce, 'I'm leaving this house', and I would go outside, close the front door, and just walk around the garden. My mother was quite indulgent with me, and if Dad refused me something she would talk him round. I never thought of myself as being spoiled – the idea of the Jewish princess fills me with horror. In any case, we never had that much money so the spoiling could never be in that way. I suppose, though, I was less disciplined than some.

Dad came from a large family, as I said – he had two brothers and four sisters, a couple of whom married money. Auntie Fanny, for instance, lived in Sunderland and was pretty well off. She had a big car and she used to get fabulous clothes made for her two daughters; when they grew out of them she used to send them to me. There were hat-and-coat sets like the ones Princesses Elizabeth and Margaret Rose wore. So I was dressed like them a lot of the time (having said I was never a princess!).

Holidays were important to us all as children, but when we went to Antwerp to stay with the grandparents, Michael and I had to do a duty call to Aunt Rosa which we dreaded. She was a very grand woman, a great-aunt on my mother's side from a wealthy family in Poland, and lived in a huge house. When Michael and I went to visit her, the bell outside was the sort you had to pull, and I was never tall enough so Michael would lift me up. Then we would hear distant footsteps that we recognised as the maid Florence approaching us, and she would say, 'Allo, allo, big boy Mikey', and let us in through the heavy wooden door. At the top of the stairs in this large imposing hall would be Aunt Rosa: she would say, ''Ello Miriam darlink', and offer both her cheeks to be kissed. This was the moment I dreaded, because on one cheek grew a mole with a bloody great thick hair sprouting out of it. Her place was gothic, but she had a beautiful garden with a glass peacock in it which I believed was real and wondered why it never moved.

My mother's family on both sides had been in the diamond business in Russia. This is why they eventually arrived in Antwerp (by way of Amsterdam), which is still a world centre for diamonds. My mother's maternal grandfather, Elias Karlin – from whom I would subsequently take my stage name – had even been a court jeweller in St Petersburg. My grandfather, Herman Aronowitz, was a diamond merchant, and diamond cutters often came to the house. When Michael and I stayed with him he would give us ten centimes for any diamond cutting we could find on the floor.

Most of our holidays were spent in Belgium, and my mother's parents would join us, with two of her brothers and their families. They would find us a house in Le Zoute by the sea, which before the war was a haven of peace. We would spend many days sitting on the sands in front of our beach hut.

One day, I remember, I suddenly looked up and said: 'Look, look, there's a flying fish!' What I saw looked like a huge great carp in the sky, an amazing sight. My parents got terribly excited and said, 'That's a zeppelin! It's the Hindenburg!' I had heard about zeppelins and had now seen the actual Hindenberg before it crashed.

We got so used to the freedom of the huts that it was difficult to adjust when we came home. My mother had become so used to emptying the teapot and slopping it out on the beach that, once, when she invited some people into the drawing room for tea, she threw the contents of the teapot onto our beautiful green Chinese carpet, much to their astonishment.

The important beach activity when we were quite young was the 'flower shop game', and it may still be going on. The first thing you did was to dig a hole for your shop in front of your hut and make a counter out of sand to stick in paper flowers. Every morning I would go to the local shop and ask for the paper and the wire to make the flowers – 'Est-ce que vous avez de papier et de fil de fer pour faire les fleurs, si'il vous plaît?' – and then I would go back to Mother who would help me make them. Everyone bought each others' flowers with handfuls of shells: 'Combien de poignées de coquillage pour cette fleur-là?' Every evening, when the tide had washed the sand counters away, we would go out and collect loads of shells. There were some grand shops and some rather hopeless ones. On the last day of the holiday we sold all our flowers for shells.

I was a glutton at the time. I ate a lot of ice cream, and there was one particular place called Madam Cisca's where you could get waffles with different sorts of ice cream on them. I once had I don't know how many waffles, loads of scoops of ice cream on them, gulped the lot down and then went on the swings. Not surprisingly I was sick as a dog and threw up everything. That experience has stayed with me and I cannot bear to see a waffle: even as I say the word I feel a kind of nausea in my stomach. The story of my unfettered appetite and its consequences would last my lifetime and become the background to decisions made without thought or knowledge. The other, deeper influence lay in my father's vulnerability, which he told me about when I was old enough to understand.

When Dad was a boy in the cadets he had been given an horrific time. Apparently the night before he went each week he would put his nose up against the wall and desperately try to turn it upwards because it was a Jewish nose. Every week some boys at the cadets used to scream at him:

> Get a bit of pork, stick it on a fork and give it to the Samuels, long nosed Jew.

Because of this shocking experience, which made me sob when he told me about it, he was naturally very protective of us, and fearful we could be hurt too. Apart from our schooling, he had been insistent, for example, that we learn to swim and had sent us to the baths in Finchley Road to learn. On these seaside holidays we naturally swam in the sea. Dad was a pretty good swimmer himself but had a fear that something might happen if we didn't have the necessary confidence in the water. His whole life as a parent was about making sure that we didn't suffer. I still find it utterly moving that his life was framed so dramatically by his Jewish origins.

I was brought up to be strong. My father's struggle had made him combative and I admired him for that. Apparently I helped him to win a case when I was still at school. It was to do with the D'Oyly

Carte Opera Company copyright, though I never found out whether he was against D'Oyly Carte or for them. He was talking about the case over breakfast, and I said, 'Per performance' – not paying for the whole lot but each performance. He rang up later and told me I'd won him the case because that 'per performance' was the most important phrase used.

Our house was full of books and newspapers. As well as Dad's law books, all the classics were there. He told me that he had read all of Dickens by the time he was twelve. I think that is why when he was dying my mother told me that he said, 'Remember this?', and mimed cutting the vein on his wrist. I am sure reading *A Tale of Two Cities* so young, with its description of Dr Minette being buried alive, must have left an indelible imprint on his mind: once you have cut an artery and no blood runs, then you can be sure that the person is dead. He must have been terrified of being buried alive. My mother asked me what he had meant because it had frightened her, so I told her he wanted her to make sure he was really dead. I read *A Tale of Two Cities* when I was young and it made a big impression on me too.

My mother was beautiful, and I still have pictures of her from this period. She had splendid legs which I later envied, although at this time I didn't have anybody that I really wanted to be, no obvious role model. I wasn't too plump as a child but I did once suddenly go on a diet for a few weeks, I can't remember why. I don't think that I was ever that concerned with how I looked, but it must have been significant in some way: maybe someone said something about my size.

Ma looked wonderful when she'd had her hair done and had on a lovely frock. It depressed me horribly when she got old and senile and indifferent to how she looked, because she was still beautiful, with perfect silver hair. Looks had mattered to her: when she first saw a couple of grey hairs she cried. As her hair got more and more grey, she refused to dye it and used to talk about people with dyed hair as 'common'. Things were different then – she would never even have had a blue rinse!

Like most normal families at this time we sat down for proper family meals. Dad had to have meat every day. Sometimes there might be fish, but always the traditional dish with two vegetables. Friday night and Saturday would be typical Jewish food. I haven't eaten meat for at least 40 years, but I don't object to free-range chicken (double standards?) and adore fish.

In January 1933, I came home from school and as was her way, Ma wanted to go out and get something for supper, so I went with her down the road. She suddenly stopped still on the pavement and burst into tears. There was one of those *Evening Standard* boards with the headline: 'Hitler is in.' Ma said, 'My God, this is the most terrible thing for the Jews.' Of course I knew about Hitler, I had been imitating him, but this was different.

The talk that night when we got home revolved entirely around what it meant that he was now in power. I think in a sort of way my family was expecting it. It would have been the same, for instance, as if we had heard that Oswald Mosley had become Prime Minister here.

I began to be aware of Dad having fights with people. In the build-up to the war he would come home after meetings with the Board of Deputies of British Jews so angry that the Sunday lunches that followed them were horrendous. He would be carrying on about certain people and I was told much later, by men who knew Dad during those days, what a fighter he was. There were some characters on the Board of Deputies who were still selling arms to Germany even though Hitler was in. Dad knew what that entailed. He was not particularly pro-Zionist whereas Ma was staunchly so, but at the Board of Deputies a lot of fights were also to do with what was then regarded as the 'Palestinian Question'. There were conversations about Chamberlain coming home from Munich with the letter of 'appeasement' from 'Herr Hitler'. Dad used to pronounce the *Herr* with sarcasm and irony, rather than in the deferential tones of Chamberlain.

At the time we had this Austrian maid named Friede. She was the most sensational maid you could ever have and used to darn my school stockings. She made fabulous apple strudel and to watch her rolling the pastry was perfection. Quite clearly she would have seen what was going on in our household because everything at the time was about boycotting German goods and there was real passion against the Nazis. One day, she suddenly packed up and said she had to go back to Austria. Dad was convinced that Friede had told on us, because, years later, he somehow got to see a copy of Hitler's notorious 'black book', which contained lists of all the people that had to be wiped out, mainly Jews or communists, when the Nazis got to England. It was compiled by Nazi sympathisers and people in Germany before the war. The list extended everywhere; I should think eventually all Jews were on the list. Looking through it, Dad found a page showing his name, the family and our address.

If you watch programmes about Hitler, he is revealed as being so thorough, meticulous and detailed. It was hideously clever the way he enlisted children and indoctrinated them to chant 'Heil Hitler'. My parents and those of their generation believed that all Germans were responsible for Hitler and had no time for them. There are a lot of people today who still feel that.

While this undercurrent continued, life went on and Michael and I had our piano lessons. Dad's brother Uncle Dave, who owned a music shop, sent Michael his first guitar. Michael taught himself to play the banjo and the guitar and then the double bass, becoming rather good. Years later up at Oxford he played double bass in a group called 'The Bandits'.

I didn't practise enough because I wanted to play Bach immediately. I loved playing Bach and hated practising scales; but the real problem was that I didn't like my piano teacher. I used to hide in the coal shed when she was coming. I knew that she was going to ring the door bell so would rush into the coal shed and leave it to Ma to open the front door, and then come out sheepishly and have to play. Later on, when I was at South Hampstead, I had a smashing piano teacher who indulged me and let me play Bach.

We were a family of frustrated conductors. Whenever we heard one of Beethoven's symphonies – usually 5, 7 or 9 – on the radio or gramophone records, Dad would start going around the huge oval mahogany dining table conducting, Michael behind him, with me in the rear. I felt I was really conducting a Beethoven symphony. Later, when I listened to Maria Callas or other brilliant singers at an opera, I could imagine that I was singing. I felt the breath in the right places and sometimes even thought, 'My God! I am singing well tonight.' It's strange that I'm sometimes inclined to drop off when I go to the theatre, which is of course embarrassing, and yet I have never been known to nap at a concert. I heard in some science programme that the spoken word is soporific whereas music isn't. That must be why I sleep with the radio on all night. When one had a huge hunk of a fellow, there wasn't any question of radio, but those days are long since gone.

Lots of German girls were coming over as refugees, and because my parents were helping to bring them over away from increasing danger, one stayed with us. She was about the same age as me, and on my mother's birthday she wrote her a little poem in German, which I still remember, but if you ask me to recite a sonnet of Shakespeare I can't. She wrote:

> Gehört hab ich mit Erstaunen sehr
> Dass heute Ihr Geburtstag wäre
> Wo jenen Ihnen wünscht das Beste
> So möcht auch ich mit frohem Feste.

It means:

> I heard with amazement
> That today was your birthday
> Where everybody wishes you the best
> So do I with all good wishes.

It makes one think, this is long-term memory, but what happened this morning? Do I remember? Well yes, maybe – but yesterday? Oh dear...

When war was actually declared, I have to admit to a slight feeling of excitement. We had been on holiday in Belgium, and when my parents knew that war was imminent we returned. My school, South Hampstead High School, had informed us that there was going to be a special meeting outlining what would happen, because it would mean us being evacuated to Berkhamsted Girls' High School. My parents didn't want me to be an 'evacuee' so they planned to take a house there. It was August and we weren't back at school yet. For some unearthly reason my parents then thought we should get out of London altogether. We took a flat in Harrogate – 97 Valley Drive – and we all got on a train to go up North.

It was Friday evening, and my mother brought an entire chicken and a whole pan of chicken soup onto the train. Later, we stopped suddenly at Holbeck and the lights went out. This porter put his head through the window and said, 'Is there a war? It's to be hoped not.' It was such a curious turn of phrase.

When we arrived at the flat, my father's sister and her family, who had found it for us, were there. Dad noticed that there was a concert the next night, September 2nd, and Myra Hess was going to play. So we went. When they played 'God Save the King' prior to the concert, Dad told us that war was going to be declared. (He knew this from the First World War, because up until then the National Anthem was always played *after* the curtain came down.) We all stood up for it and the concert began. Myra started off with Beethoven's Piano Concerto No 3 in C minor, then she played Bach's 'Jesu Joy of Man's Desiring'. The concert finished with Beethoven's Symphony No 5, the start of which ('Duh-duh-duh-*dum*, Duh-duh-duh-*dum*') was used during the war as a signature tune for the World Service. Myra Hess, of course, went on to play at the National Gallery during the war at lunchtime concerts, but the memory of that particular concert and the implications of what was about to happen I will never forget.

We didn't stay up in Harrogate for very long, only a few weeks, because the school contacted my parents and we came home.

I don't think that we children were initially affected by the war, at least not at school. We worked and played and did all the normal things, except that our school was sharing with Berkhamsted: one week we would do mornings and they would do afternoons, and vice versa. Our teachers took a big house and some students stayed there too. My parents, of course, had to have a house of their own and one of the girls, my best friend Jean Infield, lived with us there. Later, in my first job at Kew Theatre ASM-ing, I stayed with her family in Clarence Gate Gardens just off Baker Street.

It was incredible living in the country and I took to it so well, even though the thought of going into the country now fills me with dread. I suppose that's because I know I can't physically do the things I used to – going for long walks, picking blackberries, that sort of thing. At the time, however, I thought the freedom and space and the size of the sky was wonderful.

I insisted on buying a bike; I'd never had one before. I saw a bike advertised for £1 second hand, one of those sit-up-and-beg types. It was a bit big for me as I was only about fourteen. In Berkhamsted there were hills which were practically perpendicular going down from where we lived to the High Street. I wasn't that proficient on the bike, and one day going down one of these hills I realised that the brakes weren't working properly, so it became a question of how exactly I was going to crash at the bottom. It was a terrifying experience. I managed to get round a corner, skid to a shaky halt and jump off, somehow sustaining only a bloody great cut on my leg. I limped into a chemist where it was bandaged up for me. I had to pretend that I'd hurt myself by falling over something, because my parents hadn't wanted me to have a bicycle in the first place.

We never had a car because neither of them wanted to drive, so we went everywhere by public transport or taxis. This was mostly because of Dad's nervous disposition. Ma was a bit freer, but had an irrational fear of cats and the dentist, both of which phobias she passed on to me. We had a cat called Tom to whom she was less than loving.

It was during the war that Dad had a second breakdown. In comparison with his first, he apparently got over this very quickly, being one of the first people to be given electric shock treatment. He fought against it, but was given only three sessions and became completely better. Nobody ever referred to it afterwards, and it didn't affect his memory one iota. (I wish to God I had the memory today that he had when he died because he could have quoted from anybody – Plato, Socrates, the Bible...)

I was still obsessed with making people laugh, and even used to show how well I could belch. This was one of my great tricks, which Michael had taught me. Many, many moons later, when I was playing Maria in a radio production of *Twelfth Night*, I belched for the actor playing Sir Toby: when he said, 'A plague o' these pickled herrings!', I supplied the belch.

Having just started my period it was probably a good thing I had moved to an all-girls' school. I was quite advanced in Latin when I got there because I had already done some Ovid and Virgil at Warwick House. I had also learned to play badminton there because Mr Dallas had been badminton crazy. But South Hampstead did have high standards academically, and we had some wonderful teachers. It never occurred to me that women at the time were discouraged from being ambitious.

I had no interest in Maths, although now when I see young people incapable of adding up or subtracting I realise that I did learn enough to cope without having to resort to calculators. Things like geometry, trigonometry and algebra I loathed: I couldn't see the point – I mean, Pythagoras and his 'two sides of a triangle' didn't exactly fascinate me.

My English teacher was an inspiration, however, and I think now that she was probably a frustrated actress. Her name was Marjorie Barber, and when she read Portia's 'Quality of mercy' speech from *The Merchant of Venice* it was so beautiful I can still hear her. She gave me a huge love for Shakespeare. We also used to go to the Old Vic with the school before the war, and sit in the pit for a shilling to see some of the famous actors of the day. A lot of that was stopped during Thatcher's time. It's sad because schools used to go to the theatre as part of the curriculum.

The war meant all of us carrying gas masks and having ration books and of course the excitement of the blackout. This became a routine and after a while a nuisance because we'd have to stop what we were doing. Of course we knew that Hitler was a monster and had to be stopped, and we also knew that he was responsible for murdering Jews, but life in wartime was different and everyone was very alive to one another.

We knew we were in danger because we could hear the planes going over. We learned to tell the difference between theirs and ours, and knew when there were a lot of theirs coming over that the target was going to be London. We were lucky not to have had any damage. There was barbed wire everywhere. Up until fairly recently I had a scar on the back of my hand: I remember running along Gower Street from Euston to RADA and scraping my hand against some barbed wire, and it bled profusely. That was my war wound!

The radio (wireless then) was hugely important to us and of course the Winston Churchill speeches were compulsive listening. His oratory was superb and Dad, though Labour, admired him for that and as a wartime Prime Minister.

It was ritualistic, but we always had to listen to Tommy Handley's weekly programme *ITMA* (*It's That Man Again*), too. Handley was very funny; Dad particularly liked Deryck Guyler who used to do a Liverpudlian character.

I can't really remember the actual conversation that led up to it. I had been very aware of conversations going on at home about mother's family and what was happening. When Holland was invaded and then Belgium there had been some underlying panic, particularly as I could visualise the beaches we used to play on, but I don't remember anything specific being said. What I do remember distinctly is the day that my mother came to school. I was playing cricket, and she asked the headmistress if she could take me out of school specially, because she had just had a telegram to say that her mother, father, grandfather and her two brothers Max and Maurice were on a ship that had got away from Belgium: could she take me to Harwich to meet them? There was a picture on the front of an *Evening Standard*, where the photographer stuck a baby in my great-grandfather's arms: the caption read, 'The oldest and youngest refugees from Belgium.' My great-grandfather was then about 85 and he lived to be 96.

From then on there was a lot of drama because the house we lived in wasn't big enough and we had to move to a larger one. Granny, Grandpa and Great-Grandpa and one uncle, Max, lived with us but Maurice, who was married with a daughter a couple of years younger than me, went to stay with some of his wife's relations. I remember my Maths teacher saying, 'Do you need some extra blankets? Would you like some blankets for the refugees?' I don't know why this struck us as being so strange. It was a kind thought, but I suspect we hadn't come to terms with the fact that our family were indeed refugees.

Then it became a question of what had happened to my mother's sister Auntie Molly and her two children, Leni and Eddy. And what had happened to Auntie Molly's husband Uncle Sol and countless cousins in Holland? A couple of them we knew had got away early. One of them, a well-known broadcaster in Holland, went to New York. As for Uncle Sol, we heard later that he believed that Holland had been wonderful to them, a great home, and it would be terrible to desert; so they stayed. We never heard from them again.

After the war Grandpa wrote to the authorities in Bergen Belsen and had his letter returned. What we heard later was that my aunt had survived and was in a hospital but died just a few days before the war ended. If only she could have lasted a little longer.

We hadn't had any communication from any of my aunt's family or the authorities. That is something that my mother would have kept and I would have in my correspondence. I have often suspected that her dementia could have been caused by her keeping the pain bottled up for so long. She could never speak about her sister without deep pain.

I met Anne Frank's father Otto during the run of *The Diary of Anne Frank*, and every time he mentioned Anne, tears would come to his eyes. He used to get about 100 letters a week and yet he managed to cry on cue every time, which I think he did as a reflex. Although he swore that he had never seen a performance of the play, he knew exactly what business it was doing all over the world. I found that worrying. Of course, to Anne, he had been an iconic figure, in the same way that she was to all of us, and we expected him to be the character that she had described. If anyone had met him prior to the war they would have thought him a rather ordinary businessman.

The first time I was properly aware of what happened to my family in the gas chambers, I couldn't look at photos or film, I couldn't bear it. Even now as I'm talking about it, I find tears welling up in my eyes, and it's over sixty years ago. We knew they had disappeared from Holland and we hadn't heard from them, so we eventually had to assume that they had been sent to the gas chambers – otherwise where had they gone? I find it very difficult even now to think about it or to remember what the reaction was at the time. I know that each time Auntie Molly's name was mentioned, or Leni and Eddy and my uncle, there were just tears.

If *I* still have the guilt of a survivor, how must my mother have felt? She was fortunate enough to have married and stayed in England. If she hadn't met Dad then she would have gone back to Holland with the rest of her family. I wish now that I had sat down and had a conversation with her and said, 'Ma, how do you really feel?', but I never did. I suppose I knew it wasn't possible. Every year on Auntie Molly's birthday she would say, 'You know what day it is? It would have been Auntie Molly's birthday.'

My cousin Rosamine, the daughter of Uncle Maurice (my mother's brother) and Auntie Annie, came as a refugee from Antwerp and then went to live in America, settling in San Francisco. She wrote this letter to her daughter who wanted to know what happened to the family in the Holocaust.

We have more specific information about my father's side. We lost my father's sister Auntie Molly, her husband [Sol Person] and her her two children aged 16 and 19, my cousins Leni and Eddy, who I knew personally. They lived in Amsterdam, only a train ride from our home in Antwerp and I have childhood memories of them coming to visit and playing cards with them. It is fair to assume that all four of them were rounded up with other Jews in Amsterdam into the Jewish quarter. In 1942 transports were dispatched from there to the death camps of Eastern Europe. Only 10,000 Dutch Jews, out of an original population of 150,000 Jews, survived. We know little of the fate of the Person family following their deportation, except that none of the four survived the war. According to records in Jerusalem the father died early in 1945 in a concentration camp in Germany. Eddy Person, the 16 year old son, is reported to have died in the infamous Mauthausen camp in Austria. Molly and Leni were sent to the same camp as Anne Frank, Bergen Belsen. There are conflicting stories about the mother and daughter: one, they died of Typhus in the camp; another, that they died whilst being transported to Sweden after the camp had been liberated by the British. All four of the family perished only a few months before the war ended. We have in our possession a letter from my grandfather from 1945 that he wrote to British Administration in Bergen Belsen, enquiring after his missing daughter, his son in law and grandchildren. He signed the letter 'From the unhappy father, who searches for his children.'

Besides the Persons, a family genealogy chart lists ten other close relatives, mainly cousins from Holland, who perished in the Holocaust. There was an execution that I know of, a cousin in Belgium, an attorney named Regine Karlin, who was a Belgian Resistance fighter. Her husband Lucian was a Belgian army officer, also in the resistance. He was captured and executed in 1944 along with 50 others, in reprisal for the assassination of a Nazi. Meanwhile Regine, who was pregnant with their second child, went to a hospital to give birth. She couldn't register as a Jew so used a false name. Everything was done in secrecy, and she led the nuns who delivered the baby to believe that her secret was that she was an unwed mother. After Lucien was murdered, she became more determined than ever to carry on her work with the Resistance and she became one of the few woman partisan commanders in Belgium. Children especially were saved thanks to the work of the Resistance. I went to Belgium in 1940 and in mid-1942, when night-time roundups and deportations of Jews had began. About 40,000 out of 90,000 Belgian Jews perished.

I still have my grandfather's letter which was returned from Bergen Belsen.

I was getting to the end of my schooling and so I began to plan what I wanted to do next. University didn't seem to be an option, and the only other career thoughts I had at this time, being mad about languages with a very good knowledge of German, French and Dutch, were to be an interpreter. I was pretty good at playing the piano too at one time and vaguely, and very briefly, thought that that might be a possibility. Dad had always said, 'She's going to be a second Ruth Draper.' I didn't know who this was, but saw her later and realised what he had meant because she did a whole programme of different characters in different accents, very much the sort of thing that I had been doing since I first started my impersonations at home and at school.

There was still a repertory theatre in Amersham, and in school holidays I used to go over and sweep the stage – I had fallen in love with theatre. You could actually 'smell the greasepaint' around the place because people used 'five and nine' make-up, and there was that particular oily perfumed smell that all of us who used it still remember. In the beginning I went to see plays there, and then I helped out and tried to be generally useful, and my hopes gradually crystallised into a wish to join the repertory company. When I left school, however, Dad said, 'If you are going to go into the theatre you've got to have training.' He was a firm believer in training. He said that obviously the place for me was the Royal Academy of Dramatic Art. How did my father know about this? What research had he done? It is extraordinary to me that my father – working in his chambers, going on lecture tours, talking to trade unions – somehow found out about drama schools. Anyway, I was told that if I wasn't going to stay on at school and try for university then I had to go to RADA.

I don't remember applying so he must have done the application form for me. In those days RADA was delighted to take anybody who paid the money, because all the fellows had been called up. I was sent the details about the audition and I was given two speeches to do. One was a choice from Shakespeare, so I did Juliet, weighing nearly twelve stone. (Why do I remember the weight rather than how I felt doing the speech?) The other speech was a choice from various modern pieces. There was one by Dodie Smith, which I thought at the time was crap but did anyway.

June Whitfield was there at the audition, as were Patricia Lawrence, Maxwell Reed and Bryan Forbes, who had been invalided out of the Merchant Navy. There were only about three other boys. I did my audition, got in and remember going back to Berkhamsted and saying to my mother accusingly: 'There was a girl called June Whitfield and her mother was with her. You didn't come with me!' June Whitfield's mother was an amateur actress herself, which may be why June seemed to know so much about the business from the word go.

So I left school and started at RADA which meant travelling up to town and back on the train. I had been so protected as a schoolgirl and cosseted at home that the thought of being in another place altogether was exciting and grown-up. We had to do things like ballet with Phyllis Bedells. I was useless, having a lovely 'turnout' but that was it. I used to stand at the back pretending I knew what I was doing, carrying off the hand and arm movements with great style.

It was a two-year course in those days. I knew nothing about life at all, and as RADA was regarded then as a finishing school for young ladies, I suppose it helped in that respect. I didn't exactly overwork, and never realised until years afterwards what they had been trying to teach me. We had three really good teachers whom I do remember well: Molly Terraine, with whom we did improvisation which I enjoyed hugely, and Ethel Carrington and Neil Porter, who were both Shakespeare tutors. Then there was the great voice teacher, Iris Warren. She thought I had the most amazing rib expansion, and would use me as a model in lessons to show the others how to breathe properly.

I only really came into my own and started to show my mettle in the last couple of terms. In the finalists' show I was given Emilia in *Othello* with the splendid Eileen Page as Desdemona in the 'Willow' scene. Emilia was a character that was very 'me', I believed. There are two Shakespearean roles that I would have loved to play professionally but was sadly never asked to do: Emilia, and Paulina in *A Winter's Tale*. Both feisty women – feminists, I suppose.

Because it was endlessly wartime, my years at RADA became a question of finishing classes and tearing down to Euston to catch the train to get home before the blackout and the bombing started. Everybody worried until I got home. We were living at that time in a big house in the High Street, a Georgian house with a large garden with pear and apple trees. Living next door to us were two old spinsters. I remember one morning after there had been the most horrendous bombing in the east end of London. My mother was in the garden and leaned over the garden fence and said to one of them, 'Wasn't it terrible last night, the bombing, wasn't it dreadful?'

'Oh yes, I said to my sister, I said, Oh that Hitler, he is a tinker, I said, If he'd got at my bottled fruit I would have said something!'

That was the understatement of the century and it still makes me laugh.

We always found out when certain shops were going to get things that were in short supply. We heard that Woolworths were going to have biscuits on a certain day, so Ma sent me along to get some. There was a make of biscuit at the time called 'Sunshine'. I stood in this queue and in front of me was a woman with the most miserable face I had ever seen. It got to her turn and she said, 'Half a pound of "Sunshine", please.' I told the story when I got home, and we thought that line was so funny that we kept it as a family saying. Ma used to practically pee herself laughing (in fact as she got older, she did).

In the beginning of the last term at RADA my mother suddenly said to me, 'Don't you think you should change your name?'

'Why?'

'Well, Samuels is a very pedestrian name for the stage.'

I said, 'Oh. Well, what shall I change it to?'

'Well, Karlin is dying out. Why not Karlin?'

So I said, 'Miriam Karlin? Mmm? Yeah okay.'

So for the public show I was 'Miriam Karlin'. My great-grandfather Elias Karlin, who was still alive and living with us, thought it was a *chutzpah* that I'd taken his name. Then, when I got a very nice notice in *The Times* for my Emilia and Great-Grandpa saw my name in the paper, he was absolutely thrilled.

When I left RADA one of my first jobs was assistant stage managing at the Kew Theatre, which was just over Kew Bridge but is no longer extant. I was paid £3 a week with income tax deducted, which made it £2, 12 shillings. I stayed with the aforementioned friend Jean Infield from school and her family. The theatre was run by the famous Jack De Leon and his wife Beatie. She was well known for saying to actors who were going to work there, 'Five pounds it is and none of your fancy sixes or sevens.'

There I was, keen as anything and wildly conscientious. I did once, out of sheer enthusiasm, pull the fire curtain instead of the actual curtain so the theatre was flooded, but I managed to get out of that one somehow – I probably cried. Amazingly, I was forgiven.

In one of the plays at Kew there was a description of a photograph of Queen Wilhelmina on a bicycle. I immediately thought that, as my mother was Dutch, I could get exactly the right thing. So I went tearing down to my parents' house in Berkhamsted. When my mother opened the door, she said, 'What's the matter?'

'Mummy, mummy, have you got a photo of Queen Wilhelmina on a bicycle?'

She looked at me with a deadpan expression and said, 'Oh yes – trunkloads of them… What are you talking about, what do you need it for?'

I told her that one of the actresses had to look at a photo and talk about it, so it had to be Queen Wilhelmina on a bicycle. She asked me if I really thought that anybody in the audience would see the actual photograph. I said, 'But it's important for the actor, they must know that what they're looking at is real.' I was totally convinced, and I still am, that if an actor is given anything to read out on stage or screen it must be real. It's very confusing if you are not looking at the real thing, it can put you off and take you out of the reality you have created for yourself.

I must have been a self-made Stanislavski person because it was not all that well taught at RADA in those days. We did do improvisation, as I said, and we talked about Stanislavski, but it wasn't instilled into us as a basic way of working that it was good to do research or the importance of 'being in the moment' and creating your own reality.

All in all, I feel very grateful for my time at RADA, and when its 'buddying' scheme was put into action in 2000, I was more than happy to take part. The principle of the scheme is that all RADA students in their final year are allocated an ex-student as a 'buddy', who tries to see all the shows that the student does in their last year and gives constructive advice and, if possible (and if required), helps them to get an agent. I nearly always advise a student not to go with a big agency but to find a younger, hungrier agent, so long as they have a wide enough network of producers and directors to call on. There are now so many former RADA students volunteering that the students often have two 'buddies', which is of course handy as one or other of them might be working and unable to see the student's work.

I remember so little about the war ending, I think because we were so conscious that our own reality was going to be unspeakable and that we would probably hear dreaded news. There wasn't much rejoicing and we didn't have any celebrations. We listened to Churchill, but then of course Dad very soon became disenchanted with him. It was a very sad time for our family, facing the loss of all those relations.

Oddly enough, I went to Germany quite soon after the war, and was able to be an interpreter for the company of actors I travelled with. A lot of people asked me how I could face Germans. I didn't feel that every German was responsible. I don't know if I was already consciously a humanitarian person, but maybe that was the reason I knew that you could not condemn an entire population for the behaviour of that diabolical Hitler and his Nazis.

Many, many years later I did my one-woman show *Liselotte* in Vienna. I had a wonderful time; I was there for four weeks and the Viennese were good to me. They said things like, 'It's extraordinary for an English actress to bring to us our own Palatinate Princess.' I was very conscious of the fact that there was still a lot of anti-Semitism in Austria even in the 1970s – one place I went to even had a picture of Hitler on the wall.

Society always seems to need scapegoats, and anti-Semitism has been going on for 2,000 years, let's face it. Don't ask me why it's so prevalent, I'll never be able to understand it. I don't understand racism either. Why discriminate because someone is black, or because they are Asian? It's exactly the same thing. The only difference is that Jews do not generally have black skin, although I did see a new publication the other day called *Jewish Renaissance,* about the Jews in Ethiopia – the Falasha – which showed pictures of black Jews. I've always felt that I was quite lucky to only have the Jewish bit, and that if I had been black as well that would have been going a bit too far…

3

DIY CAREER

*In which Sybil Thorndike helped me get my first theatre job, I stormed
Alexandra Palace onto live television, became a funny woman on
radio with Peter Sellers, did sketches with Alfred Marks and Tony
Hancock, learned comic timing from Hal Thompson, sang in cabaret
and musicals, and was made to join Equity by my father.*

I HAD SUCH BELIEF in myself in those days: looking back,
I forged a career in television, radio, cabaret and theatre with no
apparent difficulty. By the time I was in my early twenties, aston-
ishingly enough, I had become known in all these fields. Where did
this confidence come from? Was it the blissful ignorance of youth, or
simply the determination to pursue what I most enjoyed?

A good example of this self-confidence during this period – we're
talking late 1940s, early '50s – was on one of my visits to the SF Grill
café in Denman Street. I was wearing a fabulous new outfit which
had been made for me, a sort of Dior 'New Look' suit in royal blue
jersey, gathered up at the front and a longer back and a brilliant
matching turban hat. When I made an entrance nobody made any
comment, so I went out and came back in again and made another,
rather bigger, entrance. I was noticed then!

The first thing I did on leaving RADA was to write to John Gielgud, not
having any idea that this was a bit forward, to ask him if I could work
for him. He was a huge star, of course, and was the actor manager of
a company which at that time was touring Britain with Shakespeare.

He wrote back to tell me that his company was already complete, and suggested I 'would be better advised to get some professional experience with a repertory Company, rather than try and get an engagement in the West End immediately'. Oh, how right he was. I didn't feel crushed, I just tried to take his advice.

Dad had told me to join the actor's union Equity (then based in Kingsway) which he knew about from his work as a trade union lawyer. He wrote a letter to the General Secretary Alfred Wall, saying that his daughter had just left RADA and wanted to join the union. When I took the letter to Alfred Wall, he was lovely. He asked how my father was and gave me a card, for which I paid £5 – and I was a member, just like that. That was 1943 and my number is 12268. It was so simple: now I belonged to my union and I could work in every area if the opportunities were presented to me. The exception was the West End, for which one had to have forty weeks' work on one's record.

I needed not only to work but to soak myself in my profession and I started going to the theatre in earnest, a habit that has never left me. I saw *King Lear* played by Donald Wolfit and came floating out of the Scala Theatre in Charlotte Street on a cloud. He was totally brilliant. I remember his wife Rosalind Iden played Cordelia: she had a wonderfully dead arm when he carried her on which just hung there – the best bit of acting she did the whole night. I don't think I had ever before seen a 'great' performance but just knew Wolfit's was wondrous.

I had already got to know Dame Sybil Thorndike because, amazingly and brilliantly, she had acted with us at RADA. We did a production of *Little Women* in which she played 'Marmee', and she rehearsed with us every day and played in it with us too. Isn't that an incredible idea? That would be like Dame Judi Dench or Dame Maggie Smith going to act with students at RADA in their final production. At the same time Sybil was performing in a series of plays at what was then the New Theatre with Laurence Olivier and Ralph Richardson.

I was cast to play Aunt March and also to stage manage – they didn't have a separate stage management course in those days. I was so determined that everything should be spot on that I got hold of a Western Union cablegram, the exact Western Union cablegram of the period, and wrote on it about her son being killed in the American Civil War. I was so proud of it. When she received the cablegram on stage and tried to open the envelope she said, 'Oh, they seem to have stuck it down with gum.' I was standing in the wings watching in a frightful state, because I had indeed stuck it down with gum, but afterwards she said to me, 'I think you're so good dear, so clever, but always do it with just a bit of spit, and that's enough.'

She was very complimentary about my Aunt March and said that when I left RADA I should come and see her at the theatre where she was performing. I had no compunction about taking her up on the offer. She was giving her Jocasta to Laurence Olivier's Oedipus when I went to see her at a matinee. I had the gall to go round backstage, not thinking that she might want to have a cup of tea, have a rest and put her feet up. She sweetly wrote a letter to her husband Lewis Casson for me to take to him, saying that he had to employ me. He was doing a production of *The Taming of the Shrew*, and he duly offered me the job of understudying his daughter Ann (as the shrew) and ASM-ing.

What an amazing couple Sybil and Lewis were! I admired them enormously for their compassion and their staunch commitment to justice. Despite being known as strong left-wingers, they were highly respected within the profession (and indeed the general public).

So there I was, courtesy of Dame Sybil, touring all over England in a Shakespeare play while the war was still on. When later we did a production of *St Joan* by George Bernard Shaw we were the first company to go to Paris and play there immediately after the war ended in 1945. The theatre we were to be performing in was the Marigny Theatre. The play had been written for Sybil, who had done it in the 1920s, and Lewis had directed it then and was now doing a production with daughter Ann as Joan. I played a court lady and a monk, continued understudying Ann and ASM-ing, and dressed her, put her in her armour, washed all the tights and did all the wardrobe, for £5 per week. I thought that was a lot of money in those days and happily worked my arse off.

Sybil had also been sent to Paris by the British Council to do poetry readings, and one evening there was a family reunion with her husband and daughter in the hotel where we were all staying. Because I knew her from RADA, I had the cheek during this encounter to ask her if she would like to come on stage with us the next night as a monk, telling her I had a spare tonsure in the wardrobe and a spare monk's habit.

She said, 'Oo, shall I?'

I said, 'Yes, do.'

She said, looking to Lewis and Ann, 'Oo, perhaps I shall...'

So the very next night, there I am playing a monk, true Stanislavski-style – padded up very fat, a Jewish convert to Christianity (I told myself), leching after Joan – beside Sybil Thorndike who was doing much the same, only not Jewish. It only dawned on me recently what an extraordinary moment that had been: I was sitting next to the woman for whom Shaw had written the play and she was doing rhubarb talk to me about '...disgusting...blah, blah, blah...', while we heard her daughter giving an impersonation of her – because Ann, as directed by Lewis, would have been doing it exactly as Sybil must have done it. As a director Lewis believed in giving everybody specific inflections. In fact, when he was knighted, I asked him what the correct way of saying 'Sir Lewis' would be. He said, very seriously, and just as if he was still directing me: 'Duh *Duh*-Duh! Duh *Duh*-Duh! Sir *Lew*-is!

Although I was understudying, I never got a chance to play Joan because the Thorndike family were so bloody healthy, bless them.

I started doing television at Alexandra Palace in 1946. This was something totally new, an untried medium. I didn't know anybody who owned a television set and so, although there was huge excitement, we weren't really nervous as actors. We couldn't conceive that anyone else apart from the crew and anybody in the studio could see what we were doing. Thinking back, it must have been terrifying for people who did realise, because there was no recording – everything was live.

I worked out a system which enabled me to get interviews and work on BBC television. I used to take the *Radio Times* and I'd look up and see who had directed the night before, and assume they would be in their office the next morning, which indeed was always the case. I remember the very first person on whom I tried my experiment was George More O'Ferrall, the number-one BBC director at the time. I phoned him up and he answered the phone (can you imagine directors today answering the phone?) and I said, 'Is that Mr More O'Ferrall?'

'Yes.'

'My name is Miriam Karlin. I am coming up to Alexandra Palace today and I wondered if I could possibly pop in and see you?'

He said, 'Yes, what time would you like to come in?'

'Well, I'm coming in at around twelve o'clock actually.'

'Well pop in and see me afterwards.'

So armed with the success of that phone call, I could then phone another director.

When I went in to see him I said hello and then started doing all my different accents and voices. He immediately offered me a job, maybe to shut me up. He said he was doing a production of *Alice in Wonderland* and if I wanted to be in it he could offer me a small part. Well, I was thrilled. We rehearsed for four weeks and then did two live performances – one on the Sunday night, and then a 'repeat' on the Thursday. I played the ugly cook and did all the baby noises. I remember stirring a great pot of soup, shaking pepper in it

39

and turning my back to the camera so I could make the baby noises without being seen.

It was a horrendous winter – 1947, probably – and I had been rehearsing a play which was due to transmit on the Sunday, but the snow was so deep that the mast at Alexandra Palace was almost entirely submerged. Having got to work by public transport – the thought of a taxi didn't enter my head back then – we were told that we couldn't televise that day (the wrong kind of snow!) and we were sent away. About a week later we were all contacted again to re-rehearse and then it was transmitted. I believe we got extra money for that. The payment for *Alice in Wonderland* was twelve guineas (twelve pounds and twelve shillings) which was for four weeks' work and two live transmissions. I thought that was wonderful. Afterwards it went up to 25 guineas and then to 40. I really thought I was in the money then.

I began to lead quite a life, staying up until the early hours and then going in first thing in the morning to do live television. Cables were criss-crossing the floor: I remember trying to remove my foot from a cable when I was doing a close-up with Brian Bedford. (This would have been much later, in the 1950s, when television was still live.) I could feel this bloody great cable across my foot and tried to extricate it without it showing on my face. They only had one camera live at a time and you knew exactly when they were coming to a close up because they would come trundling towards you with their red light on, then they'd switch to the other camera. For three or four weeks we had had intensive rehearsal so you knew exactly where your marks were on the floor, and you had to learn to glance down at them to see them without appearing to do so.

I did a play with Alan Bates and a very well-known East European director called Tania Lieven, who had a habit of cupping her hand over her eye as if looking through a camera lens. We had been rehearsing for only two days, and we still had scripts in our hands and she would say, 'Find me darlink, find me darlink, find me!'

I remember saying to my friend, the director Lionel Harris, 'This woman said, "Find me darlink" and we still have our scripts in our hands.'

He said, 'Say to her, "No darling, I found you yesterday, *you* find *me* today".'

Television was like doing theatre on camera, except that we were very aware that we had had absolutely no television training whatsoever. I often question why so much time is taken up doing television training at drama school. You are either a good actor or not, and if you are reasonably sane you know perfectly well that if there is a camera on you, you must not do huge gestures. It comes instinctively that one refines down one's performance both physically and vocally for the camera.

It was exciting working as part of a large team. I have always got on very well with the crew, realising how dependent the actors are on them as well as enjoying their expertise. I remember speaking at the TUC conference comparatively recently, concerning the absence of black and Asian crew members in the technical areas. I said that in all my years in television, I could not remember ever having seen a black face behind the camera. Then, only a few weeks later, I was doing an episode of the afternoon soap *Doctors* and there was a black cameraman. I got so excited and told him how I had only recently been saying I had never seen a black face behind the camera and here he was – the first. And he said that there still weren't many of them, most working on commercials.

I really felt I was in on the beginning of something back then. A group of us would meet and hang out at the Arts Theatre Club (which my mother used to call the 'Arse' Theatre Club). I would sit there for hours at a time having endless coffees and teas with people and we would talk about all the work that we had or hadn't got. When people said, 'What are you doing now?' and I said, 'I'm doing television', they would look at me with a pitying expression as if I was doing a one-night stand in some diabolically unknown fringe. I used to say, justifying what I was doing, 'But I think it's the coming thing.' It was terribly looked down on by people who thought they were 'real actors'.

I had started to use the same *Radio Times* technique to get work in radio. A radio play was rehearsed for at least a week then transmitted live. The first dramatic part I played on radio was a leading role, Anne of Cleves, for the director John Richmond – I may have been the only female actor in the country at the time who could actually do a Dutch accent. For this I got paid the princely sum of five guineas. I hadn't had any radio training at RADA either, but the people who were on the BBC Rep – I remember Norman Shelley and Gladys Young – were wonderfully helpful and showed me exactly where to stand and how to position my voice. I was very lucky.

I was particularly friendly with the BBC Rep actor Heron Carvic. I knew him from Lewis Casson's production of *The Taming of the Shrew*, in which he had played Petruchio, and we had done one of his plays when I was an ASM at Kew. I was later to work with his wife Phyllis Neilson-Terry in the revue *Cockles and Champagne*. That always struck me as the most amazing marriage. There he was, the gayest man I had ever met – he was the one who taught me how to put on eyelashes using 'hotblack', which I went on doing both on stage and in life – married to Ellen Terry's niece!

Heron and others began to see me as 'funny' because I used to impersonate everybody in the cast and make people laugh. As a result, I began to do a kind of early stand-up, made up of impersonations combined with character writing – a lot of it with my mother's help. I managed to get an act on radio, in *Variety Bandbox*, with a director called Brian Sears. Brian was very big in light entertainment at the time and thought of me as a female Peter Sellers. He had the idea of putting the two of us together.

When I worked with Peter Sellers he was still young and sexy. He was also bad-tempered and sulky, but I was very fond of him and I was in a few of his movies later, so he obviously quite liked me. One of these, occasionally shown late at night, is *Heavens Above* by the Boulting Brothers. I had quite a good part with Eric Sykes, as husband and wife in a gypsy family travelling around on a cart. I was also in *The Millionairess*, playing Vittorio de Sica's wife with an Italian accent. This was the film in which Sophia Loren falls for Peter, playing a doctor. Offscreen, Peter pursued her relentlessly – and, some say, successfully – though the big scandal during the shoot was that she had all her jewels stolen.

Peter was playing an Indian in the film – in fact, this may be where the expression 'Goodness gracious me!' originated – but I don't think we thought anything of this at the time. I now remember that in the early 1950s I played the main black character, Berenice, in a radio version of *The Member of the Wedding*. Of course, there were practically no female black actors in this country at the time, but that doesn't make me feel any better about it! (Having just seen a wonderful production of this play at the Young Vic, I have to say that the American black actor who played the part, Portia, was sensational and should win every award going.)

Peter was well known as a womaniser. He was also a 'car-iser'. Every week he had a new car and he'd say, 'Come outside, come and look at this one' – and there outside in Bond Street would be a coffee-coloured Rolls or a Bentley, just casually parked there. (In Bond Street! Can you imagine that today?)

Brian Sears got the scriptwriter that Peter used at that time, Jimmy Grafton, who owned a pub called Grafton's in Victoria, and a lot of *Variety Bandbox* was written there. Peter would write with Jimmy, but I just did what I was told. The programme went out on a Saturday evening, and we alternated with Frankie Howerd topping the bill. We did a sketch called 'Blessem Hall' ('Bless 'em All') in which we played a whole array of different characters between us – the staff, the guests and so on. It soon became a competition to see who was the funniest, really, and if I was too funny he sulked, like a child throwing toys out of the pram. Everyone who worked with him would tell you the same.

This was prior to *The Goon Show*: later I became a great Goon fan and used to be on the front row every week when they were recording the show – I've heard broadcasts and can hear this maniacal laughter and know it's me. Spike Milligan was such an unusual talent, just brilliant. The others, Harry Secombe and Michael Bentine, were wonderful too – they were all so distinctive. It was a terrific show. My connection with Peter made me feel part of the 'new wave' comedians of the time, a kind of avant-garde. In addition to working in a comedy team, I continued to do stand-up.

Stand-up is a one-person endeavour which I didn't do for very long because I found it incredibly nerve-racking. The funny thing is that I found it very different from doing a one-woman piece of drama. When, much later, I did *Liselotte*, although I was alone, I imagined the stage peopled with all the characters about whom and to whom I was talking. I could envisage Louis XIV and my husband and the children. I didn't feel as lonely as I did when doing a twenty-minute stand-up act.

I will never forget doing my solo act in Aberdeen. I opened on the Monday night, and suddenly understood the meaning of the phrase 'the silence was deafening'. There is nothing worse than being a stand-up and getting nothing at all back from the audience. I understand why people become drinkers, because, before I could go on for the second house, I had to have a large brandy. That was the first time I'd done that, and I could easily have turned into an alcoholic there and then.

I couldn't understand why they didn't find me funny. However, on the way out of the theatre I overheard a woman saying, 'She's very *advanced* in her humour', and perhaps I was. This was quite different from the metropolitan audience in London, where I had first tried out my act. The audience was in tune with me there: they understood the characters I was trying to create. They loved me at Chelsea Palace because it was a fairly camp audience – I suppose I was even a bit of a 'gay icon', not that we would have called it that then.

(In the dressing room at the Chelsea Palace, incidentally, there used to be a most delicious notice: 'Please do not stand [by which they meant pee] in the basins. Chorus girls have been seriously lacerated in so doing.' I've never known whether it was a genuine notice, or merely 'taking the piss'.)

The first time I was asked to do proper stand-up in a big theatre was after doing a 'Kosher' concert one Sunday, at the Palladium. I was seen by a casting lady called Cissy Williams. She worked for Val Parnell, the big variety boss who owned the Palladium. These concerts were for a Jewish audience, telling very Jewish jokes and playing very Jewish characters – it was another audience that understood me. Cissy Williams phoned my agent on the Monday morning and said, 'I want Miriam to open in Brighton next Monday.' I felt a bit panicked and asked what she wanted me to do: I felt it would be wrong to do the same act in Brighton. She replied she wanted me to do exactly what she had seen the night before, and even wear the same dress.

Well, I did – and I learned a lesson. I got letters from Jewish people who were in the mixed audience in Brighton, saying they were shocked to see a nice Jewish girl doing that sort of stuff on stage. I've often wondered whether Lenny Henry learnt a similar lesson, as he stopped doing send-ups of black people quite a long time ago. What you can do when it's 100 per cent your own is quite different from mixed audiences. I even find watching Jewish comics embarrassing when I'm sitting at home watching my own television. If I were sitting in an audience with only Jewish people, maybe it would be different.

After all, when Johnny Speight wrote *Till Death Us Do Part*, he created the character of Alf Garnett with the very best of intentions.

Johnny was a good old left-winger and he loathed anything to do with racial prejudice, but what he found was that Alf Garnett became so popular because people equated with him. Warren Mitchell, who played Alf, admitted it himself – it rebounded. It was the sort of thing that made me laugh hugely, but to think there were ghastly people sitting there thinking Alf was right... Satire is incredibly difficult to gauge, and audiences are so fickle.

I knew Alfred Marks from this time because he used to perform at the Sunday Kosher charity concerts too. Every Jewish comic would perform on those Sundays at one of the big theatres. Alfred was funny. He used to get Paddy O'Neil, his girlfriend at the time, to come and sit in the wings and see what jokes had gone before, and when he turned up later, she would give him a list. Alfred was one of those people that from the moment he met you would suggest some appalling impropriety, as if he was just talking about the weather. We did have quite a strange relationship.

Alfred and Paddy were starring in a revue in Brighton at this time. Their previous one had been a huge success, but while they were doing this follow-up, which clearly was not going to be as success-ful, they suddenly decided they were going to get married, so they eloped. The scripts weren't good and there was a 'panic' phone call to three people to take over from them: Tony Hancock, who had been co-starring in the radio show *Educating Archie*; a comedienne called Betty Jumel; and me. Tony had his own act that he had started working on, which he continued perfecting, literally until he died. He used to say, 'Well Sid Field took years and years doing the golfing sketch until it was perfect, and then brought it to the West End.' (I had seen Sid Field live at the Prince of Wales Theatre after he had been touring for about twenty years, finessing his act, and indeed it was an experience.) I thought Tony was wonderful, and we developed some sketches together.

Well, we opened in the show, but after a few weeks, the theatre manager Albert Rose decided he was going to close it, because we weren't doing huge business – the material hadn't had enough time to develop. It was Saturday night, and we hadn't been paid on the Friday. There we were, packed up, and no money. So I said, 'I'm not leaving this theatre until we get paid.'

Tony said, 'Oh, let's go to the pub.' (It was already 'Let's go to the pub'!) But I stood outside the manager's office, which he'd locked, and hammered on the door shouting, 'Mr Rose, I know you're in there, we're not leaving this theatre until we get paid.'

Tony was in the background and kept saying, 'Never mind, let's go', and 'Oh come on, it'll be closed'. I enacted this scene, more or less, in the film of *The Entertainer* about ten years later. Mr Rose stayed silent and didn't open the door. (We did get the money in the end, through Equity.)

It was at this time I saw the beginnings of what Tony turned into later. I could see he was a star – he was so funny – but he would become desperately depressed and sit there with his beer (it was only beer then…) and say, 'Why do you think I didn't get that laugh on that line?' There'd be a post-mortem after every performance as to why he might have lost a laugh. An obsessive if ever I saw one.

I came back to London and told everybody that I'd just worked with someone who was going to become a huge star, a second Sid Field. I absolutely adored him. His character was always the put-upon person, which I suppose he developed to mask an incredible ego. He certainly gave the impression of being very humble, but when he became a star, he never wanted any competition – hence dropping Sid James from his TV show, perhaps?

Many years later, on one of my trips to Australia, I went to see Tony one night at The Hilton in Sydney where he was doing an act. I thought he would have changed his material and be bold enough to experiment because it was such a distance from England. That's what many of us had found about Australia, that you could experiment with stuff that you couldn't do in London. I was shattered because it was identical – exactly the same act as he had done all those years before in Brighton. I went round to see him at midnight, after the show. He was now supposedly off the booze and was drinking black coffee like a crazed thing. The next time he went to Australia was when he killed himself.

I don't want to give the impression that my work in the theatre was somehow effortless, and that I didn't have setbacks. In fact, I had a bit of a scare with the first thing I did in the West End, a year or so after the war. This was a play called *Separate Rooms* at the Strand Theatre. The American actor Frances Day, a big star herself, was playing the part of a big star with a famous husband. My character Miss Sharp, who only appeared in the third act, went to their house to do a report for *Good Housekeeping*. For some reason, the character eluded me. I even had a feeling that I was going to be fired: I just couldn't find my 'green umbrella' – that elusive clue that would help me.

However, I happened to get a cold and developed a monstrous cough. The American director, Joel O'Brien, said, 'Hey, can you put that cough on whenever you want?'

'Of course.'

So, on my entrance, Frances was showing off her housekeeping skills by running around with a feather duster. Each time she got near me I would give one of my horrendous coughs, and say 'Feathers' as if I was allergic to them. Big laugh. I also decided on a piece of business with my feet on a barstool, so that when Frances and her husband said to me, 'Will you have a drink, Miss Sharp?', I said, 'No, no, no, I never drink', and went and sat up at the bar with my foot knowing exactly where the foot-rest should have been. What a give-away.

These two things helped me into a character, believe it or not, and I really enjoyed the run. I was beginning to learn that inspiration comes from wherever you can get it, even if it's the misfortune of an awful cough.

Hal Thompson was in the play too and it was from him that I discovered how to time a laugh. I call it 'the graph of a laugh'. I used to stand in the wings every night and watch him say a funny line, and as he delivered it he'd get the laugh, turn upstage, and then, as the laugh was beginning to die down…wham – he would come in, bang, with the next line. He would project more as he came back, so that the next bit of the line was heard over the laugh which was still going on. Brilliant. This, I believe, is the essence of comic timing.

A little later, the same management put on a revue called *Maid to Measure*, and I learned a quite different but equally memorable lesson from Jessie Matthews. She had been a huge musical star in the 1930s and was now making a comeback. The revue also starred Tommy Fields – Gracie Fields' brother – and Lew Parker, an American comedian, as well as three young performers: Joan Heal (who became my great friend), Johnny Brandon and myself. Jessie took numbers away from me if I got too many laughs.

One night, she came to my dressing room with a bunch of flowers and said, 'I thought you'd like these, pet.' (She always used to say 'pet'.) As she was leaving I muttered a quote from Virgil: '*Timeo Danaos et dona ferentes*', which translates as 'I fear the Greeks even when they bring gifts.' Looking back on it, this apparent erudition on my part must have made her blood boil. We did a sixteen-week tour, finishing up at the Cambridge Theatre in London. This particular year, 1948, is memorable to me because I paid my first NHS contribution – with very great pleasure!

So here I was, doing theatre, television, radio and variety. I was also developing my singing in cabaret. I've never been a good singer even though I've done a lot of it. My singing teacher Ernst Urbach said that it was going to be very hard work for me. 'If you are prepared for this, it is going to take a long time', he said, and I did work at it. I could put over a song but I didn't have a great voice (added to which, I was smoking non-stop – but more on that later). It was naturally low and strong so I could never sing soprano, always alto. Later, certainly, in *Fiddler on the Roof*, I found that it was comfortable for me to sing in the same octave as Topol.

One man I worked for in both cabaret and revue was Cecil Landau – an extraordinary character. He wouldn't be allowed to put on shows now. He had a fantastic aesthetic taste and knew what looked beautiful, but as for being a reputable employer, absolutely not. When he produced and directed a revue called *Cockles and Champagne* we had a dress rehearsal that went on until four o'clock in the morning. We opened the following night, after he'd spent four hours lighting a rose in 3D – and the number was cut after the first performance.

I hadn't been particularly happy with my material in the show. This was the time when we used to see people winning £25,000 on the pools and they nearly always said, 'Yeah but I'm going to go on working just the same.' So I got Miles Rudge, who had written a few pieces for the show, to write me a number as a factory worker. I had read about a woman who bought herself diamonds galore after winning a large amount of money. This idea was going round in my head and I thought it would make a funny number. So I started off wearing dungarees and each time I ended a verse I would finish it off with 'but I'm going to go on working in the factory just the same' and I'd roll up my sleeve and there'd be a bloody great diamond bracelet there. In the end I was covered from head to foot with diamonds and a tiara – 'But I'd go on working at the factory just the same.'

I'll never forget that first night. It was nearly midnight, and I still had a number to do. There was an extraordinary mixture of performers on that stage: Phyllis Neilson-Terry, whom I already knew through her husband Heron Carvic; Renée Houston, a famous Scottish comedienne (and alcoholic); the black singer Mildred Smith – the original Carmen Jones – and 'Lolita', a South American Carmen Miranda-type, complete with fruit on her head. The critics slated the show like crazy but that factory girl number did get some lovely notices. Before the second night I came down from my dressing room to find a running order up on the board. Cecil Landau was standing there changing things around. I had such *chutzpah* that I said, 'I think my factory girl should be penultimate to the first half finale.'

'No I can't do that.'

I insisted, because a) he hadn't given me a contract, and b) I had already been offered a smashing part in a play with Flora Robson. So something else had to be moved. (In the end I left *Cockles and Champagne* after two weeks – Fenella Fielding took over – to do the play with Flora Robson, which would not be exactly the experience I had expected!)

On the second night at the curtain call I was standing next to Phyllis Neilson-Terry. Renée Houston stepped forward and said to the audience in a very slurred Glaswegian accent:

> I jusht want you to knaw that our grreat produsher Sheshil Landoo shutting there in the bauxsh hash been faabuloush, he hash been wunnerful to ush and therre ish a grrand bunch of kidsh herre and the crriticsh, thoshe terrrible crriticsh they slot-terred that pooorr Sheshil Landoo, sho I want you all to applaud Sheshil Landoo because you're a grraand maan, Sheshil!

Phyllis and I wanted the floorboards to open up because it was the most embarrassing thing one's ever lived through, but the audience dutifully applauded. Renée was a well-known drunk – talented, but a drunk.

Everybody in the finale was wearing beautiful white lace, and Cecil never paid for any of it. He didn't really pay for anything and always had the police after him. Previously I had done cabaret for him at Ciro's Club. Audrey Hepburn was compèring, simply announcing things and singing. She was very lovely, and Cecil quite rightly thought her beautiful. I don't suppose he paid her.

After rehearsal at lunchtime one day Cecil, Audrey and some of us were standing around when two bowler-hatted gentlemen – obviously bailiffs – came up and asked Cecil if he was 'Mr Cecil

Landau'. Cecil calmly replied, 'No, he left the building actually.' We stood there and said nothing, absolutely aghast.

I was lucky enough to work in lots of areas, often because I didn't turn anything down, but also I enjoyed trying different kinds of work. Indeed, even when I was out of work I couldn't keep still. I used to run a business of sorts, making matching bath mats and lavatory seat covers – which were then a great novelty – from terry towelling. I also made and painted lampshades. I continued this when I was back in work, and I'd go on making them in whichever dressing room I happened to be occupying at the time, selling them to my friends and colleagues in the theatre.

I look back now with some pride that I tried a bit of everything (except ballet and the circus), even working with Scottish Opera in the mid-1970s. I just didn't like being out of work – who does? – so the career followed all sorts of twists and turns and was a constant surprise to me, presumably because, never having been overly ambitious, it never occurred to me to plan anything.

I was still pretty innocent about the world, but by now I had become a successful working girl – living at home, but ready to explore further afield.

4

DOING IT ALL

In which I lost my virginity, learned to gamble, widened my experience in fringe, serious plays and comedy, got involved with Equity politics, worked with Sam Wanamaker and Tony Hawtrey, almost came to blows with Flora Robson, and bonked on the Queen Mary.

EVERYTHING WOULD CHANGE for me in the mid-1950s, but there was a period before that when I found myself experimenting like a thing demented in my work, my politics, my love life and associated pleasures.

There was a great spirit of optimism around in the late 1940s and early '50s, and although we still had the remnants of rationing, we also had the National Health Service, the greatest social reform ever brought in by a government for the whole population, and class barriers were just starting to break down. On the other hand, it was a time when the death penalty was still in existence, abortion had yet to be legalised and homosexual behaviour was a criminal offence, so there was plenty to fight for.

I began to develop my own political ideas at this time, to see how political meetings worked and how debate and discussion could change things. This awareness led me to make my first vote, where I naturally voted Labour. Attlee had just been elected and I went to the celebration at Labour Party headquarters that night with my parents. It was a very exciting time personally: acting, meeting lots of people, and then going to that party. I felt really important.

I still went to the Arts Theatre Club to keep up with comedy and fringe friends, and whereas earlier we would hang onto a cup of coffee in the downstairs coffee bar, we would now sit at the bar drinking and then go round the corner and do the same at 'The Salisbury' pub. Our political views would have been thought of as quite radical and, though I hadn't become a member of the Labour Party yet, I was already starting to campaign for it.

I was also regularly attending Equity meetings and became really involved. There was something inevitable about this: not only did I have trade unionism in my blood, through Dad, but I was strongly influenced by the example of Lewis Casson and Sybil Thorndike. Lewis was Vice-President of Equity at the time, and often used to chair the monthly members' meetings at Victory House in Leicester Square. I suppose I soon became what is now known as an 'Equity activist'. (Or, as Tony Sher once referred to me, an 'Equity terrorist'!)

I was involved in setting up the first monthly branch meetings. I find now that if I go to any local branch meeting someone will make what they consider to be a radical and new suggestion, and it is something my colleagues and I tried to deal with years before. Everything goes round in cycles and comes back again if you wait long enough.

The number one issue at the time, occupying the collective Equity mind, was 'regulated entry' – in effect, the idea that in order to join Equity, you have to fulfil certain criteria. As I've already said, I had just taken Dad's note to the General Secretary and hey presto, I was in. Now, a few years later, there was a groundswell of opinion that it was all too easy. In particular, this little German woman, Nelly Arno, about four foot ten, would get up with monotonous regularity at every Equity AGM – and indeed any meeting – and say, in her heavy Germanic accent:

> I sink it's terrrible zat Eqvity can allow all zese foreign artists to come ofer here and take avay ze verk from under our Brritish noses.

Everybody would be shouting, 'That's right, Nelly! Good old Nelly! Have a go!'

Just as passionate as Nelly was a rather tight-arsed actor called Roger Snowdon. He was part of the BBC Rep and was regularly on radio, but had not just a chip, but ten bags of King Edward potatoes on each shoulder, because he wasn't being offered any theatre work. Regulated entry became an obsession with him – he could have bored for England on the subject and seemed unable to have a conversation without bringing it up. I suppose I became infected too.

So in came regulated entry. Although the principle behind it had seemed perfectly sound, it soon led to a 'Catch 22' situation which will be familiar to many actors: you couldn't join Equity until you had done enough work, but you couldn't get work until you had joined Equity. There was a more sinister side to regulated entry as well. I suppose that, almost by definition, where you have prohibition you get corruption. When I was on the Equity Council in the 1970s, I heard rumours that Equity cards could be bought. Even more shockingly, an actress friend told me that she could have got herself an Equity card by supplying sexual favours.

This had the effect of turning me totally against regulated entry, and I began to work to get rid of it. I was not alone in wanting to see the back of it, however, and found myself in a strange alliance with the very right-wing Marius Goring, who didn't want Equity to be affiliated with the TUC and was opposed to the idea of the closed shop, and Vanessa Redgrave, then a member of the Workers' Revolutionary Party, who thought that membership should be opened up as far as possible – to include performers such as strippers, for instance. Before this curious triumvirate could deal with regulated entry ourselves, along came Margaret Thatcher, who dealt a death blow to the closed shop. This action not only swept aside regulated entry but, in a sense, put into question our whole *raison d'être* as a union. Equity is still recovering from the effects of Thatcherite policies, which horribly diminished our membership. Ironically enough, having worked all those years to keep people *out* of the union, we are now desperately trying to bring them *in*!

I had never been in love by this time. I was still living at home, and although I was attracted to certain chaps, there was no one special. My parents had told me how they fell in love, but it seemed rather unromantic. Ma's family moved from Holland to Belgium when World War One broke out, afterwards coming to England as refugees. Dad came down from Oxford and the two of them met at some music group. Ma thought that he was a pompous prig when they first had a conversation. Apparently Dad's first question was 'What is your opinion of the Darwin theory?', and he was terribly impressed when she didn't try to give him an answer. She simply said, 'I don't think about it so I don't have an opinion. What is the Darwin theory, tell me about it.'

She was a very honest, no-shit kind of person and I think I may have got that from her. Sometimes I think I shouldn't have been so honest in my life but I think I'll be glad on my deathbed that I have been, never mind that I have often been noisy and outspoken. Politically I suppose, yes, it might have been better not to let people know that you thought they were idiots, bad actors or directors! Recently I was sent an orchid (which I inevitably managed to kill off) and on the card it said: 'From your friends on the Equity Council'. It was, in fact, from Christine Payne, the new General Secretary. She laughed when I said to her, 'You put "from your *friends*", because you know I have quite a few enemies on the Council'. People know I can't pretend and that was true of my mother. She would be quite cold with someone she couldn't stand or didn't trust. I think my frigidity is even more obvious than hers. Icicles can come off me on occasions.

Although we talked a great deal in my family and argued often, there were certain subjects that were never discussed. Politics, yes, art, science and literature, yes; but sex and intimate personal relationships, not at all. The press wasn't full of gossip and stories of people's private lives then, either, so I suppose it was easier to believe that everyone lived their lives in a straightforward fashion.

My mother disapproved of gays, and consequently I didn't know about homosexuality until I went to RADA. When we did Lillian Hellmann's *Children's Hour*, I didn't understand what it was about. I certainly didn't know about lesbians, and gay relationships of any sort were new to me. Once I was in the business, this soon changed! Later, Harold Lang, who by then was a great friend of mine, came to a party at our house with Kenneth Tynan. I had thought my parents were going to be out of the house and unfortunately they weren't, and Ma caught sight of Harold and Ken hugging or kissing or something in the garden and was absolutely horrified. She avoided talking about it afterwards, and I'm not even sure she would have had the words.

She never talked to me about sex at all, actually. When I was about five I asked the question, 'Where do babies come from?', and she sat me on her knee and told me, 'Mummy carries them in her tummy.' She didn't tell me how a baby comes to be there in the first place, in fact she never really explained anything about the facts of life.

One summer, on our last holiday in Belgium a month before war broke out I rushed into my mother's bedroom when I was thirteen, and showed her my pants which had blood on them. She laughed and said, 'Oh, I'm so pleased.'

'Why?'

'I thought you'd got appendicitis.'

I had been saying I'd got a pain in my tummy for a couple of days and she thought that's what it might be, but hadn't thought of telling me about the curse. She assumed I would have heard about it at school. It was pretty thoughtless, but my parents probably hadn't been taught anything about how to be parents, and they were both very young when they had Michael and me. People weren't writing books about it then and I supposed they improvised bringing us up.

Although I had no real idea of how one got pregnant, that didn't stop the urge to explore and I soon realised that my juices were beginning to work in a way I couldn't control.

There was an actor who obtained great joy from deflowering virgins, and the idea of taking a Jewish girl was fantastic to him. He was very attractive and a friend of mine was so determined that I get rid of this thing called 'virginity' that I was hanging on to, that there in her flat in Belsize Park Gardens, he and I were shoved into a bedroom and he took me, no problem at all, and that was that.

The extraordinary thing is that once you 'get rid of it' men seem to know. They kind of sense when a woman is available and ready for anything and they were like bees round a honey-pot, so I was at it like a mad thing. I didn't exactly object or even contemplate screaming 'Rape'.

I can't believe the things that I got up to. I had sex in my parents' drawing room with someone quite famous on two counts – one as a bloody good Jewish comedian and actor, and two that he would take out his willy the moment he said 'Hello'. He had given me a lift home after a 'Kosher Concert'. I think I offered him a drink or something, and he immediately took me on the carpet in the drawing room. I wonder what would have happened if somebody had come in?

I was also beginning to experiment with all sorts of drugs. I had my first reefer – we called it a 'stick of tea' – in the flat of Buddy Bradley, a famous black choreographer who was then involved with my best friend Joan Heal. As I sat there, having a fabulous time in my mind, I heard, apparently from a million miles away, Buddy saying, 'Joan, I thought you said your friend Miriam was such a funny girl. She hasn't spoken a goddam word in two hours.'

I tried to form the words to say, 'But I've been brilliant!' Nothing came out…

This encounter didn't deter me from indulging further in what we called 'high tea'. One night I was in a club in Lisle Street with the American actor Bonar Colleano, whom I had known since we worked together in *Separate Rooms*, and I went up to the all-black band and said, 'Wanna stick of tea, man?'

When we left, it was already daylight. Bonar passed out in Lisle Street and I somehow managed to get him into a cab back to his flat in Hanover Terrace. I remember seeing him stagger to his front door.

I got home at about 4.30 or 5 o'clock in the morning, and I was stoned out of my head. In addition to the dope, I must have been on something like speed (possibly 'purple hearts'), and had probably been drinking too. I had become quite used to coming home at ridiculous times and was very careful which stairs I trod on because I knew which ones creaked and which ones were safe. I would normally creep into my bedroom and close the door very quietly.

This particular time I dropped my handbag on the stairs, and began to struggle to pick everything up. My mother heard all this and came out. 'What's this? What's going on?' she said, and I looked at her and said, 'Oh bugger off!'

She was so shocked she didn't even look at me and went back into their bedroom, closing the door behind her because she didn't want to be tainted by what had just happened. The word 'bugger' had never even been used in the house.

We didn't speak for a couple of days but what frightened me most was that I realised that a whole container of pills that had been in my handbag wasn't there any longer. I didn't know what to do because they were purple hearts.

It was probably a year or two later that my mother was going out and she called to me, 'Min, I've left my gloves upstairs. Would you get them from my glove drawer?' I went to the drawer and in the glove drawer were my pills. I didn't dare take them because she would know. I left them there and never mentioned it again.

One day somebody told my mother I was having an affair with the director Anthony Hawtrey, who ran the Embassy Theatre in Swiss

Cottage. I remember her talking to me about it in the garden. I can't recall exactly what she said, but she meant, 'I hope you're not having sex with him' – she had her own way of saying it. I said, 'Oh Mummy don't be ridiculous.' She had seen my notices in the newspapers and knew I was beginning to be 'known', so I was able to make the excuse that as soon as you get 'known' people start talking about you, and left it at that.

Tony was the only legitimate son of the actor manager Sir Charles Hawtrey (no relation to the *Carry On* star!). I knew he had affairs galore, despite being married with children, and I was totally besotted with him. His wife, Marjorie Hawtrey, was a bloody good actor who knew about his affairs, so I told myself I didn't have to be guilty.

Tony directed me in a play called *Women of Twilight*, which started at the Embassy and transferred to the Vaudeville in the West End. After a few months I was taken out of the West End cast and, thrillingly, was asked to go to Broadway with the play. The only other part to be cast was the part being played at the Vaudeville by Maria Charles, so I suggested my old chum June Whitfield.

We set off on the Queen Mary: to have an affair with the director and be bonking on a luxury liner was quite brilliant. It was glamorous and delicious, and I thought I was in heaven. Noël Coward was also travelling on the Queen Mary, and Tony told me that when they met, Noël had called me 'that very clever Jewish girl'. (When he saw me in *Fings Ain't Wot They Used T'Be*, almost a decade later, he sent me a book of cockney rhyming slang.)

Arriving in New York was hugely exciting. My first sight of skyscrapers – oh! – and Times Square was amazing. It seemed to us, coming from London only six years after the war, that the place never closed. Everything and everybody seemed to stay up all night. Being able to buy food at two am was extraordinary: I'm afraid I made a total pig of myself and got fatter and fatter. It didn't worry me then – I was having such a good time.

We had taken our own set with us in breach of their union rules, so we were picketed by the Scenic Artists' Union. It was strange to have people shouting on our opening night, 'Don't cross our picket line', and having to push through them to get to the stage door. I didn't like that aspect very much, but bought the official line that it had been necessary.

June and I shared a flat in New York and my memory is of arriving bleary-eyed back at some ungodly hour after a date with Anthony to see June sitting up in bed doing the accounts, saying, 'You owe such and such for bread', etc. She had such a canny Yorkshire attitude to money. It was very funny. If only I could have had her very sensible attitude, I wouldn't have got into my future financial crises!

The play, which was all about unmarried mothers, was certainly in advance of its time in New York, despite being a huge success over here. It was duly panned, so between the critics and the picket line, we only lasted a week. I call it 'my special week on Broadway'.

We didn't come straight home and stayed on for a few weeks going to several Broadway shows. Audrey Hepburn had become an overnight star in *Gigi*. She was terrific in the show, and, as we had worked together in the Cecil Landau cabaret at Ciro's Club, we had a lovely reunion.

When we did return, it was on the Queen Elizabeth, which added to the thrill. We stopped for a very short while at Le Havre. Tony wrote a note – 'If anyone finds this please return to Anthony Hawtrey, Embassy Theatre, etc...' – and put it in an Alka Seltzer bottle, which he threw into the sea. It was about six am, the sun was just rising and there was a rather romantic feeling about being on deck and knowing that this was virtually the end of our trip together, and maybe of our relationship...

A month or so later *Women of Twilight* was playing at the Victoria Palace and I went back into the cast. Tony came round one night very excited – somebody had sent him the Alka Seltzer bottle! The affair continued.

Tony got me into gambling: he was absolutely addicted to racing and even owned a racehorse. He had a wonderful sense of humour about his own lifestyle – how he would be rich one minute and broke the next. When he picked me up and took me to my first race meeting at Kempton Park it was in his Rolls Royce, which he frequently put in hock for a few thousand so that he could gamble. On the way to Kempton he drove like a maniac, having had quite a few drinks and taken amphetamines. At the time I was a racing virgin and thought 'each way' meant 'there and back again'. He showed me how to go to the tote window and what to do, giving me £7 to bet with. I came away with £25, which was fan-bloody-tastic. Of course that started me off, and I found myself looking up runners and riders. Within a few weeks I was totally addicted, not something I'm very proud of. One day I would win a stack and the next day lose it all and more. (It is very true, you never meet a poor bookmaker.)

Tony died very young. When somebody phoned to break the news to me at home, I was distraught and Ma was incredibly *simpatico* to me. I realised then she had known all along that we had been having an affair.

After Tony died, it took quite a long time, but I did move on to the next one, as one does. Survival instinct, I suppose.

The next was also a compulsive gambler and this time got me into dog-racing as well, which I had never done with Tony. He was a very talented musician and often used to accompany me when I did cabaret. He was a composer as well as a pianist. I knew he was brilliant when I first met him and, indeed, he later won an Oscar for Best Film Score.

We had one extraordinary bank holiday weekend, a 'lost weekend'. We went to Kempton Park on the Saturday, got rid of a load of money there, came back and decided to go to the dogs at the White City in the evening. I cashed a cheque in a local shop, knowing it wouldn't get to the bank until Tuesday at the earliest, so I had money to play with. Then we came back, phoned up people and asked them to come round and play poker. We played all night, survived on coffee, a great big tin of biscuits and other bits of food. We gambled all through the Sunday and on the Monday went back to Kempton Park and did it all over again.

Next day I phoned my mother, sounding rather pathetic. She wanted to know what was the matter and I said, 'Nothing, nothing.'

'You sound terrible, what's the matter?'

Then I lied horribly: 'I just got this bill for income tax.'

She said, 'I'll speak to Dad', and he saw me out of it every time. I think now that he may have understood my problem because when we were in Belgium he used to like to go to the casino. My mother tried hiding his evening clothes, but there weren't many places she could hide them in our holiday flat and he'd find them easily. One evening at the White City, I even caught sight of him at the tote window. He was pretty embarrassed actually, and made out he was coming to see what it was like because I had talked about it; but I did think back to that time in Belgium when I was a child and wondered whether he too had had his own addiction problem.

I became really irresponsible about money, completely relying on my father to get me out of trouble, and ironically, I'd lie quite easily about how I got into debt in case I worried them. There were times I'd just let debts accumulate, not even open envelopes that I knew contained bills. I was capable of being in complete denial about the amount of money I owed: if I hadn't seen the bill, I didn't owe it.

The first time I went to Australia in 1964, I had a secretary who had a key and would come in and sort out my post – anything financial went to my father. I was away for nearly a year and he discovered that I was in real financial schtuck with my income tax, owing a hell of a lot. He got me out of the mess and paid all the outstanding bills, but when I came home from Australia this time he really read me the riot act, telling me how much I was in debt, and that if he hadn't helped me, the bailiffs would have come and taken my possessions. He made me swear that I would never ever let an envelope go unopened and even if I couldn't pay the income tax or whatever I was owing that I must send them a little something on account. This is the promise I have kept and have characteristically gone the other way now. My friends think I am totally mad because the moment a bill comes through the door I write a cheque, instead of getting interest on the money, keeping it until the last minute. It frightened me so much to realise how easy it was to get into debt and how lucky I was to have a family who could help me at the time. I am deeply ashamed to say that I didn't learn to stand on my own two feet until I was 50, when my father died. I say I learned, but I still have had to call on my darling brother, who has always been stingy with himself, but incredibly generous to me.

One night around this time, when we were doing a production at the tiny fringe theatre The Boltons, there was the worst smog in London that we had ever seen. (It became known as 'The Great Smog'.) How the cast got to the theatre I will never know. We had an audience of two, so we had a little meeting about going on. I said, 'If two people have bothered to come out on a night like this, we have got to do the play.' So we did.

I don't know how I got home, either. The family had stayed up waiting for me because they were worried. Then, after I had gone to bed I woke up at about four am to hear my mother talking anxiously on the phone, so I got up to see who she was talking to. She was phoning the doctor to tell him that my grandfather had been taken ill. It was Dr Britton (Leon Britton's father), a brilliant doctor who adored my grandfather. He put on his clothes over his pyjamas and walked over a mile to our house, but by the time he got there Grandpa had died. He couldn't have driven – you couldn't see your hand in front of your face.

Dr Britton and Grandpa were both originally from Russia and they used to talk Russian to each other. My mother adored her father and

I used to get upset because I thought she was rude to her mother. She got irritated with her mother, I suppose in the way that I would get irritated with her later on. Perhaps it's always like that with mothers and daughters. Ma was in real grief when Grandpa died. He had been an amazing man.

A whole forest was planted in my grandfather's name. I often wonder whether it is still in existence. The trees would be huge now. They were pines, and when I last saw them, a long time ago, they had grown much taller than me in the space of ten years. When you are in Jerusalem, you actually feel as if you are opening the Bible. It is a green and fertile land. How do they manage to make things grow in the desert?

In those days when the evening's performance was finished, that was that: you took off your make up, got changed, and left the theatre. However, on tour at the Abbey Theatre in Dublin, I had my first experience of a theatre where the actors were expected to come out and drink in the theatre bar with the customers.

This was in the play for which I had left *Cockles and Champagne*, and I had really been looking forward to working with Flora Robson. Flora, who always used to tell me how awful it was to be plain, was very helpful at the beginning, saying in rehearsals, 'This is your scene, darling, just take the stage'. The play was set in the country, and Flora had one of those rather boring and difficult roles to play, which she could do splendidly. However, after she had worked very hard for an act and a half, I appeared as a tart from London, wearing amazing clothes and very high heels, and had a lot of funny lines. When she found that the audience laughed at my character she would sometimes kick the furniture to upstage me and behave in a really extraordinary manner. Once at a party she got very pissed and pulled my hair. I couldn't believe it that this was the famous Flora Robson, behaving in this way to a young actress. It was unbelievable but true – even worse than Jessie Matthews had been almost a decade before.

After each show, the audience, depending on how much they liked you, would find out what your tipple was and would line up drinks for you. Because the character I was playing was very sexy and seductive, the chaps thought I was terrific. In those days I actually drank scotch, so the first night I came out front there was a line of about eight scotches, all for me. I started talking away and after about five scotches I was pissed out of my brain and saying to this chap in very slurred speech, 'You see the reason you and I get on so well we're both fucking persecuted; you're fucking Irish Catholic and I'm fucking Jewish.'

He said, 'Oh she's right you know, we're all fucken porsecuted.'

The next morning I remembered what I'd said. I was deeply embarrassed and thought this must not happen again – and then of course the next night, four scotches later, because I was trying so hard not to say it, I was off again: 'The reason you and I get on so well…', etc, etc, *ad nauseam.*

It got to the Saturday night and I'd hardy taken a sip and I was already at it: you know that thing when you are so determined not to say something…

Dublin was great. I used to do my gambling in the day and acting, flirting and drinking at night. God did I have a ball, apart from the dreaded Flora.

After my experiences with Flora, and with Jessie Matthews, I swore that I would never be jealous or spiteful to younger actresses, and I hope I have been true to that pledge.

Fortunately, I have also known talented women who were wonderful to work with. One of the best was Evelyn Laye, whom everyone called 'Boo'. She was a lovely woman, and I admired her professionally and as a woman. I worked with Boo in a weekly revue at Wimbledon Theatre when she was the guest star for a number of performances. Weekly revue is very difficult and stressful, because, as the name suggests, you are changing the material every week. Finding that we were constantly let down by our incompetent stage managers, I spent a great deal of the rehearsal period losing my temper and swearing at them.

After one of my outbursts, Boo called me into her dressing room. She said, 'Why do you do it?'

'Do what?'

'Carry on the way you do, throwing temperaments all the time.'

I interjected, 'You see the incompetence, the inefficiency? They're all such idiots!'

'Yes, but you're doing it all the time, it's as if you're crying wolf, and nobody's going to pay any attention. I used to be a bit like you when I was young, but I learned very quickly that people take no notice if you keep doing it. But now I only have a blow up once every two years, so when I create a scene, people fly!'

I didn't really take on board what she'd said, but when I reconsidered six months later, I realised how right she'd been. I have tried, not always successfully, to follow her advice.

Many years later this more relaxed approach was to backfire spectacularly. I was playing Davis in Pinter's *The Caretaker*, directed by Annie Castledine. For this production the caretaker Davis became – with Pinter's permission – an old woman; the other two parts remained male, which allowed for some interesting sexual tension. The set had been designed with my bed nine feet above the stage. We'd rehearsed in London, but when we got to the Sherman Theatre, Cardiff, where we were going to play, I saw that the bed was raked as well as being so far off the ground, and asked if it was safe. 'Oh yes,' they said. In the old days I would probably have gone crazy, but I said nothing. Then two-thirds of the way through the technical rehearsal I was standing on the bed and calling to the actor playing Mick, and slid off – the bedsheet was nylon, which was pretty bloody stupid – and my eye caught the edge of a shopping trolley underneath the bed. It was a horrendous moment: I wasn't even sure I was still alive. I caught sight of Annie Castledine's face, which looked just like a vast green moon, and gathered enough strength to call out: 'Arnica! In my handbag! In my dressing room!'

I was taken to hospital in a terrible state – not least because I was in my costume for the part. I was wearing old men's trousers and six layers of underwear full of holes, which the nurses took forever to get off. My face was a fright, too: very white with a gash of red for lipstick (a bit like Marcel Marceau), and hair in ten little ponytails done up with rubber bands. Fortunately, no bones were broken (perhaps because I was on HRT at the time), and I was able to continue the tech the next day – but now with the bed straightened out!

I was lucky enough to work with Sam Wanamaker, who directed me in a beautiful production called *The World of Sholem Aleichem* at the Embassy Theatre. This consisted of two stories by Sholem Aleichem himself and one story by Y L Peretz, another Yiddish writer of the period. In the first of these three plays I was playing a mother, and I remember Sam saying to me: 'I don't want to see any Mama walk or Mama gestures, I want to see a beautiful, upstanding model of Jewish womanhood, and if I have to tie your hands down, that's what I'll do.'

He was a splendid director because he constantly sought the truth of the situation. It was a tough experience for me but he gave me the freedom to find Jewish characters not based on any kind of stereotype.

Directors are so important to enable one to use one's full potential as an actor. There are many who have no knowledge of how actors work. In the early days I had to develop my own methods and survival skills. The Stanislavski technique of 'What is my objective?' which makes the work active – not just self-admiring, polishing what you're saying, but actually knowing what the character wants – I don't think I came across this way of performing properly until I worked with Joan Littlewood. Then I instinctively knew that it was the right way. I didn't give it a name and call it 'my objectives and super objectives', but I would go home after rehearsal and work out what I was doing and why. Directors I worked with in the earlier years told you where to move, where to sit, when to drink a cup of tea, and so on. I would work out my own motivations, to make it true for myself. I didn't realise then that directors didn't have to be like that. They didn't have to work out beforehand where one was going to sit and so on because that becomes restrictive. Even so, one still saw some bloody good acting!

Looking back, I was extremely lucky to have been offered such a range and variety of work and can see now that whatever you learn in one field can directly transfer across to another discipline and experience becomes accumulative.

I am talking of work experience here, not sex, drugs and rock and roll, although…

5

BODY SWAP

In which, whilst playing a mermaid for Peter Hall, I halved my body weight, consumed lots of pills and went from farting to depression; had my first abortion, worked with Joan Littlewood at Stratford East and played in The Diary of Anne Frank.

UP TO 1955 I WAS a big girl – I was fat. I had been around the eleven and a half to twelve stone mark since my late teens. I had 38-inch bust and 42-inch hips, and was very curvaceous. I did have a fairly good waist but I had big tits and a big bum, big thighs (*very* big thighs) right up until I was cast to play Lina, the Polish airwoman, in Shaw's *Misalliance*. This was directed by Lionel Harris, who was very short, totally rotund, and always talking about some new diet that he had discovered and which he only stuck to for three days.

At the first rehearsal we were shown the costumes, designed by Hutchison Scott, and I saw that mine was for someone with a Garboesque figure. It was a very male trouser suit, and I'd never worn trousers even for myself, let alone for the public. I said to Lionel: 'You know that doctor you were telling me about?'

He said, 'It's Dr Goller', gave me the telephone number straight away, and handed me the tuppence for the phone. Before we even started the read-through I'd made an appointment to see him that lunchtime.

His surgery was in Harley Street, just a few houses away from where I was living at the time. When I went in he said, 'What can I do for you?'

'I want to be two stone lighter in four weeks.'

He said, in his North-country accent, 'Why did you come to me so soon, why didn't you leave it another couple of weeks!'

I said, 'Never mind the funny stuff, let's get on with it.'

He gave me the diet sheet plus a whole bottle of funny-coloured pills – a different coloured pill with each meal. I was allowed only four teacups of liquid a day, no fruit, no carbohydrates and no alcohol of course, but one could eat as much protein and vegetables as one liked. It was a sort of early Atkins diet. This was a huge turning point in my life, though I didn't recognise it as such, merely that I was doing what was required to play the part, rather as some film stars put on and take off weight to play in films. Of course, I can see now that the speed with which I embraced the diet and the pills was significant, and realise that the pay-off – being slim and elegant – was something I really wanted.

You could practically hear me deflating because at the time I was rehearsing *Misalliance* in the day and performing in a show at the Arts Theatre Club at night. It was called *Listen to the Wind* (which I renamed 'Hark, hark, the Fart') by Angela Jeans, with music by Vivian Ellis. The director was a very young Peter Hall, who ran the Arts at the time. (I was to work with Peter again in *Separate Tables*, 47 years later – so he must have liked me!) I was playing a sexy mermaid with a tail, a very thick, very tight tail. I had a huge comb and as I was fished up from the orchestra pit by some child actors, I was saying 'Oh shiver me flippers' or something like that.

One packed matinee, I noticed with my peripheral vision that one of the young actors, Mavis Sage, was holding her hand to her mouth. I thought, 'She's laughing, I'll kill her.' Then she let her hand go and threw up right out front – *macedoine* of vegetables everywhere – and rushed off stage. Nora Nicholson, who played the grandmother, lifted her crinoline above her ears and exited, and all the rest of the kids followed her, leaving the stage decorated with a mass of mixed vegetables, and me having to sing a number and make the audience believe they weren't seeing what they were actually seeing. So I sang with as much conviction as I could muster:

> Did you ever see a mermaid walking?
> Did you ever meet a mooch like mine?
> I lost my tail in a North Seas gale
> And now I've got a flat in Maida Vale.

I was strutting up and down on stage and leant up against the proscenium arch in my high button boots. I then looked back and could see the outline of my boot silhouetted in diced carrots.

I finished the number and went off stage and the chaperone said, 'What happened, dear?' When I showed her my soaked fishy tail she said, 'Oh, that would be her lunch dear! She threw up her breakfast earlier but she is such a little pro, she would go on.'

My tail had to be cleaned before I could go on again, and it was hard to get the smell out of it.

As the run progressed the costume used to be taken in nearly every day because I was losing so much weight, with accompanying sound effects. I opened in *Misalliance* four weeks later, weighing nine stone six pounds. I had been eleven stone eight when I was cast. During the course of *Misalliance* my character Lina is required to pick up the young lead. In this production he was played by Peter Barkworth, who was the same weight as I was before I started my diet. Lionel told me: 'I want you to throw him over your shoulder like a fur stole.'

The pills I was on were a mixture of diuretics, appetite suppressants and speed, to which I became addicted. I developed an 'eating disorder' although I didn't realise it at the time.

It was because of the actor's need for another identity that I had always felt more comfortable being another character. When I lost weight I got nearer to being able to be the me I believed I was. When I was big I was cast as much older, which necessitated getting inside a really different skin. When I was slimmer, I managed to use myself more, which meant I could think of myself in a different way as an actor.

Now I was able to play different younger parts, I am sorry to say I became a bit narcissistic, which I had never been before. I had always been rather ashamed of my body although blokes apparently liked it, and a couple of chaps said to me after, 'You used to be so wonderfully sexy when you were curvy.' But I didn't think so and felt much sexier when I was slim. It felt like a kind of evolution. I had been clothes conscious when I was big, and was thrilled that I could now buy different kinds of clothes. I became much more extravagant because it was easier to find elegant clothes for my new shape. The main advantage, however, was that I was able to play different parts.

I kept on going down and down in weight, and lost so much that when I had a nervous breakdown, it never occurred to me that this could have been partly because of my diet.

My mother had a fur coat which I used to borrow to go and see people because it made me feel good. It was a black Persian lamb coat trimmed with mink around the collar. Whenever I wore it for an audition, I got the job.

When I went to audition for H M Tennent in the mid-1950s, I was wearing the coat. Hugh Beaumont, known as 'Binkie', phoned me at home because I was between agents, having left one and not yet found another. Beaumont ran H M Tennent and was the biggest employer in straight theatre: for him to phone me at home was a big deal. When he asked me to come in and talk to him I got in a panic, and every pair of stockings I put on laddered, but I borrowed Ma's coat to put on top. I got her to phone and say I had been delayed and would be a bit late.

I got there and I had to talk money, which was quite frightening. I was sitting across the desk from Binkie Beaumont, and he said, 'I think we'll pay you £40 a week.'

I said, 'I think £50. I got £40 for the last show I did. So I think it should be £50.'

He said, 'No. £40.'

Somehow I knew about negotiation because then I said, 'Well, shall we meet in the middle?'

He agreed, so we made a deal for £45, which was a lot of money then. I thought myself very wealthy. I heard later that the wardrobe mistress, Lily Taylor, who was very famous in the business, had told everybody, 'I hear we have a very smart actress coming to work with us.' That was me in the fur coat.

Of course I kept on borrowing my mother's coat from that day on. Eventually, when it came to my being in *Fiddler on the Roof* in the late 1960s, she said, 'Isn't it about time that you got your own fur coat?'

She suggested I get on to the Pragers because they were the people who made all fur coats for theatres. We knew the Prager brothers, Sidney and Morris. I ordered a mink coat and they made it for me. It was beautifully tailored, with the fur going round instead of straight down, and they made it with a zip in the centre in the waist, so that I could unzip the skirt part and wear it as an evening jacket. Later on, when coats became longer they put a lot of extra mink at the bottom so it became a long coat. Fur coats became a kind of *Leitmotif* for me.

I was still going to my singing teacher Ernst Urbach. He knew Maria Callas and when I went on the diet he said, 'You are going to do what Maria Callas did.' She eventually lost her voice through severe dieting. The story, true or not, is that she put a tapeworm inside her and that was how she lost her weight. I wasn't shocked when he said that – perhaps I was also prepared to pay a price for my new body. Callas became very beautiful when she'd lost the weight, but I think it does affect one's nerves and one's whole metabolism. I know it did with me. (Of course, I'm not equating myself with Callas vocally!)

I am always thrilled to hear her voice and feel very privileged to have seen her Tosca and her Medea – incredible. I remember how in *Medea* she climbed a flight of stairs, dressed in this fantastic cloak. She'd obviously rehearsed it over and over and knew exactly where the cloak was going to fall and how it was going to spread. She grabbed her two children, one under each arm, and she sang her aria with her back to the audience – it was sensational.

I still thought of myself as part of the alternative comedy scene: my politics were known to be quite radical even though I was working in the West End and others thought of me differently. I have gone through various stages politically; at one time I did lose interest. I revolted against everything as one does when young, but came back to it even stronger, more left-wing than ever. A lot of people at the time believed I was a member of the Communist party, and I did lots of work for Unity Theatre. Reggie Smith was a wonderful radio director and a communist, as was his wife Olivia Manning, who could be a rather difficult woman. They got me to do all sorts of things for Unity and for the CP. When the BBC did Olivia's *Balkan* and *Levant* trilogies as *The Fortunes of War* (in Alan Plater's adaptation), Kenneth Branagh played the Reggie Smith character splendidly, and Emma Thompson the Olivia part quite sensationally – so like her.

One day one of the group, Alex McCrindle (at one time Vice President of Equity), asked me something, assuming I was a member. I told him I wasn't a CP member, and he told me I had to join. Something stopped me, although in theory I agreed with so much of what they were saying and doing, and the things that I talked about were very CP, very pro-Russian, a mixture of Trotsky and Marx. I was never Workers Revolutionary Party, although I have to say that I agreed with a lot of their policies too. Their analyses were absolutely right in the end and everything they prophesied did happen, but I still never quite wanted to join.

So I was working hard and playing hard, and of course I got pregnant. I asked various girlfriends for help, and found out about a fellow in Half Moon Street called Teddy Sugden who was quite well known. When I went into his office, he was sitting there smoking a cheroot and asked what he could do for me, so I told him I was pregnant and asked if he could help. I discovered that his fee was 100 guineas. We are talking about the 1950s, which was the time of back street abortionists. This chap would have done it under anaesthetic and it would probably have been done correctly, but at the time I couldn't get hold of 100 guineas, so I went lower down the scale and found Auntie Phil who lived in Brighton. The deal was you paid her fare from Brighton and gave her 25 guineas and a large gin after she'd done it.

It was organised that it would happen at my friend Joan Heal's flat in Eaton Square. I was not only in a show but was doing cabaret after the show, so I was really busy and absolutely petrified. Auntie Phil got out this instrument, whatever it was, and got me to squat and as she was shoving this thing up me she said, 'Don't be nervous dear.' She named a couple of really famous stage stars of the time and said, 'I did the same for them in between the matinee and evening shows.'

Afterwards, I ran a temperature of 104 or 105 degrees, and I remember making an excuse to my mother as to why I didn't come home, because 'it got so late and it was much more convenient, and Joan was right here in town', so I got away with it. When I ran this high temperature Joan said, 'Now I know it's all great fun to have one's friends having abortions under one's roof, but there comes a time when one is going to have to call a doctor and I am going to do that right now.'

She phoned Patrick Woodcock, a well-known doctor who dealt with all the stars – Noël Coward, John Gielgud, Marlene Dietrich whenever she came over – and he was absolutely lovely, got me sorted and then became my doctor for many years. (I used to call him 'Timbertool'.) Having been NHS he then went into private practice: this is how my double standards began, because he persuaded me to join BUPA. He said that it would be sensible because, being in the theatre, if you need to have surgery it has to be done when you are free. I still feel deeply ashamed of it.

When I thought it was about time I left home, I didn't know quite how to say it. I had said that I was going to stay until I got married of course, but I was leading a double life, having affairs, and I had already had one abortion. The woman who ran the bar at the Embassy Theatre used to let a flat in Montague Place and she told me she had one that was about to become free so I thought I'd take it. I remember telling my mother that I was going to leave but for some reason I was terrified about telling my father. I didn't tell him until the morning I was going. Surprisingly, he wasn't that upset. I couldn't tell either if he was pleased, but he didn't give me a bollocking which I think I'd half expected.

Eventually I came to the conclusion that he quite liked my living away because he had this addiction to auctions and once I'd left home he would ring me up after he'd been to one and say, 'Can I come over? I've got a couple of things that you might like and perhaps if Mummy doesn't like them you might want them.' He'd come round with huge sets of beautiful china dessert services. It wasn't the money, he just liked beautiful things. He couldn't seem to stop getting dessert services and my mother used to say, 'How many more dessert services can a person use?' It was ridiculous, but I must admit they were always beautiful – Copeland and other well-known makes.

I discovered that some dealers who were 'gallery first nighters' (actually these were the ones who had turned up on the night when the big smog happened) thought Dad was a dealer too, and when I went to an auction with him and they saw us together, my revelations that he was a barrister totally messed it up for him, because he never got such good stuff thereafter. Dealers apparently have little rules amongst themselves, and because they always thought china was

Dad's patch they had left that field open for him. They felt betrayed, and he never did so well after that.

I got pregnant again the following year. Can you believe that anybody could be so idiotic? I called up Auntie Phil again, as if she hadn't done enough damage the first time. I had moved into my own place then in Montague Place, my first flat. This time she did it there and once again it was horror, horror, horror.

Years later Gerald Croasdell, the then General Secretary of Equity, rang me and said, 'Oh Miriam, I've had the police on and they wanted to get in touch with you. Do you mind if I give your phone number and address?'

I said, 'I don't mind, but I've got a matinee this afternoon at the Garrick, so if anybody wants me they can come there.'

He said, 'I don't know what you girls have been up to, but they wanted *****'s number as well', naming one of the other performers Auntie Phil had mentioned. The penny dropped.

After the matinee I was sitting in front of the mirror taking off my make-up and there was a knock at the door. Two plainclothes policemen were there. I said, 'What can I do for you?'

'We want to talk to you about Auntie Phil.'

'Auntie who, is that an aunt of mine or something? I don't know an Auntie Phil. Who is she?'

They said, 'She's an abortionist.'

Shock horror from me – 'An *abortionist*?!' (This was me being a very bad actor, completely over-the-top – I didn't do it very well.)

'Well she's asked for your case to be taken into account along with several others, because she's been arrested.'

I didn't realise the implications of all this and I thought they were going to cart me off because I had committed a crime. They said, 'Nothing is going to happen to you but she's asked for your case to be taken into account.'

I said, 'Look this is slander, it's libel, my father's a barrister' – I had a phone right near me, in my dressing room – 'I could phone him now and get legal advice.'

They said, 'No, no, you don't need to do that.' (I am sure my father went to his grave, bless his heart, convinced that I was a virgin).

So I just went on pleading my innocence, nothing to do with me, I don't know her, and eventually they said, 'Oh well, don't worry, nothing will happen to you', and started to leave. Then at the door one of them turned around and said, 'Incidentally, if you do want an abortionist, we know someone much better than Auntie Phil.'

I had considered getting married earlier, but hadn't thought about it for a while. There had been a chap around who had been around forever and I remember saying to him, 'If I'm not married by the time I'm 30, I'll marry you.' But when I got to 30 I'd found someone else and finally pushed him into the arms of another woman. I was quite relieved then because I thought, well that's all right, that's that. There had been another that I got close to marrying, around the time that my brother got married, but then the man in question let me know in no uncertain terms that he didn't want me to go on with the business and that I'd have to give up the theatre. My Dad – totally out of 'archetypal Jewish father' character – said, 'Anybody who wants you to give up everything that you've worked for, is not worth having.'

I remember too, a conversation with Edgar Lustgarten, a very well-known barrister who wrote crime books and recorded famous criminal stories on radio, TV and film. He was very successful, and used to send me flowers. He was rather like a 'stage-door Johnny', inviting me to dinner at the Caprice restaurant where he would dine regularly and buy me champagne. One day when he took me for dinner we were talking about Ruth Ellis, who was due to be hanged in a few days. There was much agitation then about the death penalty and there were campaigns at the time to have it repealed. Most of my more radical friends certainly didn't believe in it. When I said that I didn't believe in capital punishment, Edgar, who was supposed to be a Labour lawyer, started going on about how it is essential that there has to be a deterrent to deal with serious crime. This turned into a huge row. He started getting personal and said something like, 'I just can't understand you…you enjoy the champagne and everything and then repay me with extraordinary rudeness… I give you so much and you treat me like this.'

So I told him I would rather sit having a cup of coffee in the Express Dairy (which used to be next door to the Arts Theatre Club) with one of my chums with whom I had a real affinity, than have all this fucking champagne with him, and I walked out. I enjoyed the feeling of strength it gave me, strength in my opinions, the ability to know my own mind and express it forcefully. He wasn't a boyfriend, and I didn't eventually enjoy his buying my time. I certainly didn't love him.

I was in a play, *The Bad Seed*, at the Aldwych, directed by Frith Banbury, and the day Ruth Ellis was to be hanged I had a matinee. The character I was playing had became a lush during the course of the play because the child who was the 'bad seed' had killed my little boy and I turned up at the front door of her mother's house crying and carrying on. That afternoon I was in such a state about the woman who was being hanged that I didn't know whether I was grieving for my little boy in the play or Ruth Ellis in real life.

That particular day I had placed three bets on one of the big horse races, and, coming offstage, I heard the commentator on the stage door radio: my three bets came in one, two and three. (I think this was the race where 'Nicholas Nickleby' won at 50/1.) For me to win over £100 in one day was the equivalent of more than two weeks' salary, and yet I didn't even raise a smile, I was so upset about the hanging.

When I made an entrance during the run of the same play, Diana Wynyard had to embrace me, and after the performance she said, 'Have you had what I think you've had? An abortion?'

I said 'Yes, how'd you know?'

'Because it was something I felt about you when I embraced you.' That was really weird, but she was wonderfully *simpatico*. We became great friends. She was a beautiful woman and a splendid actor, but sadly died when she was still quite young. She and Peggy Ashcroft were great mates – both Croydon girls – and it was through Diana that I first met wondrous Peggy.

I then went through this phase of thinking what a strange thing it is to go into a theatre, put on make-up, put on some clothes, and then go onto a stage and pretend to be somebody else. What the hell kind of life is this? Why does one do it? It seemed to me a totally worthless way of living. What good was I doing in the world? I wanted to be of some use to the world and felt useless.

I felt compelled to accept the part of Mrs Van Daan in *The Diary of Anne Frank*: not only was it a splendid part, but the subject was so very close to me personally. Far too close – I identified so closely with Anne Frank. If my mother hadn't stayed in England and married my father, she could have been me. As it was, I felt she represented my cousin Leni, her brother Eddy and their parents, Ma's sister and brother-in-law. The task I gave myself was that if my mother's family had suffered but hadn't survived two and a half years in Amsterdam, the least I could do is to suffer and survive two and a half hours every night. I took it so personally and couldn't think of the play objectively at all. It got so bad I couldn't even bear to hear laughter in the theatre backstage because I felt that any laughing was at me. Even now I can't stand anybody asking me, 'How are you?', and this stems from that time. If anybody said, 'Good evening, how are you?' I wanted to say, 'What do you mean how am I? I am a sick woman.'

The play told the story of how the Franks lived until the Nazis caught them. To the audience watching it, it was a sad experience not an heroic one, because everything was from Anne Frank's perspective, but the actors were playing brave people. My character, Mrs Van

Daan, was a greedy woman, whose husband used to steal food from the Franks while they were living with them. Mrs Van Daan wore a fur coat (another one!), and I had to pad up for the first act because she was a big woman, gradually losing some of the padding for the second act; by the third act, the clothes were hanging on me.

The actor who was playing my son, Harry Leuckert (with the stage name Lockhart), was married to a girl called Jean, who was then window dressing at Liberty's. About a decade later, in 1967, I went to a preview of an Erté art exhibition at the Grosvenor galleries and Harry was there with Jean. Erté, that superb artist, was alive then, and I met him – a charming man – and I bought six of his paintings, designs he had done for the Folies Bergère in the 1920s.

Anyway, Harry said to me, 'Miriam, you remember my wife Jean?'

I said, 'Oh yes. Are you still at Liberty's?'

He replied, 'She's *Jean Muir*, you know.' I felt like such an idiot.

There was a very good female stage manager for *The Diary* called Mary Allen, who was wonderfully understanding and could see what I was going through. The only thing I lived for each day was the performance at night; there was a certain point in the play when it was perfectly legitimate to cry, which of course was easy for me. The actor playing my husband, Max Bacon, was certainly not my favourite person. I would hear him coming through the stage door and just saying, 'Hello. Good evening', and I'd say said to my dresser, 'What did he say? What did he say?'

'He just said good evening.'

'Yes, he would.'

I then got Mary to put a notice up on the notice board to say that nobody must ask me how I am, which must have seemed pretty bizarre now I come to think of it.

For some reason I thought I was dying of cancer of the womb. I have no idea why. I'd already had two abortions and they were so dreadful maybe I felt I had damaged my body. So this maniacal thought came to me. During the period that I was playing in *The*

Diary, I didn't have much of a social life which would have maybe given me another perspective. I used to go tearing home after the show and had these terrible ritualistic things I did, almost hearing voices in my head. I'd make myself some food and then say to myself: 'You have to wash up by the time you count to ten, otherwise you're going to get some bad news…a phone call to say Mother or Father is dead.' This was pure obsessive-compulsive behaviour, though I didn't know it at the time.

Mary must have realised help was needed because she made an appointment for me to see somebody at St Thomas' Hospital. I thought I was seeing a gynaecologist. I went in, and there was William Sargeant. I sat and didn't speak, and he sat and he didn't speak.

After the fourth appointment of silence he suddenly said, 'I've done some television programmes.'

'Oh really, on what?'

'My subject, the "Hurt Mind"'.

I said, 'What? Is that what's wrong with me?'

'Well, yes, just a slight case of manic depression.'

I said 'Good God, I know all about that. My father's had two nervous breakdowns.'

Suddenly he started writing, and wanted to know all about my father and his two nervous breakdowns. He made me see that in some way my father's breakdowns were like mine. He put me on a large dose of Drimamil – the equivalent of two 'purple hearts' daily – and was responsible for me staying on it. 'You could have one of those a day for the rest of your life, it won't harm you.'

I learned later that Sargeant was a Pavlovian psychiatrist who disapproved of psychotherapy and promoted pharmaceutical solutions. He was also a lech. He came to see me in *The Diary of Anne Frank* and invited me back to his house for supper after the show. He and his wife lived in Hamilton Terrace (funnily enough, I moved to Hamilton Terrace myself, years later) and I'll never forget that particular night when he knew what I was taking, and still plied me with alcohol, loads and loads of it. He got me pissed out of my head and at around about one am he said that the couple next door were coming in. I suddenly realised what he was after: he had an orgy in mind. I sobered up incredibly quickly and insisted that I go home.

The next time I saw him professionally, a few days later, he said, 'It was very interesting watching you the other night', and I thought 'You shit!'

I heard years later from another actor that he tried the same thing on her. Here was a man who was supposed to be an impressive psychiatrist, and he turned me into a drug addict. Of course, I wanted to believe him about Drimamil because it suited my purpose. Being in *The Diary of Anne Frank* was very disturbing for me and I felt that the drug gave me the help I needed to continue to play the part.

I was pleased with my new shape but the whole experience of *The Diary* devastated me and took me a while to recover. Even so, I must be a masochist because many years later I took part in a film for television written by Miep Gies, the woman who looked after the Franks when they were in hiding. She had been Otto Frank's secretary, so it looked at these same events from a totally different angle. It was directed by John Erman, an American, and the splendid Mary Steenburgen played Miep Gies. I was engaged to play a small part and also teach her a Dutch accent. Most of it was set in Amsterdam and just to go there was pretty harrowing for me, knowing that not one of the family had survived. The director said he wanted me to walk along the street carrying a shopping bag with just a couple of pathetic things in it like some carrots or a turnip. He said, 'I just want you to walk along and stop when you see this jeep.' He didn't tell me what was going to happen.

So we did the first rehearsal, and as I walked along the street this jeep stopped and two SS men got out, went into the building next door to my house, got an old Jewish man and dragged him into the jeep, chucked him in as if he was a piece of meat. I stood there with tears pouring down my face and the director, who knew about my family, came over and said, 'I thought that might happen, so I won't rehearse again, we'll just go for a take.'

I kept thinking, 'My God, that's what actually happened to my uncle.'

The other day I had tea with Frith Banbury, an extraordinary man and the director of both *The Bad Seed* and *The Diary of Anne Frank*, who was 95 this year. He told me that George Voskovec, who played Otto Frank, had been very worried about me and my weight, and had told Frith about his concern. I don't think Frith realised quite how closely I was relating to the play, so all these years later I was able to tell him.

At around this time I got to work with Wilfred Lawson, who was a notorious drunk – he and Trevor Howard were known as the two famous drunks in the theatre. In the end I worked with him on three occasions, and I have often said to people: 'Look, I would rather work with Wilfred Lawson pissed than a hell of a lot of actors sober, thank you.'

First we did Gorky's *Lower Depths* on television. The director Michael Elliot used to let Wilfred rehearse in the morning, and then he was free in the afternoon. He was just superb in the production. The next time I worked with him was at the Arts Theatre Club, in a play called *All Kinds of Men*. I had a big part in that, and at the dress rehearsal Wilfred was clearly pissed. I got myself into a great state about it, and at the end of the dress rehearsal I was sitting in my dressing room taking off my face, carrying on and screaming that it had all been a disaster. Suddenly Wilfred was at the door, and he said, 'Are you going to apologise to me?'

I said, 'What for?'

'Well I think you should apologise to me.'

'What for, Mr Lawson?' I said. 'I have always been your greatest fan, I think you are a great, great actor, but I cannot take what went on tonight, I can't take it from you or from anybody else.'

He said, 'Give us a kiss then.'

Every night thereafter he used to hand his wallet to the barman at the Arts, and the most he had was a light ale.

The last time I worked with him was a play called *Gorillas Don't Drink Milk*. (I mean, no one should do a play with a title like that.) The American producer, who had previously written a musical about Henry VIII, was also playing the leading part. We started rehearsing and he phoned me up one night and said, 'Oh Miriam I gotta tell you, I fired Wilfred.'

'What for?'

He said, 'Well, didn't you know he was drunk today?'

I said he wasn't. He insisted that he was, and being the producer I suppose he pulled rank.

I should have left then, and I didn't, and I hated myself for staying. But I managed through Equity for Wilfred to be paid. We remained friends and he used to send me Christmas cards. (People were amazed that Wilfred even knew it was Christmas!)

I was so unhappy about Wilfred going that I reverted to taking some Nardil and Librium, which had been prescribed by my doctor for depression. One lunchtime I went out with other cast members. I only wanted coffee, but was persuaded to eat something. 'All right,' I said, 'I'll have a bit of cheese.'

A little later, on our way back to the rehearsal rooms, I had a truly splitting headache, so bad that I had to be taken home. My mother, obviously worried, came round to see me – as did my doctor. It turned out that he had forgotten to mention that if you were on Nardil and Librium, eating cheese (of all things) was very dangerous. Apparently the same thing went for Marmite! Not long after there were stories in the paper about people dying after eating the 'wrong' foods with this drug combination – so even though I felt as if I was having the closest thing to a stroke, I suppose I should count myself lucky…

I still continued to do cabaret and revue whenever possible. For example, I worked with Ron Moody and Hugh Paddick in a revue called *For Adults Only*. This led to an unexpected bonus when I was shopping in Fortnum and Mason.

In the revue I did a lovely number about supermarkets which I had had written for me. This was when supermarkets had first come into the country. In the sketch, I wore a headscarf and had a fag hanging out of my mouth, and came to the checkout with a shopping basket and a huge trolley, both packed high with stuff. The first thing I said was, 'Oh, I just popped in for a loaf,' which got a big laugh. I had this terrible cough – because I smoked in those days, I was able to produce one at will – and as I was coughing, I took a second fag out of my pocket and lit it from the old one. This produced still more coughing, at which I said, 'Oh, it must be the sawdust off the meat counter!'

So I was in Fortnums that Christmas, having bought a load of presents, and as I sat writing a cheque, a chap came up to me and said in his North American accent, 'Excuse me – Miriam Karlin?'

'Yes?'

'I just wanted to tell you I've seen the show and I think you're just wonderful and I just wanted to congratulate you.'

I said, 'Oh, that's terribly sweet of you, thank you so much,' and continued writing my cheque, while he hung about.

He said, 'Actually, I've seen it twice.'

I sort of laughed and said, 'Fabulous.'

Then he left, or I thought he did, but as I went down the stairs I found him waiting for me. It transpired that he had been particularly impressed with the supermarket sketch: 'You know, I was the first person to set up supermarkets in this country.'

I thought, 'He is mad, this creature!' So I humoured him while we walked down the stairs.

He continued, 'I brought my daughters to see your show the second time, and I'd like to give you a present from our store.'

I thought, 'Poor soul, how sweet.'

At the bottom of the stairs he called over one of Fortnum's black-coated gentlemen and said, 'Would you get Miss Karlin one of our gift packages of honey?'

The man reappeared with three amazing pieces of beautiful Italian pottery: each jar contained a different kind of exotic honey. I thanked them hugely, went home and rang my mother.

I said, 'Mummy, the most extraordinary thing has just happened at Fortnums...' and told her the story.

She said, 'Oh well, you know you that was? That was Garfield Weston.'

'Who's he?'

'He's just bought Fortnum and Mason. He's got three daughters.'

'That's right,' I said, 'he said he'd brought them to the theatre.' Well, my mother knew everything – I mean, she knew it all. It was incredible.

Having discovered who he was, of course, I speedily returned to the store. I went to the jewellery department, I went to the fur department. (This was in the days when one could still wear fur.) I never saw him again...

For a long time, the State of Israel was something I had been campaigning for, and I gave talks about Zionism to women's groups because I felt that I was representing everything that my grandfather had worked for.

The first time I went to Israel, I actually stayed on a kibbutz – Kfar Hanassi, one of the largest. I was highly emotional as the plane touched down in Tel Aviv airport, and did all the things that the archetypal Zionist would do, including literally kissing the ground. It was something that all my life I had been hearing about and it had only been in existence for a few years. It was, let's face it, the most socialist country that the world had ever seen. There was no class difference whatsoever. You'd get a taxi and you'd be driven by someone who was studying to be a lawyer, or a head teacher. There was no question about tipping anybody because that would be insulting.

There I was, working on a kibbutz which had actually been started by some people from England and it was so invigorating and exciting. A few years ago, when I saw Mike Leigh's wonderful play *Two Thousand Years* at the National, it was like watching my life unfold before me. They even referred to the same kibbutz, Kfar Hanassi. It was extraordinary. On the kibbutz we would be woken at about five am and taken out in a truck to an apple orchard. We would be cutting off the shoots, pruning, working away till about seven am – a good two-plus hours' work – and then a truck would come to take us back for breakfast. I have never ever enjoyed breakfast as much as those. Huge, wonderful, tasty tomatoes, eggs, cheese: it was fabulous, and we had worked hard so we deserved it.

We went back again and worked for another couple of hours before lunch, and again after a little siesta in the afternoon. It was hard work but it was organised and civilised.

I went back several times throughout the late 1950s and '60s. There was one time I went back and I stayed with the Topols. I remember waking up and hearing Galia, his wife, banging about and I wondered what on earth was going on. Next morning when I went into the bathroom there were a whole load of cockroaches on the floor and she had been busy killing them. That's something you get in hot climates, of course.

On a later visit I was staying in Eilat, which is in the south, and I met some journalists who were going to be doing a tour of all the kibbutzim from Eilat to Tel Aviv. Because I had booked into a hotel in Tel Aviv the next day, they asked me if I wanted to come with them in their jeeps.

I remember the heat in the Negev desert was mind-blowing: we were completely soaked through with sweat and covered in desert sand. Apparently it was regarded as a really good thing to be arriving in Tel Aviv covered in sand, because it meant one had seen the real country. I had seen flowers actually growing in the Negev.

I had all the pro-Israel arguments in those days and believed in them passionately; in fact I remember defeating a motion put forward by Vanessa Redgrave (we are now very friendly and I respect her enormously) at the Equity AGM that we should boycott anything to do with Israel, including Israeli artists. I hadn't written the speech until that morning but my argument was about all those Palestinians living in camps and my belief that if they had been Jews, we wouldn't have allowed that. Jews all over the world would have put their hands in their pockets and made sure they had somewhere to live. I maintained that all those wealthy Arab oil sheikhs kept them in those camps intentionally, as pawns. I still think to a certain extent that is true.

The most important thing about Israel in the beginning was that it was exhilarating to see real socialism in action, which we'd never really seen before. I mean, one had got the NHS in this country and all of that, but to see socialism working as it did there at the time was truly wonderful. That's what people like Vanessa didn't realise. Unfortunately it allowed itself to be prostituted in a way I suppose, because they needed money – and where did they go? Once you start getting into bed with Apartheid South Africa, you're never going to get out.

About this time, the early '60s, Peter Sellers sent me a poem from Israel. Having totally forgotten I had it, I was amazed to come across it recently. I was so pleased that I'd kept it. Clearly Peter was aware that I had been to Israel and had become obsessed with it, so when he found himself in Haifa he thought he'd write to me. He was only half-Jewish: his mother was Jewish and his father was a very silent

Yorkshire man. They couldn't have been more different. His mother was much more of an archetypal Jewish mother than mine.

It is quite a surprising poem, written in the famously atrocious 'McGonagallian' style so beloved by both Peter and Spike Milligan.

> Oh beautiful TEL AVIV, situated in ISRAEL,
> To sing its praise I must not fail,
> The Jewish Government Tourist Office are most kind,
> In aiding the traveller places of Biblical interest to find,
> Also the Zionist organisations and the Jewish youth clubs,
> When visiting them one does not receive snubs.
> The KIBBUTZIM are a delight to behold,
> Full of Jewish SABRA's, some young – some quite old,
> Of course THE WOMEN'S ARMY is a most thrilling sight,
> Hundreds of young Jewish ladies drilling with all their might.
> Ready to defend their country from the rebel hand,
> And to kill any turbaned devil of brown
> Even if his name is Claude.
> David Ben Gurion is an excellent man, I have no hesitation in
>   saying,
> And when released from his PRIME MINISTER's chores,
> He goes straight to the SYNAGOG and starts praying.
> And I think ABDUL NASSER ought to be ashamed of himself,
> For I consider he has acted the part of a silly elf,
> Thinking to invade the Promised Land,
> He should stay where he is, in his Arab sand.
>
> Oh wonderful ISRAEL, I will now conclude my muse,
> Although I hate to, for I love you and your Jews,
> They are a wonderful race, that no one can gainsay,
> And I hope they stay like it – and don't get fey
> Because they start a state without delay,
> It was sometime in 1948, the exact date I cannot say,
> When they politely told the British to...go away.

And when the brave British Tommies left,
They went with good cheer because as they got on the boat
  one said –
'I'm glad I'm fucking off out of 'ere.'

Faithfully Yours,
Sellers McGonagall, Poet and Rabbi

When I first worked with Joan Littlewood in *Fings Ain't Wot They Used T'Be* it was the first time I had experienced a director working with actors to develop character and relationship through improvisation. She rang me up and said, 'Miriam, this is Joan Littlewood here'. I know my heart leapt with excitement. She said, 'I'm sure you don't want to come and work for me in my old theatre, 'cos I know you're a West End actress.'

I had been offered a job taking over from Joan Greenwood in some play or other at £100 per week. This was 1959 and that was a lot of money, so when I rang Ken Carter, my then agent, and said, 'I've been asked to do something with Joan Littlewood', he said, 'They pay nothing.' When I said I thought it was £15 a week, he replied, 'Well don't expect me to pay your Fortnum's bills at Christmas!'

Frank Norman, who wrote *Fings*, had initially sent a few pages to Joan, and she had realised that his rich cockney was so good that a whole show could be made of it. She asked Lionel Bart to compose some songs, and they started work.

We had a longer rehearsal period than I had ever been accustomed to. For the first couple of weeks we just sat around playing poker and getting to know one another, but it was amazing the relationships that grew out of this exercise.

One of the characters was a burglar called Redhot, played by Ted Caddick. Ted and I got on well. There was nothing in the script to say there was any relationship between Redhot and my character, Lil, because my written relationship was with my boyfriend Fred (played by Glynn Edwards) whom Lil married at the end. Joan sent me to a bridal place to get a wedding dress, and I was surprised at how senti-mental she became. She said, 'Oh, I do like white weddings' – which was so unlike the way I thought she'd feel!

For one improvisation she brought loads of props from home. She put them in a couple of suitcases for Redhot to bring on, having done a burglary – a 'screwer' in cockney. She said to us all, 'You have got to pick out something for yourself that you want and then get rid of it as soon as the copper comes in.' We didn't know when the police were going to come, so we were playing cards and handing round tea and when Redhot came in with his cases we all pounced on him. I found a huge silver fruit bowl. When I got it out, she obviously cued the copper, because I was in the middle of saying, 'Oh this is lovely.' So I quickly put this thing underneath me and sat on it like a piss pot. Joan laughed so much that it stayed in the script. It stayed in every night until a friend of mine came round and said, 'Oh Mim, your face when you sat on that bowl, I laughed so much I could die.' Then, of course, I couldn't do it: I'd become self-conscious, so left it out till I could come to it fresh. This taught me a bloody good lesson: never ever congratulate an actor on a specific piece of business or on the way they say a line.

Joan's notes were extraordinary, all of them written on exercise book paper with a red biro. One night, we'd been running in the West End for about three or four months and I got a note from her which said, 'Darling Mim, you're so bleeding marvellous and you're being fucked by that arsehole, Glynn. Tonight I want you to come on wearing something different and enter from a different place!'

They had already called the quarter, so I ran up to the wardrobe and found a different blouse and made an entrance from the opposite side of the stage. Then, so help me, Glynn came on from another completely different part of the stage wearing the most outrageous tie that I had ever seen. We were suddenly listening to each other and we must have sounded different because gradually the rest of the cast listening over the tannoy gathered in the wings to see what we were doing. When we finished the scene I said to Glynn, 'Did you get a note from Joan?'

He said, 'Yes', and showed it to me. It said: 'Darling Glynn you are so wonderful and that cunt Karlin is fucking you up. Wear something different tonight and make a different entrance.'

It worked and she knew it, because we were once again really listening and relating to each other. It had all become so easy that we were on automatic responses.

Encouraged by Joan, I decided to put in some ad-libs in certain places and bought an *Evening Standard* every night so that we could be topical. I remember when the Common Market was first being talked about, opening the paper and saying, ''Ere Fred, what's this then, the Common Market, is that Berwick Street? Is that what they are talking about?' This was probably one of the first times that topical news was used like that. Frank Norman was furious because he really didn't like losing control of his script.

I used to do warm-ups before every show, going through the exercises Ernst Urbach had taught me. Barbara Windsor and Toni Palmer, who were playing the tarts, would be yelling 'My old man's a dustman' and sending me up rotten about it, but I didn't care. I haven't seen Barbara for years except on telly of course and she's become really terrific. Joan recognised her stellar quality all those years ago. I have seen Toni, though. I was able to use a line of hers not so long ago, which I thought terribly funny. She was sent a script by a young director who had been an assistant at Stratford East. It was a massive part for her and was to be done in some fringe theatre. After she had read the script the director phoned her and said, 'Did you read the script?'

'Yeah.'

He said, 'What do you think?'

'Very good. Very good.'

'So, you'll do it then?'

'No.'

He said, 'But you said you liked it?'

'Yes, I think it's very good.'

'Well why don't you want to do it?'

And she said, 'I can't be bothered.'

I was longing to use that line for myself, and was finally able to do so about six months ago when a similar thing happened to me. It was somewhere very, very fringe with a huge great part which would have required six or seven weeks' rehearsal – and we would have been given three, max, because it was a two-hander. I was able to say to my agent, 'I can't be bothered.'

During the run of *Fings* in the West End Lionel Bart phoned me in my dressing room after a matinee and said, 'Oh Mim, I just want to tell you I'm coming in tonight with Judy Garland.' Can you imagine? I went into a catatonic state. I had seen some doctor a few days before and he'd given me pills, though I don't really know what they were for, slimming pills or maybe beta-blockers. Out of sheer panic at the thought of Judy Garland coming, I took one of these. I felt I had to have outside help, but I'd been playing in this show for months and I think I was pretty good in it, so why would I suddenly be in a blinding panic?

When the show started I spotted her, and when I had to sing all I could think about was how could I possibly sing in front of Judy Garland. I forgot about relating to anybody on the stage, the whole performance became about me performing in front of Judy Garland. At the end of the show she came round with Lionel and her husband, whom she called 'Circles' because he had round eyes with circles underneath, and asked us to join them at a party at Douglas Fairbanks Junior's.

I had a pretty awful standby frock to put on and my mother's fur coat, which had been the 'lucky' fur coat, but was now looking pretty naff in comparison to all their glamorous ones. When we got to the party the door was opened by a butler and I could see, out of the corner of my eye, a pile of minks and sables. I handed this thing that looked like a hearth rug to the butler and he put it carefully with the others. Despite my awful performance, Judy was very sweet to me and we talked for some time and she invited me to join them at Les Ambassadeurs, a very posh nightclub, which I had previously frequented with Tony Hawtrey. The whole night was torture for me. There were any number of stars at Douglas Fairbanks' party – Jimmy Stewart was there; all big, big names – but because I was in such a state I didn't recognise anybody. I got home at three or four am.

The next morning, it can't have been more than 9.30am, Lionel Bart phoned me and he said, 'Mim, what was the matter with you last night, I don't know what the hell kind of performance you were giving. Judy didn't say anything did she?'

I said 'Oh please don't go on…don't go on telling me, I know it was horrendous. You should not have told me that she was coming. I know it was ghastly and if only you hadn't *told* me she was coming…'

It took me quite some time to get over it. That was the most horrible night on stage I can remember.

I'm afraid I wasn't quite as star-struck a little later, when I performed in front of Princess Margaret. This was again at Stratford East, in a play by Ted Allen called *Secret of the World*. It was very dramatic and I had a wonderful part in it. One night Princess Margaret came to see it with the recently ennobled Lord Snowdon, and I and John Bury, who played the lead and directed it, were asked to go to meet them in the interval. I knew that the next act had my hugely dramatic part in it, so after we chatted I said, 'I'd better go back now.'

She said, 'You can't start until I've finished, and I've still got this much', and she showed how much scotch she had left in her glass. I still went, though: my preparation was more important than her drink!

I was recently reminded of a wonderful event I used to take part in at this time, when I went to a luncheon to honour Richard Attenborough for his work for theatrical charities. In his speech Dickie mentioned *The Night of a Hundred Stars*, which had started when Noël Coward and Laurence Olivier had got together and decided that they had to find a way to make more money for theatrical charities. They devised a series of variety shows which took place on a Sunday. The chorus line always consisted of people like Joan Sims, Dulcie Gray, Sylvia Syms – all the women who were currently known and working. There are pictures of me with my new slim body being madly enthusiastic, dancing with my two left feet.

These *Nights* went on for years and there was one particular night when Judy Garland was appearing. It was at the time she'd had a lot of publicity for overdoing drugs. The Beatles were also appearing, and I was sitting half on stage, half off, with them. When she came on they started shouting stuff like, 'Oh shut up you druggie', and stuff like that and I kept telling them to 'Sshhh'. I was rather shocked, because although they were great, this was bad behaviour and some of the things they said were quite vicious. I think they were just being silly and they'd had lot to drink themselves.

The *Nights of a Hundred Stars* were terrific. We had a lot of fun but took it terribly seriously, rehearsing like mad, as none of us were professional dancers. The audience paid a lot of money for their tickets, but they got their money's worth – amazing stars, basically anyone who was not working that Sunday, doing unexpected things. For the first time ever I was able to wear black fishnets and be quite pleased with my legs. (Thank you, Dr Goller!)

6

PISS ELEGANT

In which the new slim me became successful, blowing the whistle in
The Rag Trade, *giving up smoking on* TV, *was militant, socialist,
hedonist and addicted to Australia. I appeared on the* Celebrity
Game *with Zsa Zsa Gabor, on platforms with Harold Wilson,
the Anti-Apartheid movement and the Equity Council, worked
with Bing Crosby, Topol and filmed with Laurence Olivier in* The
Entertainer.

I JUST BEGAN TO DO more and more of everything. My new
slim body and face, with its cheekbones looking back at me from the
mirror, were something I'd worked for, like everything I had done,
so I felt I'd earned it and wasn't going to slip back to indulgent food
habits. I didn't want food to stay in my body for any length of time,
and I didn't find the idea of being sick very appealing, so I purged
my body using laxatives. I must have come to some sort of balance
between eating and getting rid of food at some stage because I didn't
become over-thin, and because I worked out and did yoga, my fitness
levels or at least flexibility levels seemed all right. I persuaded myself
that I was healthy because I stuffed quantities of vitamins down
myself (even though they must have gone straight through me), and
after I'd finished *The Diary of Anne Frank* the paranoia seemed to
diminish, so I felt good.

I have never had a personal agenda for the pursuit of work. If I had I
would probably have got further in the career. I just wanted to enjoy

myself and develop all my other interests. If there is an opposite, the antithesis, of a networker, I am that person – a de-networker, an anti-networker – and if there was anybody important in the offing work-wise or romance-wise I ran a mile. If I discovered that a chap was wildly wealthy, I would disappear because I wouldn't want him to think I was only after him for his money, which had been my experience with Edgar Lustgarten. So instead I began to pick up stray dogs and chaps who were broke and would take them for a meal, pour the *vino* and look after them, wanting to be in control. This is probably the reason I never married actually, because when I was considering it, I don't think I could have been subservient.

There is a contradiction, though, because I did admire a few distinguished men – mind you, only because I liked their politics. I really admired Harold Wilson, for example, who became a friend. I thought he was terrific. I will always think of Tony Benn as an amazing, iconic figure and also, luckily enough, a friend. I suppose that talent is the ultimate inspiration to me. When I had affairs with fellow actors, if I then saw them on the stage being bad– I'm sorry, that was the end of it. (I have also always said that I would never go to bed with a Tory!)

My political involvement became all-encompassing during the 1960s and '70s: this was the period that I began to really take part and speak publicly on platforms of all kinds. My energies were completely divided between my work commitments and campaigning for Equity, the Anti-Apartheid movement, Israel and the Labour Party.

Having come back from a holiday in Israel very brown, seriously chocolate-coloured, I was asked to do a 'Bing Crosby Special'. On the first day of rehearsal all the people who were involved in sketches were called and we sat around a large table and read the script. Shirley Bassey was going to be in the show, but as she was only singing she didn't have to come to this rehearsal. The well-known casting director Rose Tobias Shaw was there, and she told me later that Bing Crosby's manager – who, stereotypically, was smoking a cigar – sat listening to the reading and looking at me, before turning to Rose and saying, 'Shirley Bassey looks a little Jewish, doesn't she?' I told Shirley about this and she thought it was hugely funny. From then on, I used to send her little telegrams and sign them 'From your black friend' and she would write to me as 'your kosher friend'.

This show was the first time I had worked with an important American star. However, I was soon working with quite a number of big American names, as my agent at the time, Michael Sullivan, was part of the Grade organisation. Every time they brought over some big American star, one of their clients got to work with them.

I had recently come out of *Fings Ain't Wot They Used T'Be* so they wanted me to sing the title song with Bing. Lionel Bart had to rewrite some of the lyrics, because it wasn't suitable in those days to talk on television about 'ponces killing lazy whores', a line from the original lyrics. So when he wrote some new lyrics I had to learn them. Bing Crosby, however, had everything written on boards: he did not learn one line of anything he said, or any of the lyrics. I was staggered, rather shocked actually. I was briefly disillusioned with big stars and felt much more of a pro, but he was used to doing this. It was what all American stars did, I later realised.

The programme that would make me 'known', *The Rag Trade*, started in 1960. It was written by Ronald Wolfe and Ronald Chesney – the 'two Ronnies', before Messrs Barker and Corbett came along. I am often asked whether it was more than a coincidence that I was cast as a militant in *The Rag Trade*. I didn't realise the importance it had to women until much later when many women trade unionists and other women told me that I had been their role model. I thought I was just being rather a tiresome person blowing a whistle. However, the success of the show did give me access to some politicians like Harold Wilson.

I remember bumping into Denis Norden in Harley Street and he was pleased that I was going to do *The Rag Trade*. He and Frank Muir were tops at the BBC at the time, so it was nice to get this encouragement. The director of the show was Denis Main Wilson, who had an amazing capacity for picking the right people. He managed to get the chemistry right in every show he was connected with, and his instinct was quite brilliant.

We had a studio audience. It was a weekly turnaround which seemed very quick in those days, because I had been used to doing plays on television when one rehearsed for three or four weeks. I had done one-offs with comedians – Tommy Cooper and people like that – but this was the first time I was engaged to do a series.

The Rag Trade was recorded when I was living in Harley Street and I didn't have a telly, and I'd never watched myself. There was one week when I thought it was quite good, so I asked Mrs Price the caretaker, who lived in the basement, if I could come down and watch her TV. She said, 'Oh, would you, Miss K?' That would be lovely.'

What I hadn't known was that when *The Rag Trade* was on, all the Harley Street caretakers foregathered downstairs in Number 113 to see 'her lady' on the box. There they all were, with beers and snacks, and they all stood up, in a crazy sort of deferential way, when I came in, looking like shit, not expecting anyone apart from Mrs Price. When it started I swore and yelled at myself, the faces I pulled, the way I moved, but worst of all the way I looked. I am sure I absolutely ruined their evening!

Having seen myself, I decided I had to be totally different. So for the first two days, I quite evidently *was* different. One of the Ronnies came up to me and said, 'Are you all right, Mim?'

'Yes, why?'

'Well, you seem very quiet this week.'

I said, 'Well, I saw the last show and I was horrified.'

He told Denis Main Wilson who came over and, accentuating every stress by banging his fist on the table and stamping his foot (as was his wont), he said, 'We've decided – you must never watch yourself again.' The very things I hated about what I was doing were the things the audience loved!

Although it was a sitcom, I suppose I thought of it as a drama, simply because the people I was working with, the backbone of the show – Peter Jones and Sheila Hancock, in particular – were real actors. I'd known Sheila a bit before but I had known Peter for much longer and we got on very well. We were huge friends and remained so until his death a few years ago. I still miss him.

That was the interesting thing about it for me, the experience of being in a company. It was only when I got to the second production at the RSC almost 20 years later that I fully realised the value of a company, in that when one has established a relationship with a character in one play, there are no boundaries: one doesn't have to keep breaking down barriers and forming new connections in the next production. Of course, it was the same episode to episode in *The Rag Trade*.

The audience adored Esma Cannon's character 'little Lil'. Esma always played bizarre little old ladies in films as well as TV, but in reality she was the very opposite of that. She was about four feet something and used to come to rehearsals in a mink coat down to her ankles, a matching mink hat, and a large handbag filled with all her jewellery. Although I suspect she was pretty well off – better off than the rest of us, at any rate – she was a shrewd little businesswoman, and was apparently the first in the cast to quibble about her salary.

My relationship with Peter Jones, the boss, was meant to be one of antagonism – a militant shop steward against the Boss. Because we liked one another, we built up a love/hate relationship safely and strongly. The moment the boss asked us to do something additional, my shop steward character Paddy would say, 'Wait. I have to call a meeting', and I'd blow the whistle and shout 'Everybody out' and call a strike. Of course I was very much into the trade union movement at the time – not only because Dad had written books on the Factories Act and trade union law (sometimes I would quote from them on the show and Dad would get excited) – but also because I was becoming increasingly involved in the Labour Party.

It is really difficult to do a performance for an audience and a camera. I don't think I ever learned to do it properly. We had a warm-up comedian first while we got ready; then, if anything went wrong, then the warm-up comedian would come along and explain to the audience what was happening.

I think a lot of the skill rested with the director knowing exactly when to cut, how to cut and whether to stay on the face or not and let the laugh happen. I think a director of comedy has to be rather like a comedian themselves in that they know the 'graph of the laugh' and when it is going down, you cut. We did play to the audience more than we would have done in a play for television, but then as several of us had done a lot of comedy, I think that we were well aware that the relationship with the audience was most important.

I was still doing *Fings*, and Sheila was in *Make Me an Offer*: on Saturdays we both had matinees. Around midday one Saturday, during the *Rag Trade* rehearsals, I wandered into the kitchen attached to the rehearsal room to take a pep pill surreptitiously, only to find Sheila, standing at the sink, doing exactly the same thing! We fell about, and from then on we went through a ritualistic routine every Sunday, when we recorded the show. The routine had three ingredients: champagne, which I brought in a 'cool bag'; a bubble bath (all the dressing rooms had baths in those days); and a half or a whole pep-up pill. Sheila has mentioned in her book that I was the instigator – she would ask what the 'recipe' was for each Sunday, and she followed me religiously. Unfortunately, I don't think I ever got the mixture right: I was never happy with my performance. I always thought Sheila was great, though.

When I embarked on *The Rag Trade*, I never envisaged that I would so quickly become associated with a catchphrase – 'Everybody out!' People would shout this out in the street when they saw me. Then there was that bleeding whistle. It got so bad that at one point

I moaned to Denis and the Ronnies that I was sick and tired of blowing the whistle. It was pointed out to me, however, that my sole *raison d'être* as a shop steward was to do just that. Even the Queen seemed to have caught the habit. I was introduced to her in Glasgow at a Royal Variety Performance and she actually said, 'Where's your whistle?'

I looked down at my very low-cut dress and said, 'Not on me, Ma'am.'

I don't mean to sound ungrateful; I simply hadn't anticipated what would ensue when one was tied to a successful series. When *The Rag Trade* was brought back after a 15-year interval, Sheila (wisely) didn't want to do it any more, and Diane Langton came in. She used to sit in the same place as Sheila in the workroom and we became great mates too. She was very much given to putting on weight and was neurotic about it. In fact, she was neurotic, period – very much of a hypochondriac. One day when she was sitting opposite me she leant across and said, 'I've got a lump! I've got a lump! Look, look, look, look, look!', pointing at her neck. I said, 'It's the shit rising.' That gave us a jolly good giggle.

One had heard how brilliant she was in *A Chorus Line*, the hit musical of the time, but she often didn't appear because of nerves. I said I wouldn't tell her when I was going to see it, but booked a Saturday matinee. We were rehearsing on the Saturday morning and I didn't tell her I was coming. I simply said, 'See you tomorrow.'

I had arranged with a friend from Leicester that we would go together. As soon as we were in our seats we heard, 'Unfortunately, Diane Langton is indisposed…' I was furious. The next day, recording day, I leant across and said, 'Where were you yesterday?' She looked at me and said, 'You weren't there? O God, I was in Regent Street', and she gave me a whole load of crap about being stuck in traffic in Regent Street and when she had got to the theatre they said it was too late because they had gone past the half and the understudy was ready.

I adored her and she should have been a huge, huge star because her voice is fantastic. The reason that she hasn't become a big star is that people were frightened of employing her, which is a great pity. She had so much more talent than quite a few I will not name!

I was going to say that I don't think a great deal of talent goes to the grave unrecognised, but that is bollocks. A hell of a lot of brilliant talent goes to ashes without ever being recognised and it is a great pity. It is a question about being in the right place at the right time and you are either fortunate or you are not. I don't want to sound in any way envious of those people who have got to the top, and as far as the general public is concerned, I suppose they think I have. I don't think so. I perceive myself as a working actor who is fortunate to have worked quite a lot, probably more than quite a few people of my age. On the other hand, it is my perception that I haven't done as much as I could.

I don't think I am really terribly good in movies – much better on stage. Theatre would be difficult now because of my physical condition, though sitting-down or lying-down parts would be fine! The best thing about theatre and of course a studio audience is the unpredictability and immediacy of the response, being able to make an audience laugh or cry at will. *The Rag Trade* had that unpredictability.

I didn't realise it was going to be such a huge success because as far as I was concerned it was just another part. When we first did it in black and white we had to learn about the trade and we went to several rag trade factories but I never did learn how to work the machines properly. Every time there was a break in filming I would scream for help with my needle threading.

We didn't feel that we were doing anything unusual or that the programme was doing anything new from a working class perspective because there had already been a film – *I'm All Right Jack* – with Peter Sellers, and I was playing the female equivalent of Peter's character. This was particularly relevant at the time because, let's face it (and one can only say it in retrospect), trade unions had gone a bit too far. One wouldn't admit it at the time.

People did, however, have a fairly satirical attitude towards the sanctimoniousness of some union members, and I still cherish a marvellous notice that was reprinted in a paper at the time:

> When 'Music While You Work' is being played, Brothers are requested not to leave their benches to do the twist, as it causes considerable interference to fellow Brothers who are conscientiously playing Bingo.

I suppose it was because of *The Rag Trade* that I was cast in the film version of *The Entertainer*, although I had also worked in revue with Ronnie Cass, the musical director on the film. I played this chorus girl who was also a shop steward. There were several things that were fascinating about doing the movie. First of all was meeting Larry Olivier.

We were shooting it up in Morecambe at The Winter Gardens, the old derelict theatre, and on my first day I came into the theatre and he was on the stage so I just sat in the auditorium and watched. He was doing one of his numbers and when he saw me – and I couldn't quite get over this! – he actually came down from the stage, came over to me and said, 'Hello, nice to meet you. Now tell me, do you think it's a good idea for me to bring the mic on when I sing or should the mic come up?'

I was so staggered that he should be asking my advice I said that being the character that he was, he should bring the microphone on with him. And that's what he actually did. I was very flattered.

We didn't really rehearse that much, but Tony Richardson, whose first film this was, was fortunate enough to have the best camera and lighting man in the business, and of course Olivier knew quite a lot about movie-making. Tony used to say, 'What are we going to do today? How are we going to do this today?'

Sometimes he would suggest that maybe Larry should be upstairs and Larry would point out that from the continuity point of view it wouldn't work because he should be downstairs.

One night Tony decided he wanted me to do a number, and it was decided I should sing 'Put Me Amongst the Girls'. I sang the number while the old boy was dying offstage. They told me to keep going so I had to keep on reprising the number.

It turned out to be rather a marvellous film, based on a bloody good play, of course. A lot of interesting things happened during the course of doing it. This was at the start of Olivier's relationship with Joan Plowright. Alan Bates was in the movie, and every evening around about five o'clock, Larry would come to me and say, 'Dinner tonight. Eight o'clock, at the hotel.' The first time I was asked I was so thrilled. He would also go to Alan Bates and invite him too.

We were all staying in one hotel; Larry and Joan were staying in another. We had this dinner arrangement for a couple of weeks. We would go back, get showered and changed, and Alan and I would be terrified in case we were seen by Brenda De Banzie who played Larry's wife. Larry loathed her, wonderful actor that she was. Every night at dinner, after Larry had had two large scotches, he would say, 'Brenda De Banzie is my idea of an *ordinary* woman.' She was known as Bingo Da Bongo and would have been furious if she had known that we were having dinner with Larry and she hadn't been invited. Alan or I would go downstairs in our hotel and see if the coast was clear and we'd creep out, because otherwise she would ask where we were going. She was really strange – quite a plain woman, but thought of herself as being beautiful. If one went to rushes at lunchtime, she would say, 'Did you go to rushes? Tell me, did I look too pretty?'

'No Brenda, you looked right…right for the character.'

'You know they have such trouble trying to make me not look pretty.' Extraordinary to have that delusion.

What neither Alan nor I realised at the time was that we were the cover, and we only found out when we got back to London. The whole place went up because the newspapers had got hold of the fact that Larry and Joan were now an item. It was terrible, because Vivien was still married to him at the time. Then there was the divorce, and Joan and Larry decided not to see one another for a year to see if they would both feel the same way after some distance, which of course they did.

I met Vivien Leigh a long time before all of this on one occasion at the theatre. She was so beautiful, and I thought a bloody fine actor. I remember going to the first night of *Streetcar Named Desire*, directed by Larry, and she was absolutely wonderful. Funnily enough, someone who sent me love the other day, which I thought was very sweet, was Renée Asherson, who is now ninety-one and was also amazing as Stella in that production. I'll never forget it.

Later I wrote to Larry and Joan after seeing them both perform in *Saturday, Sunday, Monday*. He replied in his lovely way, 'Thank you so much, darling, for making us so happy.'

Harold Macmillan was in power at the time of *The Rag Trade*, but there was a general tide turning towards Labour. I've always rather despised people who couldn't see the difference between themselves and the role they were playing but here I was in that position myself, and because of playing this militant shop steward, I was perceived to be an activist and it was through that that I got invited to a Labour Party meeting. At one of those meetings I met Harold Wilson. He looked at me as if I was an old friend. I'm sure it was because of knowing me from the telly, and I suppose my familiarity with him came from the same thing. Up until Wilson, there hadn't been anybody who I thought was a truly fine potential socialist Prime Minister – that is, since Attlee.

It wasn't long before I got involved in actively campaigning for the Labour Party, and was called by Transport House and asked to speak. The subject was why I was involved with the Labour Party and what I thought Labour could do for the country. I wasn't yet a member, even though I was committed to it. I made the speech, which went well, but then I was asked to speak again, and the thought of writing another speech filled me with horror. So I phoned Dad:

'Hey, do you think that I could use the same speech I gave last week?'

He was surprised that I should even ask such a question and said, 'Of course – what do you think all those MPs do? They make the same speech over and over again. They do it in the house, then on radio, on television, it's constant repetition. Of course you can do it.'

Up to this point, 1964, I had never had a television set in my home and was rather snobbish about it. I always said I had better things to do with my time. However, it was election time, so I hired a TV set from 'Multibroadcast' (which later became 'Radio Rentals' and is now 'Boxclever') just for the night. I'm still renting! I watched the election with some friends and some *vino*. When Harold won, there was huge excitement, one felt it was the dawning of a new era, rather in the same way as people felt in 1997.

The 1964 election brought in the nearest thing we have ever had to a Socialist cabinet, but unfortunately it only lasted a short while. There were people like Michael Foot, Tony Benn, Barbara Castle and of course Jenny Lee (widow of Aneurin Bevan – father of the Welfare State), who became the first Arts Minister. A great liberalisation began: homosexuality was legalised, hanging and stage censorship abolished and Britain heralded the start of the 'classless society'. There was great turmoil with the Grosvenor Square protests, and Enoch Powell's 'Rivers of blood' speech hit the headlines.

I had a pretty extraordinary relationship with Harold Wilson, and did find him rather attractive. He had that wonderful way with him: he made you feel as if you were the only person in the world, even though the room was crowded. It's a rare quality, and not surprisingly, I believe Bill Clinton has it too. My friendship with Harold lasted throughout his two terms in office, from 1964 right up to 1976.

By 1964 *The Rag Trade* had become huge in Australia, and I was asked to go to take part in a revue called *Is Australia Really Necessary?* I had some really funny stuff to do in it, my best number being Princess Anne opening the Sydney Opera House – at the time the Opera House was seen rather like the Millennium Dome: the talk was that it would never happen. So I did a piece about how Princess Anne might open it in 1984, and I dressed like the Queen. Because I had been campaigning for Harold Wilson I got involved in Australian politics while I was there and got to know various leaders of the Labor Party. In Melbourne I remember going to a late-night sitting at Parliament House which was fun. At that time the ghastly Sir Robert Menzies was still in power. The way they spoke to each other was quite hilarious, very informal and not at all like our House of Commons. In the 1970s the Labor Prime Minister Gough Whitlam wrote to me after he had been elected:

> It was not, for our opponents, quite a case of 'Everybody out', but at least enough went out to allow us to come in with a real mandate for change and renewal.
>
> I trust you will find your hope for a transformed Australia justified on your next visit here.

Through my connections with the Labor Party in Australia I discovered that they had had a break-away group, called the Independent Labor Party, who split the Labor vote totally. This was the reason that Menzies' Liberal Party (the equivalent of our Tory Party) stayed in power for twenty years. I was frightened when I heard about it, and when I came back to England I wrote to Harold Wilson and told him about my fears, suggesting that it could happen here. He wrote back:

> It was most encouraging and reassuring to have your letter and particularly its comments on the Australian election in relation to the situation here.

However, it is a difficult time and I should very much appreciate hearing from you again with your comments on the issues on which you were going to write before the results in the by-elections were known. I would greatly value this, since I know your political judgement is good.

Of course, my fears proved to be valid, because in 1981 the so-called 'Gang of Four' – Shirley Williams, Roy Jenkins, David Owen and Bill Rodgers – broke away from the Labour Party to form the SDP.

During the 1970 election there was a newspaper strike. (Actually, it's quite a good thing to happen before an election because it means you can't be fucked up by newspaper headings.) I was rung up by Transport House and they asked if I would address a meeting that night – the penultimate night before the election – at Walthamstow Town Hall. Harold was supposed to be giving the speech, but was meeting union representatives to deal with the strike. (These meetings were always referred to as 'beer and sandwiches at Number 10'.) I had by now given quite a few speeches for them so I wasn't unduly panicking and had prepared what I was saying.

Fortunately, my speech was very well received, and every time I saw Harold Wilson afterwards, he'd say to people, 'Oh do you know Miriam? She's my understudy.' He knew everything I'd said in that speech because when we were talking he'd say 'And when you told them about this…' I was staggered.

However, Harold lost this election, and there was a big wake to which I was invited. Everyone got pissed. I said to Harold, 'Look, you've had a flop, it's like first night, you've got to go on giving performances, you've just got to get on with it. You've just got to win the next one.'

All the polls had said that Labour would get in and of course Harold thought they would win, or he wouldn't have called the election. They voted *en masse* for Heath. It was pretty bloody disastrous, because he was already prepared to bring in draconian, anti-union laws. This was going to challenge my political Labour Party views about the relationship with the unions and Equity's union intentions.

To think that Harold ended his days with Alzheimer's – that was so frightening, because he had a memory that was astronomical, there was nothing he forgot. I can't bear to imagine him wandering around the House of Lords not knowing where he was, really. The people there used to take pity on him and humour him. It's a cruel world, isn't it?

As a trade unionist myself, I felt that Heath extracted some teeth; when Thatcher got in, she took out the lot – molars and all! When Callaghan was PM, we had the 60th anniversary of women getting the vote, and there was a celebration performance at the Palladium. *The Rag Trade* boys wrote a sketch for me to do which was pretty derogatory about Thatcher, who happened to be in the audience. (She was already known by the general public as 'Thatcher the milk snatcher', because as Education Secretary under Heath she had cut the free milk children got at primary school.)

The next day I went to a party at Number 10, and she was there too. We nearly bumped into one another, and you have never seen two pairs of eyes looking at one another with such total frigidity. I saw Marcia Falkender and said, 'What's she doing here?'

'We have to have one-third them to two-thirds of us.'

I suppose I had become what we would call nowadays a celebrity because I was asked to be on shows as myself. I met Zsa Zsa Gabor on a game show called the *Celebrity Game*. It was sort of an early reality show and there were about nine or ten people who were placed in three rows and asked questions. One week Tommy Trinder was on with me, and Zsa Zsa Gabor was supposed to be on as well. We were there on time but she hadn't turned up: the reason was, they had sent an ordinary car for her and she wanted a Rolls Royce. Everybody was getting pretty pissed off and Tommy Trinder had to keep the audience entertained, which of course came naturally to him.

She finally turned up, but then she had to go off and have her hair done. The poor audience were kept waiting for nearly two hours. When it came to play the 'Celebrity Game', I was asked some question about dangerous meat. Suddenly Zsa Zsa Gabor, sitting just below me, made some comment out of turn. I was starting to speak and she took out her powder compact and, very busily started powdering her nose. The camera went straight to her, so I said, 'Camera…camera, come to me please, I'm very lovely and I was speaking. So stop flitting to that one down there.'

Everybody behind the scenes went apeshit because they'd never seen anything like it, and they couldn't cut it out because it was live. The next day I was doing my shopping at Church Street market just off Edgware Road and all the market people said stuff to me about it – 'Ohh I thought you was going to put your cigarette ash down her back' (because of course in those days you could smoke on TV), and they were saying 'Ooh, Zsa Zsa Gabor – hate her.' There was quite a contrast with my persona at the time which was 'piss elegant' and her, a 'fluffy bunny' type.

I had somehow managed to save a bit of money, enough to buy my first place, rather than renting. I remember opening an account at Liberty's because I wanted a Georgian dressing table. I don't know why, but I had to have one and I had looked everywhere in the Kings Road and all the second-hand shops. At that time Liberty's had a second-hand department and I came across the very thing, and I just had to have it. It was £120. That was a lot of money to me then, but I bought it and they asked me if I wanted to open an account, which of course I did. I'm ashamed of this now but I fancied a crocodile handbag and so I bought one and had a pair of crocodile shoes made to match. So that is a kind of 'piss elegance', but I just thought that was how one had to live.

By now I had become independent and because I had loads of friends, used to have dinner parties, rather good ones, and people knew they could drop in on a Sunday morning for drinks. I had a special drinks party on Christmas Day, and sent Christmas cards to everybody and wrote inside 'Champers as usual, midday.' I'd get crates of champagne and bits and pieces to nibble. Over the years there were a number of people whose turkeys were ruined on Christmas day because they'd stayed too long at my place and got pissed. This particular year I had just moved to Hamilton Terrace, so not only was it the usual champers, but they would see my fantastic new pad as well.

On Christmas Eve I got a phone call from John Jacobs at the BBC to say that a dear friend of mine, Vida Hope, who had been rehearsing for two weeks with him in a play, had been killed in a car crash and would I take over, where was I going to be and could he bring over the script? I told him I was going to be at the hairdresser, so he brought the script there and I read it. It was a smashing part but how the hell was I going to do it in the time?

The play was *Stray Cats and Empty Bottles* by Bernard Kops, with music specially written by Larry Adler. It was with Irene Worth, James Booth and Ronny Fraser (the 'British' Ronald Fraser) and the part that Vida had played was enormous. My agent had the BBC over the proverbial barrel in that, of course, at this late stage they had to have me, so he could ask quite a lot of money. (This actually went against me in the final analysis, because they didn't employ me for a few plays afterwards as I was too bloody expensive.)

John said that on Christmas Day they would come round and Larry would teach me the music and he'd show me the moves. I didn't know how many people were coming to have champers, because I didn't RSVP or anything, so when people arrived I told them I was afraid that they were going to have to leave by about 2.30pm and told them what was happening. I did manage to get rid of most people, but there was a load of debris around still and when John Jacobs and

Larry Adler arrived I still had my beautiful old square piano so he played on that amongst the rubble of the party. I had to open the play singing a kind of Brechtian song, in close up, which was frightening. John Jacobs promised me that if I made the slightest mistake he would stop and retake, and I could do as many retakes as I wanted, and I suppose that because I had that safety net I didn't need any retakes and managed to learn it somehow and do it. The part was one of a hag: the whole cast played down-and-outers, which after the Christmas drinks party and the subsequent dramas, I felt quite able to do. Quite a dramatic Christmas.

I was delighted when the director Charles Marowitz asked me to play three different types of desperate American female in the Saul Bellow 'Trilogy'. This was a two-hander, with just Harry Towb and me. However, I then encountered a huge problem with one of the characters. The first one was a young Jewish New Yorker, desperate to get married to the chap I was taking home to introduce to my parents on a Friday night. He was obviously not keen to meet them and managed to get the car stuck and have problems with the jack. It was called *Out from Under*. No difficulty with that character for me.

The second one was fascinating: *Orange Soufflé*. She was a Midwestern whore who serviced a captain of industry, a very old bloke who used to visit her regularly every week. This particular week she decided she wanted him to marry her and make her a respectable woman, so was going to show off her expertise and cook an orange soufflé. I actually made an orange soufflé during the performance – I am never happier on stage than when I'm doing some business. He just kept sitting there waiting for the usual, probably a blow job. When he left without the requisite proposal, I was so furious that I chucked the soufflé after him.

The third one was a play called *The Wen* (a kind of mole). This is one that I should have been able to do easily but somehow I just couldn't get hold of her. This was someone much, much older, a typical Jewish mama from Miami. She was meeting someone who had become a famous nuclear physicist. They had been kids together at school, and he had a kind of fantasy about her, which had built up in his imagination, because when they were young he had once seen this wen she had in her nether regions. It had become a fixation, and although he had had world recognition for his work, he just had to see it again. A really interesting story, and it all took place during a hurricane in Miami.

It was driving me insane that I just couldn't inhabit this character. We were getting towards production week and I remember my mother phoning me and saying, 'You know Auntie Annie's over here.' She had been living in Miami, but had come to London because she had sisters living here and her husband Maurice, my mother's younger brother, had recently died. 'Come over and see her.'

I said, 'Oh I can't, I've got a technical rehearsal tomorrow, I have no time.'

'Please, just for half an hour.'

Well, when I saw Auntie Annie whom I hadn't seen for a number of years, it was a revelation. I watched her movements. She sat in such a way that I could not only see she had elastic kneepads on her knees, but also the way she put one hand under the opposite armpit. Suddenly everything clicked into place, because everything about her was the character I was trying to find. It's kind of heartless in a way that actors, like writers, use their friends and family in this way. It turned out that this performance was the best of the three. Sometimes a certain prop can give you the access to the character (the proverbial 'green umbrella'), but this time it was Auntie Annie and I could develop and internalise the pain she had, but also use it for comic effect.

Looking back I think my Auntie Nora must have had peripheral neuropathy, which is what I have now, because she used to say: 'You know I can't stand – me legs!'

Top: Miriam Samuels, as I was then, as a baby (*left*) and a very small child (*right*).

Left: My great-grandfather Elias Karlin (*above*), pictured in 1925, the year I was born. He and my grandfather Herman Aronowitz (*below*) – shown at the same sitting – were staying at the King David Hotel in Palestine when they got the telegram announcing my birth.

Right: With my mother, Celine Samuels née Aronowitz.

I

II

All photographs in author's collection

Opposite, top: Antwerp, 1927. My baby cousin Eddy, my mother's sister Molly, Dad (Harry Samuels), Ma, me, Molly's husband Uncle Sol, Grandpa, my brother Michael and my mother's younger brother Uncle Maurice. Molly, Sol and Eddy would die in the Holocaust.

Opposite, middle: Michael, me, Ma, Dad, during an apparent beret-craze. (What is my mother trying to do to my father's ear?)

Opposite, bottom: Another seaside snap. Me, Grandpa, Dad, Ma, Grandma, Michael.

Top: Warwick House school. Mr Dallas the Headmaster is in the middle; I'm just behind his right shoulder. Famous old boys include Geoffrey Finsberg (on the right, second row down), who was in Mrs Thatcher's Government, and Arthur Boyars (on my right), poet and publisher.

Bottom: Two portraits from my late teens. (I suppose I ought to apologise for the furs on the right.)

III

Elm Croft - Elm Grove
Berkhamsted - Herts
5th September 1945

The Autorities of the
Bergen Belsen Camp.

Dear Sirs,

I have read in the News Chronicel that in
the Belsen Camp the inmates men, women
and childeren of many Nationalities are
being now restored to health.

Pray be so kind to inquire if by good
chance there is among them a Dutch family
by name of Person. In June 1944 I have
been told by the Dutch Governement in
London that they were deported from Wester-
bork, Holland, to Bergen Belsen.

I am the unhappy father who searches for his childeren.

Yours very sincerely
H. Aronowitz

Sal Person, age 52/53
Malwine Person-Aronowitz, age 45
Lena Person, age 20
Eddy Person, age 16

IV

Opposite: A page from my grandfather Herman Aronowitz's letter to the authorities at Belsen, enquiring about the fate of his daughter and son-in-law and their two children (Auntie Molly, Uncle Sol, and my cousins Leni and Eddy).

Above: In Israel in the early 1960s, at the forest planted in memory of my grandfather.

V

Author's collection

Photographer unknown

Author's collection

Top, left: Michael's daughter Vivien, Dad, me, Michael, Ma, in the early 1950s. (Since she is not in it, I imagine the picture was taken by Michael's wife Hilary.)

Top, right: An early professional portrait (possibly my *Spotlight* picture).

Bottom: With Reggie Smith and Olivia Manning (the *Fortunes of War* novelist) in a pub.

Opposite, top: A triptych from *Women of Twilight*. *Left*, with Mary Matthews and June Whitfield on the boat train for the Queen Mary; *middle*, an artist's impression of me as Olga; and *right*, a photograph from the production.

Opposite, bottom: In *Listen to the Wind* (aka 'Hark, Hark, the Fart') as the Mermaid from Maida Vale. My female supporter is Mavis Sage, who would later spatter me with a *macedoine* of vegetables. The boy is Robert Palmer; they were both from the Corona School for stage children.

VI

VII

Author's collection

Houston Rogers / V&A Images / Victoria and Albert Museum

Photograph by J Vickers

Photograph by J Vickers

Top: Nicely varied roles from the revue *For Adults Only* – *left*, my impression of Kim Novak; *right*, the chain-smoking supermarket shopper who 'only came in for a loaf'.

Bottom: From *Fings Ain't Wot They Used T'Be*. *Left:* In the wedding dress that made Joan Littlewood sentimental. *Right:* In rehearsal with Paddy Joyce, Glynn Edwards and Ted Caddick.

Opposite, top: Singing with Bing Crosby on his UK special. I'm looking at Bing; he's looking at the autocue.

Opposite, bottom: *The Rag Trade* – enough said. Sheila Hancock, Reg Varney, Peter Jones, me, Esma Cannon. (That's Wanda Ventham laughing her head off at the back.)

Photographer unknown (Associated-Rediffusion Ltd)

@ BBC Photograph Library

IX

Top: From one of the *Nights of a Hundred Stars* – Susan Hampshire, Anna Massey, me, Hayley Mills, Barbara Windsor.

Bottom, left: With Harry Towb in the middle play of the Saul Bellow trilogy, *Orange Soufflé*.

Bottom, right: With Topol in *Fiddler on the Roof.*

Opposite, top: In the Australian TV programme *The Mavis Bramston Show*. There's Ron Frazer ('the Australian Ronnie Frazer'), Barry Creyton, Gordon Chater, me, and guest star Barry Humphries – in drag, of course.

Opposite, bottom: Some of the paintings I had in my old flat. The portrait of me is by June Mendoza.

X

XI

@ Mirrorpix

Photographer unknown

Photographer unknown (Westminster Press)

Top: With Clive Dunn and Harry Fowler, on an anti-Vietnam War protest outside the American Embassy in Grosvenor Square, 1972.

Bottom: Two ceremonies at Buckingham Palace – *left*, with my parents when my father got his OBE; *right*, with Wendy Hiller some 15 years later. (She was getting her DBE; I was a humble OBE.)

Opposite, above: In *A Clockwork Orange*, about to meet an unpleasant end from Malcolm McDowell as Alex. Operating the camera on the extreme left is Stanley Kubrick himself.

Opposite, below: Some stage roles. *Clockwise from left:* Two portraits of *Liselotte* – young and old; with David Stoll in *The Bed Before Yesterday*; as *The Witch of Edmonton*, for the RSC; as Martha in *Who's Afraid of Virginia Woolf?*, with Bernard Horsfall.

Photographer unknown

Photograph by Ray Abbott

Author's collection

Author's collection

Author's collection

Opposite, top: The cast of *Torch Song Trilogy*. I am next to Tony Sher in the middle.

Opposite, bottom: With Peggy Ashcroft at the first night of the Women's Playhouse Trust production at the Royal Court.

Top: With Paul Barber and Neil Kinnock. The Kinnocks had seen our play *Not Fade Away*, by Barrie Keefe, at Stratford East: here we are in the bar afterwards.

Bottom, left: With Tony Benn at the Shaw Theatre, after one of his talks.

Bottom, right: My brother Michael, at his doctorate ceremony in 2006.

Author's collection

Photograph by Nick Wall (Ugly Duckling Films)

Top: With Glenys Kinnock at my eightieth birthday party. The party's instigator, theatre producer David Pugh, can be seen lurking at the back.

Bottom: A still from the film *Flashbacks of a Fool*, starring Daniel Craig. Here I am showing off my state of the art teeth (or tooth?) from 'Fangs FX'.

Then I worked with Jerome Robbins. Extraordinary genius of a man! I was asked to play Golde in *Fiddler on the Roof* opposite Chaim Topol (better known simply as Topol). Actually it's funny, because I think I was the only person in this country who already knew Topol: I had met him in Israel on one of my trips in the early 60s. Then he had come to see me during the Saul Bellow plays which were done in 1966 – I remember it was 1966 because that's when we won the World Cup and Israelis, being football-mad, came over in droves to see their team play. Topol had come and visited me in my dressing room after the show and we chatted about this and that. Six months later he rang me up because he was in London and having heard his voice I immediately knew what he was here for. I said, 'You're here for *Fiddler on the Roof.*' He was, and he already knew I had been cast to play his wife.

We started rehearsing and they'd sent over an assistant director who had worked on the original Broadway production, which had been on for four years and was still running. This assistant director's brief was to mount an identical production.

We'd rehearsed for about two weeks and I was getting more and more depressed, because I was being told that on a certain line I had to do this and on another, that. So at the start of one rehearsal, when I'd made up my mind I was going to leave, I went to this assistant and said, 'Look I'm terribly sorry but I can't work in this way, I have to find my own way. I can't be told to sit down at a certain place, stand up at a certain place, clap my hands at a certain place, I can't do this. I'm sorry, I have to find it myself.'

He said, 'Please, listen, I am here to do an exact copy of Broadway. Wait till Jerry comes, and he'll probably change the whole thing. Don't worry, please stick with it.'

So I stuck with it, and then Jerry Robbins arrived, that amazing little man. He hadn't even seen his own production for about two years and he didn't give a stuff about it. He became very aware quite soon that the chorus were unhappy. Not only did he learn everybody's name within about twenty-four hours but he gave a talk to the whole cast:

> Every man of this community in a way is a Tevye and every woman a Golde. You each have your own story, you have a history, you have a family. I want you all to go home tonight and write down who you are, where you come from, all about your family, everything.

He even gave us books to read.

What a difference! Within no time at all the cast, who for a while now had been a miserable bunch, became very excited: it was extraordinary to watch this little dynamic man who had created *West Side Story* showing the difference between a click by one of the Jets and a Jewish click, transforming himself from being a Jet to a Jewish man. He is Jewish, although I didn't know that. But my mother, who knew everything, told me that Jerry Robbins' real name was Rubenstein because she read all about it. (My mother always knew everybody's background.)

We improvised. Jerry absolutely believed in improvisation and in one of the most moving scenes in the whole piece, when I had to tell Tevye that our daughter had gone away with a non-Jew, we tried it every which way until we found the right one. We tried different words and it freed us up. Eventually, when it came to it, I even found the right place to do the clap that the assistant had wanted – but I found it for myself and could own it, I didn't have it imposed on me. When it came to the opening night, as far as I was concerned the only person I wanted to please was Jerry.

I didn't think the show was going to take off. I thought we were going to get a Jewish audience for a few weeks and that'd be it. I didn't think anyone else would be interested in the show, but they were.

We'd had technicals that went on forever, dress rehearsals that went on forever, a whole week of previews, and then we opened. We had the press and on the Saturday we had two shows, we'd been going right the way through and on the Sunday we were to record the show. In those days musicals were always recorded the Sunday after the opening night. (Could it be fear that the show might close before the week was out?)

Anyone who has seen *Fiddler on the Roof* knows that at the end of Act One the Russians come in and break up the wedding scene. We have given our daughter some very special goose feather pillows for her wedding but before it is over, the Russians arrive and everything gets beaten up. At the start of Act Two on the Saturday night, Topol says to me, 'Golde, do you love me?', and I sing, 'Do I *whaaaaaaaat?*' with my mouth wide open. As I was doing it, there was nothing I could do, I could see a feather floating down and it went into my mouth on the 'What?', and I choked. Somehow I managed to finish the show, I don't know how. I hardly slept a wink I was in such a state. We were recording the next morning round the corner from where I was living, in Abbey Road, and I rang up my singing teacher Ernst Urbach at about eight am. He told me to come round and he worked on me, but there was nothing he could do.

I went to the studio and I tried and tried. They let me go home and I rested a bit and then I tried again and I couldn't do it. So what did they do? I think it was one of the first times that this happened: I actually recorded all my stuff about two weeks later. I listened to Topol on the headphones and sang my stuff as if he was there and it worked, it was extraordinary. But God, that feather – will I ever forget?

With Jerry I had felt able to be totally creative. My performance couldn't have been more different from the woman who played the part on Broadway because she had been a ballet dancer and was a very high soprano. As I have said, I sang in the same octave as Topol and have two left feet.

Fiddler on the Roof was a turning point for me in a way because it was the most successful musical in Britain at the time. It was a great show, a show about racism – a kind of beautiful folk-tale.

One night during the run, my mother phoned me up to say that Dad had been taken to Middlesex Hospital with a heart attack, double pneumonia and thrombosis. This was in the middle of a performance. I finished the show, and Topol and my dresser came with me. My dresser stopped off at a Catholic church and lit a candle and we went on to the hospital. My mother and I were eventually called in by the consultant and he said he didn't think that Dad would live through the night. Ma and I stayed in a visitor's room, and my mother just sat there crying. I sat in a corner literally saying, 'Breathe, Daddy, Daddy, Daddy, breathe, breathe, breathe.' He had to live.

Well, at about 4 o'clock in the morning they came to us and said that they didn't think there would be any change so we might as well go home. I went with my mother to her home and stayed the night. At about eight am the phone rang and we thought, this is it, this is it. Ma answered the phone, and it was someone who lived down the road. This woman's husband was in the same ward as my father in Middlesex Hospital and she phoned to say that Dad was sitting up reading *The Times*. He lived for another nine years.

Around this time, in 1968, there was a huge concert for the 20th Anniversary of the creation of the State of Israel in which I took part. It was a huge show at the Albert Hall, directed by Toby Robertson, and there was loads of publicity about it. Immediately after that show I was banned from Arab territories. I did a reading, and made a statement about never giving up Jerusalem. When I had visited Israel, I could see the Golan Heights and knew that it was very easy to bomb. At the time I thought Israel was right, but I realise in retrospect that this was the time when they should have been magnanimous.

My political activism continued throughout this period. I never was a 'feminist', as it were, but I did believe in equality of opportunity for everybody, and I would carry on more about the rights for black and Asian artists and Jews, than about women. (One umbrella for equality.) I was lucky enough never to really suffer much inequality as a woman, so I didn't do the bra burning or anything, and I thought at the time that it was rather silly. I did take up the women's struggle in Equity because women were being paid less than men up until pretty recently. Around this time I also became a member of the Anti-Apartheid movement and I used to stand outside South Africa house with placards protesting.

I was talking to a cab driver recently as he drove me home from St John's Hospice because I could smell smoke in the cab. I was moaning on about the sort of day I had had and told him what was wrong with me. I said to him, 'Do you smoke?', and he said, 'Yes.'

I said, 'You don't want to end up like me.' Mark you, if anyone had said that to me years ago!

I had become addicted to smoking, addicted to gambling, addicted to pills, addicted to bloody everything, and I realise now, looking back, that my first addiction was going on stage – attention, that was the first.

My father had tried to bribe me and he offered me money if I would stop smoking. Although I took money off him all the time, that was something my conscience wouldn't allow. My relationship to smoking had been a torturous one. All through my early years, I had never attempted to put a cigarette in my mouth because we were a non-smoking household. There were always some rather posh cigarettes in the house for visitors, kept in a smart box, and Dad had a rather lovely silver cigarette case. He very occasionally smoked cigars, but there was no smoke allowed in the house itself and my mother went to her grave having not even tried a cigarette.

Up to the late 1940s I had never smoked, but I was doing one of those ghastly Esther McCrachan plays in rep at Colchester, either *Quiet Wedding* or *Quiet Weekend*. The character I was about to play I thought would be a smoker. I was staying in digs and the woman who ran them was a Mrs Ferguson, known as Auntie Fergie; and, almost too conveniently, she had a cigarette and sweetshop downstairs.

Dora Bryan had stayed in the digs prior to me and Auntie Fergie said how funny Dora Bryan was because she always wanted ice cream for breakfast. (Well, Dora has always been a funny woman.)

Having decided that the character should smoke, I said to Auntie Fergie, 'Could I have a packet of Gold Flake and a box of matches?' She sold me ten Gold Flake which were in a yellow and orange packet. I took them up to my room and took out a cigarette. I knew that I had to smoke convincingly: I could always tell when watching anybody on stage if they were smokers, because they inhaled properly. I thought it was very sophisticated and very smart, and think I had secretly always wanted to do it.

So I took out a cigarette, lit it and inhaled. Luckily I was sitting on the bed, because I momentarily passed out, more or less. Then I came to, and instead of stopping, proceeded straight away to finish the cigarette, and having smoked that one I became addicted. It is the first puff that is so terrific, even if it makes you faint. Very often I would light a cigarette, smoke half of it and put it down somewhere, then go and light up another one in another part of the room. I would sometimes have four or five going in a rehearsal room, depending on where I was.

So after that first cigarette I carried on smoking more and more. A decade or so later I was in a play, *The Egg*, with Nigel Patrick. This was a French play, by Felicien Marceau, so the appropriate cigarette was a French one – Gauloise or Disque Bleu. Although my character in this play didn't smoke, 'Paddy' Patrick's did, and he was given packets of Disque Bleu cigarettes which he used to pass on to me. They became my cigarettes of choice and I used to get through 30 to 40 per day, inhaling so deeply that I swear I had yellow toenails. You never saw smoke coming out of any top orifice!

January 6th 1970 is deeply imbedded in my mind because it was the day I gave up smoking. I was doing yoga at the time, and yoga and cigarette smoking are not ideally suited. For the sake of decency I didn't smoke for at least an hour before a yoga class or for an hour afterwards, and told myself this was all right.

I was coming from class, and stopped to pick up an *Evening Standard*. The headline read 'Smoking and Lung Cancer'. This was the second report by the Royal Society on the relationship between smoking and lung cancer. The first one had been ten years previously in January 1960, and apparently some doctors who had given up smoking then had now found that their lungs had regenerated. Reading all this I went home and put on the television. All the channels were showing programmes about people dying from smoking, with graphic descriptions.

I decided I had to stop and that the cigarette I had had an hour before the yoga class was the last one. I was watching non-stop television and at the same time I kept putting my hand in the fridge and taking out loads of vegetables and stuffing myself with them. I couldn't eat enough. My jaw was aching from eating so much, but being a member of Weight Watchers I was determined, at least, that I wasn't going to put on weight. I was also going to Australia the following week, my fourth visit. I went to bed with this aching jaw, but I was a non-smoker.

When I got up the next morning I thought, 'Oh shit', because the first thing I used to do was light up. I tried getting on with life, walking around in circles in an agitated fashion, and then fortuitously the phone rang and it was Thames Television, from Eamonn Andrews' current affairs programme *Today*. They said, 'Miriam, we were wondering, have you thought about giving up smoking in light of yesterday's report?' I said, 'It's funny you should say that, because I did last night.' They said, 'Oh good, would you mind coming on Eamonn's programme tonight and talking about it with some others who are doing the same?'

I went on, and there was darling Georgia Brown who was also a Disque Bleu smoker and smoked about the same as me, about 40 a day. We went on that programme every night until I went to Australia the following week. I rang my mother and said, 'Mummy, you will be pleased to hear I have given up smoking.'

'Do you think it wise, just when you are going off to Australia?'

'Christ Almighty, this is what you have been carrying on about for years!'

I still don't know whether she was being very clever in that she knew that whatever she was advocating, I would always do the opposite.

On the way to the airport to go to Australia, what was worrying me most was the little light over the seat in an aeroplane which went out and meant you could smoke when you were in the air. I was travelling first class, because I didn't have to pay my fare. I got on this Qantas plane and the cabin staff were lovely Aussies, and when they welcomed me I said, 'Would you do me a favour? I have just given up smoking. When you come to put that light out, don't, leave it on the whole time please, and when you come round with the free cigarettes, please don't come near me.'

A couple of them had seen me on the Eamonn Andrews programme so they knew what I was talking about and how difficult it was proving to be.

The only other person that I could see there was a very good-looking black guy just a few rows behind. Just after we took off, I was getting into a state because this was the time when I would normally have a cigarette. I looked around and said, 'I am getting so nervous, because I am a smoker, you see, and I have just given up.'

He said, 'I have never smoked myself. It must be very difficult for you.' We had a few conversations and I found myself more able to cope.

It was announced that we were going to be stopping in Dubai. I had been banned by all the Arab States because I had taken part in that anniversary show for Israel. Even though this was two years later, I was still banned, and when I heard we were going to be stopping in Dubai, I told one of the stewards I was worried. They had a meeting with the captain and when they came back they said I need not get off and that they would see that no one came on board.

Well, this lovely black guy came over and said, 'Look, if anybody comes on the plane, I'll sit here and I'll tell them you're my wife.' He was the Sierra Leone Ambassador and was going to a Prime Ministers' conference. Ted Heath had just become Prime Minister and when my new friend got off in Singapore I said to him, 'Give a message to Ted Heath for me, will you?'

'What?'

'Just kick him in the balls!'

We arrived at Sydney Airport at about 7 o'clock in the morning and were greeted, as ever, by unshaven reporters. They said, 'Welcome back to Australia, Mim', because over there they all knew me as Mim Karlin. For the sake of something to say, I said, 'I've given up smoking.'

They said, 'Oh no! I don't believe it!' – they knew me from *The Rag Trade*, when I always had a cigarette in my mouth – 'You, without a fag, I don't believe it!'

I said, 'No, I have. I gave up on the sixth.' It was now a week later. There must have been a paucity of news, because it got onto the front page, with pictures of me when I was smoking in *The Rag Trade*. It even made television and radio.

I then got a letter from the head of the anti-cancer council, one Dr Nigel Grey, in Melbourne. That was actually where I was going to be working on that occasion, opening in a play there. He said he was delighted to hear about me giving up smoking and that he wanted to meet me and would I consider making some anti-smoking commercials? I thought, goody, that could be therapeutic.

I started rehearsing the play *Butterflies are Free* in which I was playing the mother of a boy who was blind. There was just three of us in the play – the boy, the girlfriend and me – and I thought that if I could get to opening night without a cigarette then I would have made it. I wasn't to know that both of the cast and the director smoked Disque Bleu, and the rehearsal room was filled with that wonderful aroma. It was agony, although I pretended it wasn't. When we later became friends, they told me what a cow I had been during rehearsals, even though I thought I'd been so cool and thought I'd hidden it well. I was amazed. I think I am now far more lenient with people who behave badly because I wonder whether they have a problem they are hiding.

At rehearsal one day, I learned that the Ambassador had phoned to say he was in Melbourne and had given his number for me to call. When I did he said, 'I just wanted to tell you that I gave your message to Ted Heath.' So we met up, which led to a really good time and helped me over the smoking quite a bit...

I was away for nearly a year and when I came back to England there were loads of messages from him waiting for me. He was now the Sierra Leone Ambassador here in London and he invited me to lunch. When I arrived at his house, which was in 'Millionaires' Row' in Hampstead, I saw a diplomatic car outside with a special number plate and crown, and found that I was being treated like the hostess. He saw me home in this amazing car. A boyfriend of mine had been sitting outside my house in his old battered car waiting for me, and I had to give an explanation which may not have been entirely convincing!

That New Year's Eve, I was getting ready to go to a party when the doorbell rang and standing there was the Ambassador, saying, 'I just came to wish you Happy New Year.' I invited him in for a glass of champagne. He said that he couldn't because he had people waiting in the car. I said, 'Well bring them in', full of hospitality. In came the wife and about three children of varying ages. Of course I was charming and sweet to the children, but I often wondered, how did he explain me away?

I did see him again afterwards but heard about six years ago that he had died. He was a lovely man.

In that year in Australia not only did I take part in the anti-smoking commercials, I wrote some of them and more or less directed them because the director didn't know what to do and although I'd never done it, I had picked up enough to know what would work. The best thing was that we were actually able to get them on television while Australia was still showing cigarette commercials. That was quite a political breakthrough.

That anti-smoking doctor, Dr Nigel Grey, turned out to be quite something too!

I loved Australia, but had a few problems with some of the politics. For example, when I was in Melbourne on my first visit, it was ANZAC day and the Premier of the State of Victoria, a Mr Bolte, was on the radio the next day saying that some disgraceful person had written a five-letter word on the ANZAC memorial in Melbourne. What was the filthy five-letter word? PEACE. I couldn't believe it.

The one thing I really disapproved of, indeed loathed, about Australia – and let it be known when I first went over there – was their 'Keep Australia White' policy. As far as I was concerned it was still a racist country. It had already taken in some of immigrants, and there were many Hungarians, Greeks and lots of other Europeans; in fact, the management that I worked for was Hungarian and had arrived in Australia after the 1956 uprising. However, there were very few black or Asian people.

I did notice a difference over time, and gradually there were more people from different nationalities. Once there was a Labor Government, albeit for a short time, they introduced legislation and the situation improved. I was questioned about it by an English magazine before one of my visits to Australia. Like a twit, I said that there were so many gays in Australia – all these great butch-looking blond surfers in Sydney – and perhaps there could be some sort of wonderful exchange. There was an over-population in places like Asia and Africa where people had large families, and would it not be better to send some of the gay Australians over to Asia and Africa and bring some black and Asian people over to Australia? That would even it all out and Australia would have a population, because it is wildly under-populated and always has been. I got bollocked quite severely for that!

Still, I did have wonderful times there. The Australians were so open. There were no class barriers, the weather was just heaven, and being able to get into that surf was gorgeous. I felt so well physically when I was there and made really good friends. An actor that I knew, Patsy Lovell, was in a cab going to the station at Channel Seven where I worked, and the cab driver said to her, 'Have you met Miriam Karlin?' and when she said she knew me very well, he said, 'I think it's great that she's come back home.'

She said, 'No, no, she's English', but he insisted: 'No, no, she went overseas to do *The Rag Trade* and now she's come home.'

Pat couldn't get it into his head that I wasn't Australian. I took that as a great compliment.

I suppose I was accepted because I played so many Australian characters on TV over there. In particular, I appeared on a very popular show called *The Mavis Bramston Show*. This was rather like an Australian version of *That Was the Week That Was* and created quite a stir. There were questions asked in Parliament House about the terrible things that were being said on the show. I think I did the Queen several times on television, which was not possible to do here at that time. There was a sketch that I introduced (prior to Peter Cook and Dudley Moore doing something very similar) and this involved Gordon Chater and me sitting on a park bench every week. It was a sketch about a non-relationship and it caught on.

One of the guests on *The Mavis Bramston Show* was Barry Humphries, whom I had met on my first visit to Australia. In those days he was drinking like a fish and he had fucked up I don't know how many marriages. He had also made himself bankrupt, but did he make me laugh. I remember coming home to England saying, 'I've just met the funniest man in the world.'

Barry had lived in Britain for quite some time, but people hadn't realised quite how brilliant he was. I'd seen his 'Dame Edna Everage' in Australia but he had not done her yet in England. He had even taken over in *Oliver!* at one time and played Fagin when he was here.

After it became news that I had given up smoking, I was going to the Playbox Theatre in Melbourne for *Butterflies are Free*, and bumped into Barry outside. We had a reunion: he had seen all this publicity and said, 'I've got to give up smoking too.' I knew that he had joined AA since I had seen him last, so I told him not to try giving up smoking, and to stick with his thing because it would be too difficult to do both. He said, 'I love going to the meetings. I go to two or three AA meetings a day and the place is blue with smoke and people are getting up and coughing and saying, "I've never felt so good (*cough*) since I gave up the devil drink (*cough*)", I love it!'

He sent me a letter after I had been playing in Perth, but I'm not sure I believe what he says.

> We are still attracting a largely 'Butterflies are Free' audience, to the extent that we have been obliged to distribute Braille programmes.
>
> I hope you realise that in Perth you are at present being confronted with the stiffest challenge so far, to your resolve to live a life free of drugs. While I was up in the Cairns I discovered that the local hippies smoke the dried skin of cane toads, which apparently gives them a charge!
>
> This undoubtedly accounts for the expression often used by heavy smokers, 'Pardon me but I've got a frog in my throat...'

Apart from being a brilliant comedian Barry also happens to be incredibly knowledgeable and articulate about art and painting. He certainly knows paintings and has got quite a collection himself. I went to a private view of the artist Ray Crooke in Sydney and fell in love with a certain painting. I just had to have it, and the red sticker was put on it. The next day they phoned me from the gallery and said, 'Miss Karlin, are you sure you wanted that painting?'

'Yes. Why, why are you asking?'

'Well, the National Gallery of Western Australia was interested in having it, as is Barry Humphries.'

I bought the painting and had it at home until I moved to the flat I'm in now, when I had to sell loads of paintings because I just didn't have the wall space. I remembered that Barry had been after that Ray Crooke painting and he was in London, because he had a show on at the Strand Theatre starring Edna. I dropped him a line and he arrived with a friend with him who clearly was also an art person, maybe a dealer. I brought out the painting and they both loved it. Barry said, 'Christ, I should have got in quicker!' In the end his friend actually bought it.

Even though I haven't been to Australia for many years, I'm still in touch with friends there. I was recently having a phone conversation with an ex-critic for the Melbourne paper *The Age*, who has had similar medical problems to me. As usual, I quickly got onto politics and, having carried on about Blair, I said, 'And what about *your* arsehole of a Prime Minister, that bloke John Howard?'

He said, 'You know what we call him?'

'No, what?'

'Bonsai.'

'Why?' I asked.

'Baby bush!'

Brilliant – that could have applied just as well to our dearly departed Mr Blair...

I don't think I have ever given newspapers cause to print any scandal about myself. I've done plenty of things but I have never been chased. There was one story that the *Evening Standard* ran, in which they made out that I was having an affair with an Australian Labor politician, Don Dunstan. Don, whom I absolutely adored, and who was very fond of me, later became Premier of South Australia. I remember telling my friend Peter Noble, who used to write for the *Evening Standard*, that I was going off to Australia. I said how thrilled I was that Don had phoned from Adelaide, suggesting that we should meet and that I should stay in Adelaide for a day or so, even though it wasn't on my itinerary. The day I left London there was a piece in 'Londoner's Diary' in the *Standard* implying that I was having an affair with Don, which I certainly wasn't. I was so horrified when I read it that I decided that I would not go to Adelaide after all. Don was very upset, as was I.

When I was asked to play Mrs Patrick Campbell in the television play *The First Night of 'Pygmalion'*, I told my then doctor Patrick Woodcock about it, and he said, 'Ooh Johnny G' – that was John Gielgud – 'worked with her and does the most wonderful impersonation of her. I'll invite you both to dinner and if he's in a good mood he'll do it.'

A dinner date was set. John was indeed in a very good mood and did the impersonation, so I found myself doing an impersonation of John Gielgud doing an impersonation of 'Mrs Pat'.

We rehearsed a lot. The director Hal Burton was a great one for detail because he had also been a designer and made certain that all our clothes were wonderful, totally right for the period. In the production Max Adrian played George Bernard Shaw and John Osborne Sir Herbert Beerbohm Tree. One day at rehearsal John arrived in hysterics, having just seen John Gielgud on the Kings Road. Gielgud had shouted across from the opposite side of the road: 'Oooh, John, don't tell anybody, but I've just recorded Larry's obituary. Don't tell a soul.' (Larry Olivier, who was very ill at the time, went on to live for another twenty years, thank goodness.)

My creative experiences at that time were really varied in terms of style and technique. You somehow create a store or blueprint of all the people you've worked with over the years and the different things you've learnt and hope to take the good bits and sift out the rest. I am very much an instinctive actor, that I do know, and know when something is truthful. I think when I had real difficulty with the third Bellow play it was the first time in 20 years that I encountered real problems with 'finding' a character – since Miss Sharp and her allergy to feathers in *Separate Rooms*, in fact. Charles Marowitz was pretty tough with me and I was in a panic, but once I had got her, the relief was huge.

Even at this time, which in retrospect was one of the most 'successful' periods in my life, I still approached each new role as a potential disaster, pathetically enough. I've always felt (and I've heard other actors say this, so it's nothing new) that I'm going to be found out and people will realise that I can't do it. I've been afraid for all these years that they're going to discover I'm a phoney: I still have that sense of unease, whether I am giving a performance or a speech.

I suppose this is what 'piss elegance' is all about, really. I'd been in a couple of 'hit' musicals; been able to buy somewhere rather grand to live; become what is now called a 'celeb', courtesy of *The Rag Trade*; found myself an honorary Australian. What the hell does any of that mean, though? It was all show, liable to disappear at any moment. – just a superficial *folie de grandeur*.

That feeling extends out into the wider context nowadays and I perpetually think that disaster is just around the corner. There is an advantage to this, of course: when one does see good things, one does realise how really good they are. For instance, Nelson Mandela coming out of prison – that was the most glorious moment. I have never actually met him, but I went to a huge reception at Commonwealth House in Kensington when he was released. I was overwhelmed. Not that he should have been in there, of course, but to see him coming out with no feelings of bitterness, that was just extraordinary. Now *he* had, and has, true, real elegance.

7

GOOD STUFF

In which I worked with Stanley Kubrick in A Clockwork Orange, *campaigned with Peggy Ashcroft for the release of the Sharpeville Six, received my* OBE *at the Palace, spoke at the Oxford Union Debate, and played huge roles in* Mother Courage, Hay Fever, The Seagull, Who's Afraid of Virginia Woolf?, *and my one-woman show* Liselotte.

PROFESSIONALLY AND PERSONALLY I was having a really good time, and after the 'summer of love' the world appeared to reflect my optimism. Everything around me seemed to be opening up: the culture, the music and the politics.

I had never really looked my age, and so hadn't owned up to it. Back when I was only 20, I had this form to fill out for *Who's Who*. I was sitting at the bar in the Embassy theatre, Swiss Cottage (now the Central School of Speech and Drama), and someone said, 'Oh, don't put your birth date.' I was very proud of the fact I was only in my twenties and already being asked to be in *Who's Who*, so I wrote down my real birth date. He said I'd regret it later, and he was right.

My great friend Peter Noble (he was the one who had gossiped about my presumed affair in the *Evening Standard*) used to write for *What's On* magazine and knocked five years off my age whenever he wrote about me, so for a long time I was assumed to be younger than I really was. When I was at the RSC, my real age of 57 was published in the *Guardian*. I remember coming into the Barbican green room and people saying, 'You're not, are you?'

I said, 'Unfortunately I can't sue them 'cos they're right.'

Just after the 1970 election, when I'd been campaigning for Harold Wilson, I was at one of Peter's parties. Harold himself was there, and the room was filled with people from all walks of life, including Stanley Kubrick and his wife Christiane. At the time I did a lot of yoga and was sitting cross-legged on the floor talking to Harold. We were asked to go down to eat and, as we were walking down the stairs, Christiane said, 'Stanley's been looking at you.' I thought, oh really, and didn't take much notice.

The very next day my agent called me and said, 'Stanley Kubrick wants you to be in a movie, *A Clockwork Orange*.'

Stanley used to make one movie about every four or five years. Nowadays when you are considered for a movie, you first of all have to go and meet the casting director, then you do a video and then maybe the producer, 5,000 miles away, might see it in three weeks' time and you'll never hear another thing. In those days it was different.

When I got the script I went into a kind of catatonic state. I was being offered the part of the 'cat lady' and would be surrounded by cats. I had never told a living soul that I had a phobia about cats. I used to tolerate them when I went to friends' homes, but cats always knew – they sense it if you don't like them and come to you.

I agreed to the movie, of course – you don't say no to Stanley Kubrick – but I became more and more neurotic as time went on. About four or five weeks before we started they were making the costumes and I was sent to see Thea Porter, a top designer of the day. I had about three fittings for an amazing black chiffon cat-suit with very wide legs, to be worn with a huge great belt, which I think in itself cost about a thousand pounds. They were also making two identical outfits because, as they said, 'If a cat scratched me, there would need to be another one'. This made me even more nervous.

One day they phoned up from the studio and said, 'Oh Stanley hears you do yoga.' (Well I had been sitting in the lotus position for about two hours when he first met me.)

'What do you wear when you do yoga?'

'A leotard and tights.'

'Oh right, we'll call you back.'

When they did, they asked, 'Would you mind wearing an emerald green leotard and white tights?'

As I was in a very thin period at the time, I didn't mind at all and said it would be fine. They also wanted me to wear a wig so I had to go and have fittings for a bright red wig.

It was about two weeks before I was going to be called and my neurosis was building. Not only was I going to be terrified by the cats around me, the cats would know, an audience would know, and most important of all Stanley would know. What the hell was I going to do?

From out of nowhere I had the sudden idea: hypnosis. I had a doctor in mind – Joe Robson, whom I'd known all my life because our families had been great friends. (Indeed, he was the son-in-law of Emmanuel Snowman, with whom my father had set up the West Hampstead School.) He was a proper GP but had taken up hypnosis a few years earlier. He looked after all the Goons. I'd never before wanted to go with anything personal, but something as ludicrous and illogical as a phobia of cats – fine!

I phoned him up and told him I'd been asked to be in a film and had to play a character surrounded by cats, and I was terrified of them. He said his mother-in-law, whom I knew very well, was exactly the same. I already felt better because it was the first time I had uttered the words out loud.

I went to see him in Harley Street the next day and because it was the middle of winter I'm ashamed to say I was wearing my mink coat. As I was sitting there, he noticed how I was enjoying the feel of my coat, so when he got me down on the couch, he referred to cats as 'little minks'. I saw him three times and I truly felt cured.

Having read the script, I then bought the book and read that. I realised it was an extraordinary and brilliant piece of writing, and to be doing it with Stanley Kubrick – well obviously it would be important, but I never envisioned it reaching cult status.

When it came to shooting, he asked me to go down to the studio a few days before, because he wanted to see a typical yoga routine. I did 'salute to the sun' and a few other combinations. One never knew with Stanley whether one was rehearsing or shooting because he kept the camera running, and on my first day I was so deeply into my yoga doing all my deep breathing, that when he said 'Cut' and I opened my eyes, there was a little white cat with a ginger nose nestling in my crotch and licking my knee. It was so sweet. Stanley had enjoyed it so much that he had just left the camera running although it wasn't supposed to be in the movie. The cats didn't bother me at all now – I loved my 'little minks'.

Later, I was doing my yoga routine and when I was in a position where my legs are over my head (the 'plough') I heard a doorbell ring. Again, I was so deeply into it I said, 'Oh shit!' and went to open the door. I had no idea, until I saw the movie, that the sound was on. The line got a big laugh in the cinema.

This was the scene when Malcolm McDowell's character Alex comes in and picks up one of my sculptures, a three foot phallus, and proceeds to try to kill me with it, whilst I pick up a small statue of Beethoven with which I try desperately to defend myself. The shooting of the scene went on for hours. We were in a fairly small room and Stanley was running around with a handheld camera. We just went on and on and improvised the entire thing. We seemed to do it for an entire day and night, over and over. The scene had been scripted, and I had learnt my lines, of course. With Stanley, you had to learn your lines. If you didn't, you were out – people were fired over it. Then, once we'd learned the lines, he let us improvise: in fact,

I don't know that I actually said any of the scripted lines in the end. We talked about it and we rehearsed and played around with it and then rehearsed on camera – he was shooting all the time anyway.

Nearly a year later when the movie was being shown, Stanley asked me to go to Australia, America and Honolulu to promote the movie, along with Adrienne Corri, who played another of Alex's victims. Adrienne didn't last the entire time because she got pissed off and went home. I stayed the course, and worked my arse off. I realise now when I see American stars coming over to promote their movies just how hard it is. I used to be up at about six in the morning, having my hair done, getting dressed, maybe putting my leotard and tights underneath whatever I was wearing so that I could demonstrate the yoga on camera for breakfast television, and then doing all sorts of programmes right through the day and night. Sometimes I'd work fourteen hours a day.

This lasted for four weeks. I didn't get paid for any of this, but got all my expenses and stayed in the best hotels and glamorous suites everywhere with champagne in fridges. The film had opened and was already being misunderstood. One of the reasons for my promoting and talking about it was to correct people's misapprehensions and correct the false belief that it was just about violence. The point was that it was an indictment of our generation and that of our parents. These monstrous tower blocks and concrete jungles in which kids were bought up, trapped at the top of some ghastly high-rise building with nowhere to play. What do they do? They go out and beat up old ladies.

I took the task very seriously. I really believed in what the film was trying to say, and this was a time in which I wanted to do work that mattered and that said something. I had some fascinating discussions trying to explain what the movie was saying but I found that the people who understood it best were young people. The underground papers really knew what it was saying, but the over 45s were hopeless. I remember there was a gigantic shopping centre outside Brisbane, the Indarapilly, with a huge great cinema complex. The fellow who was compèring said, 'I'd like to introduce you to someone who you know and love. It's great she's come here to meet us, Miriam Karlin.'

Then he said, 'You've taken part in this new filum *Clockwork Orange*. Tell me about the filum.'

I said, 'Actually, it's really about a place like this.'

He didn't understand what I meant, so I said, 'Well, it's about a sort of a plastic society', and I looked around at this place which was so phoney, where everything was plastic – even the plants. I talked as articulately as I could, but after I had finished a load of women with shopping bags came up and wanted my autograph because they loved *The Rag Trade* and asked when I was going to do some more of that. They hadn't understood a word I had said.

After a month of this I was worn out. They gave me a week to myself in New York at the end, which was fine, but I came home absolutely knackered. I thought that there might be some flowers or something from Stanley to thank me, but there wasn't anything, not even a letter. I waited a few days – nothing, so I went to a greengrocer and bought about six Jaffa oranges, cut them in half, squeezed them out and put all the pips in a little plastic bag, put the twelve shells of half oranges in another, wrapped the whole lot up in a bigger plastic bag, and wrote a little note on one of my visiting cards saying, 'Dear Stanley, they have sucked me dry.' I sent the whole thing to Stanley.

I got back my visiting card, with this added: 'Dear M, don't get the message, love S.' Here is a man who has an incredible sense of humour when it comes to his movies, but absolutely none about himself. So I wrote him a letter and enclosed a sheet of my typical day's schedule. Then I did finally get the letter I had anticipated, but I had had to chisel it out of him.

> Sorry I didn't get the symbolism but I do appreciate the tremendous job you and Adrienne did. The cuttings have been terrific. I hope you have recovered.

After all that he withdrew the film, ostensibly because he received death threats, and there was a copycat killing. I think it was possibly also to do with Stanley himself having second thoughts about it. It was the very first film to look at gang violence. I did have second thoughts about it myself because I hadn't considered then that young kids could sit in front of a television and watch the sort of violence people imagined they were seeing (although you didn't actually see it, because it was all suggested). I hadn't considered at all that a mother might sit her kids down in front of the television and go out, leaving them to get a video. I think that none of us could have predicted the impact the film had on vulnerable people, even though we felt then, and I still feel now, that the film had a really honourable purpose.

I suppose we rarely think about the future consequences of what we are doing. While one part of me can't help marvelling at the miracles of technology, another, fiercer part of me kicks in and is horrified by the filthy can of worms that technology has opened up with the internet. I think technology moves so fast nowadays that our brains can't keep up with it. When the internet started, few people thought in advance that it would be used to show horror, so there weren't any safeguards put in place. Now it seems too late to change things. It's no good saying we've got to stop children watching horror, the genie is out of the bottle and it is there to be seen. China gets criticised for putting restrictions on democracy and I don't approve of censorship, but I know this is again where I am full of double-standards. I suppose I want children to be brought up so that they would be protected from pornography and horror. I sometimes wonder what kind of kick people get out of manufacturing it. Is it all just about money?

I suppose one is asking for a utopian world, but that is what I have always dreamt of and wanted: a ridiculous utopian idealistic socialist world. I remember saying to my mother, 'Mummy, wouldn't it be wonderful if everybody said at the same time, say 12 o'clock, they are all going to love one another. Wouldn't that be lovely?' There was that incredible day that Bob Geldof organised in 1986, when people all over the world were running at the same time to end world poverty. I watched it on television and thought, 'This is what I said to my mother when I was a kid – and they are all doing it.' It looked like the nearest thing to Utopia and it seemed that for a few hours people were all capable of loving each other. There didn't seem to be any hate anywhere, and all ethnicities, races or colours and classes were just people, running for the same thing.

I still hold onto my utopian sentiments. During one of my recent chats with my brother, I was saying in my naive way, 'You know, if it weren't for religion and oil, the world could be a wonderful place.'

Ever the realist, my brother replied, 'Knowing us, we'd soon find something else to fight about.'

Stanley asked me to be in his next film, *Barry Lyndon*. In fact, I got paid for being in it, but then he got more death threats when he was in Ireland shooting, so he had to come away, and I didn't end up doing it. I trusted him totally and whatever he had asked me to do, I would have done. When we were working we weren't looking at clocks, because we went way over time, even though we had very definite unionised hours in those days. We just went on working even if it was freezing cold and wet in the most unpleasant surroundings, but no one was complaining because it was Stanley Kubrick.

I enjoyed the fact that I could do work in theatre or film that was politically interesting, combining my two most important passions. Soon after *A Clockwork Orange* I went to Watford to play *Mother Courage*. Rob Walker directed it and, as it was at the time of the Vietnam War, we talked a lot about whether I should do it in Vietnamese clothes and be surrounded by drunken American sailors and soldiers. We threw that idea out because we realised that Brecht had known there would always be a war going on somewhere – bloody right, of course. At the first act curtain I said 'Fuck the war', thinking of Vietnam, and I believe the audience knew what I was talking about. It would be the same today of course, except one would be thinking Iraq.

I was also working on a one-person piece called *Liselotte,* which wasn't politically motivated at all but was a part which would give me such satisfaction to play. She was Elizabeth Charlotte of Hanover, the daughter of the Elector of Hanover. The material came to be in my possession because I had been asked by the BBC to do some readings of *Letters of Liselotte* on Radio 3 (or the Third Programme as it was in those days). I knew nothing at all about her, but there had just been a translation of her letters by Maria Kroll, and so I did three consecutive weeks of readings of them. I became absolutely fascinated by the woman. I got so interested in her that my father bought the rights of the book for me, so I 'owned' *Letters from Liselotte.* I did nothing about this for about a year until Dad got annoyed with me and said 'Look I didn't buy that for you to just sit on, get on with it, do something.'

Having worked with Frederick Bradnum who was a director and writer at the BBC, I asked him if he would do a dramatisation of the book. He did, but somehow it wasn't quite right. At the time I was working with Peter Watson (then a very young director) on a play about the Kray Twins, *Alpha, Alpha* by Howard Barker. I played Dolly Kray and talked about 'my lovely boys' all the time. This was at the Open Space Theatre that Charles Marowitz was running. I discovered that Peter had a great knowledge of French and German literature and history and spoke both languages very well. As my German is pretty good too I could see that he was the perfect person to direct *Liselotte,* so I asked him if he was interested.

Peter was amazing, so conscientious, sitting in the British Museum day after day doing research. He used to come to my Hamilton Terrace pad nearly every day and when we finally agreed a script, he thought that the Theatre Royal in York would be the best venue to give it a first airing, as he'd worked there for Richard Digby Day.

Liselotte was a wonderful character to play. Her father had decided when she was nineteen that she would probably never get married because she was very plain, so he married her off to Louis XIV's gay brother Philippe duc d'Orléans. There she was in the French Court having her first sexual experience with a gay man. She wrote copious letters and diaries all about the goings on and the mores (or lack of them) at court, some of it quite filthy and explicit. I thought she was a wonderful woman. She always referred to sex as 'the business' and she said things like:

> After the birth of my third child, my daughter, in 1676, he left my bed and I never enjoyed the business sufficiently to ask him to return. […]

> There are those who don't mind what they have, human or animal, they take whatever comes along. I know someone here who brags he has had relations with everything under the sun except toads. Since I heard this I can hardly look at the fellow without feeling sick.

I believe she was secretly in love with Louis XIV and loathed Louis' mistress Madame de Maintenon whom he later married. Liselotte, who called Madame de Maintenon 'ze old hag', was determined to outlive her. I started off playing Liselotte at the age of about 40, gradually ageing throughout the piece. Finally, in my seventies, I entered very excitedly and announced with glee: 'I have outlived ze old hag.'

We realised on the opening night that we had something pretty good – except that it ran for two and a half hours. So we went to work cutting it. We took it to the Edinburgh Festival Fringe for four weeks, where it went well and after that we took it all over the world, so it became one of my most successful pieces of work. Ernst Hanover, a young member of the Hanoverian royal family, was living in London and saw me doing an excerpt on a TV programme from the Festival

Fringe. He got terribly excited and came down to see me when I was playing it in Brighton. He thought of himself as producer, and talked about filming it in Versailles. Because of his name and his connections, he managed to get us the Palace of Versailles – a pretty good venue for my *Liselotte*.

The most extraordinary thing is that in 1974 the one room in the Palace of Versailles that was still extant from Liselotte's time was Madame de Maintenon's room. So I actually performed the play in the room of Liselotte's arch-enemy. What happened on the night made me wonder whether her ghost was hovering over us, determined to get the better of the production.

The palace was absolutely freezing, I remember, and prior to the performance I was desperate for the loo (naturally). In a very flimsy dressing gown I went down this grand staircase in search of a lavatory and can still feel the panic I was in on my return, lest I bump into any of the royals entering. When I saw them take their seats, I realised that the audience consisted entirely of Liselotte's descendants. There was the Comtesse de Paris in the centre, surrounded by all her family: it was incredible to see them all together in the palace. If the royal family had continued, the Comtesse would have been the heir to the French throne.

It was one of my best performances. By the number of handkerchiefs on view, I could see the family were actually crying when I was talking about Louis' death. They gave me a fantastic supper afterwards and I was given all sorts of gifts, but the shock news was that the sound had given up after the first few minutes and our 'producer' didn't have the guts to tell anybody, letting me go through the entire thing without sound. He hadn't got the balls to stop the show and tell us so we never got any film at all.

Peter Watson was furious. We had some wonderful music which he had chosen for the production – Lalande, Lully and Rameau, right for the period and very much my sort of music. Even though it was such a disappointment not to have a record of the event, it had been an extraordinary experience to have performed it in Madame de Maintenon's room. I thought of them as 'my' ancestors, which sums up my empathy for them at the time.

I saw in the paper only about a year ago that the Comtesse had died in Paris. She had told me, 'You know, we have the same sense of humour as Liselotte. We also all talk about farting.'

Around 1975, out of the blue, I received my OBE. I was just about to do my Liselotte in London. Cameron Mackintosh had phoned me up and said he'd got a few weeks at the Phoenix Theatre and would I like to do the show there? He insisted on calling it *The Diary of a Madame*, which I felt was wrong, but he was the boss. He has since admitted his mistake because it gave quite the wrong connotation. She was known as 'Madame' because anyone who was married to the King's brother was called 'Madame' – she was anything but a *madame*!

The first day I came to the Phoenix to rehearse, a guy brought me a long, very grand envelope which said on the back 'From the Lord Treasurer's Office'. I realised I must keep *schtum* about this because it was an official letter offering me an OBE. So I just pretended it was nothing, and when I finished rehearsing I phoned my dad, because he had already had an OBE. Ma and I had been to the Palace to see him getting his. I went tearing home and he helped me fill out the forms. It was asking what charitable work one had done and I had indeed done quite a bit. It was thrilling to be recognised as someone who had done something for the 'British Empire'. I thought back to the game I used to play as a child and felt quite humble. Harold Wilson was responsible for me getting it and as it was him, I was hugely pleased. One part of me doesn't really approve of this honours system (my double standards again) and I would certainly not have accepted it if it had come from Thatcher, but then she would hardly have given me anything.

At the same time as I was offered the OBE, I moved from Hamilton Terrace to Clapham. Everybody thought I was bonkers – moving 'south of the river' from St John's Wood? As it was my fiftieth birthday, I organised a house-warming and birthday party in my new house, though I secretly knew it was also an OBE party. The routine was that as the guests came in, I gave them a drink and then showed them the house. Amongst the guests was Fenella Fielding who came with Stella Tanner. Stella had already seen my house and thought she knew the way there, so she gave Fenella a lift, but they got lost and it took them an eternity to drive to South London. Once they arrived I showed them round the house as usual. When Fenella came down the stairs after her viewing she said in her inimitable husky voice: 'The house is a great success, are you bringing it into town?' Kenneth Williams actually quoted that on a television show as if it was his!

I hadn't had the time to get myself any clothes for the OBE presentation because I'd been working doing a season of plays at the Gardner Arts Centre in Brighton, finishing with a couple of weeks of *Liselotte*. There was a wonderful costume woman working there and I suddenly wondered if she could make me something. She said, 'I thought you'd never ask', and made me a beautiful outfit, with a hat to match. I managed to find the time to get the shoes and the handbag myself.

My friends the Clarks drove me to the Palace. One of the courtiers came and gave instructions on what one must do when one meets the Queen, walk backwards from her and so on. My parents were there, and once I had been given instructions, one of the courtiers told me that my father wanted to talk to me. The funny thing was that Dad never knew that when he got his OBE he forgot to walk backwards, but he said to me very earnestly, 'Now listen you mustn't start the conversation with her and you have to walk backwards.'

I said, 'Yes I've been told, Dad', and caught my mother's eye.

Time was getting on and I hadn't been called yet and was getting very nervous because I knew I had to catch a train back to Brighton in order to be at my dress rehearsal. It was opening night and I was meant to be there for 3 o'clock.

Finally I was called at 12.15. When the Queen gave me my OBE she said, 'I'm very pleased to be giving you this. Are you working at the moment?'

'Yes Ma'am, I'm opening tonight playing one of Your Majesty's relatives.'

She looked rather frightened – perhaps she thought it might have been her sister or mother – and said, 'Oh, which one?'

'Elizabeth Charlotte of Hanover.'

There was a total blank across her face and she said, 'Oh I do wish you much success.' She didn't recognise the name, although she has some of the best portraits of Liselotte in her gallery.

My commitment to Equity and various international causes continued to preoccupy me. In the 1970s the International Committee for Artists' Freedom (ICAF) was formed. This was a sub-committee of Equity with Paul Eddington as the Chair. Peggy Ashcroft was also on the Committee. Its work became very important during the Pinochet period when a group of actors were going to be executed in Chile. We used to go to the Chilean embassy, stand outside and protest: I remember Julie Christie handing in a letter to ask for their reprieve. We got the Equities all over the world to become involved, and Christopher Reeve actually went to Santiago himself. It was through our combined protests that those artists were saved. We're still in touch with some of them. Over the years many other people have been helped.

About seven or eight years ago we realised that each time we appealed for money to theatre people with trust funds, like Trevor Nunn, they would ask, 'Are you a charity?' If you've got charitable status it's much easier to get money out of people, so we decided we had to become one. We went through all the hoops, and it took us about three years of hard work but we managed it: our charitable arm is the International Performers Aid Trust (IPAT), which cannot campaign politically. I am a trustee and we've got some wonderful patrons; Alan Rickman is now our President. The ICAF remains as our campaigning organ.[1]

I think it was through Glenys Kinnock and the One World Action charity that I first got involved with Burma Campaign UK, which works to restore democracy to Burma and in particular to support the Nobel Peace Prize winner Aung San Suu Kyi, who despite winning an election remains under house arrest, a prisoner of the illegal military junta which rules Burma. I remember going to a demonstration outside British Home Stores back in 1996, trying to stop people going in and telling those coming out that the shop was buying products from Burma. (The BHS was doing nothing illegal, unfortunately – no British government, Tory or Labour, has imposed effective sanctions on this regime, which is something that that amazing lady is constantly calling for.) Then, a few years later, I learned from a mole at Thames TV that their holiday show *Wish You Were Here* was doing a programme about holidaying in Burma. I went berserk on hearing about this, and told everyone I could think of – Glenys, Jon Snow, John Pilger. They bombarded Thames with messages saying how monstrous it was even to contemplate putting out such a programme, which, I am delighted to say, was then pulled.

Aung San Suu Kyi is far from the only victim of that dreadful regime, of course. Helen Lindsay, a friend and fellow member of ICAF, heard from her contacts at Amnesty about two jailed Burmese comedians, 'The Moustache Brothers'. Working with both Amnesty and Burma Campaign UK, ICAF conducted a frantic campaign on their behalf, sending letter after letter to the Burmese Embassy, and thankfully they were released in 2001.[2]

As I write this, however, one of the 'Moustache Brothers', U Pa Pa Lay, has been rearrested, along with a leading Burmese writer and comedian, Zaganar, whose 'crime' was to give water to the monks demonstrating against the regime. I have high hopes that Gordon

1 'Some Speeches and Letters', page 237.

2 *ibid*, pages 237–9.

Brown, who has expressed such admiration for Aung San Suu Kyi in his book *Heroes*, will bring real pressure to bear on the Burmese rulers. How strange that only recently the First Lady Laura Bush and her arsehole of a husband, no less, have been expressing their concern to the UN about the generals' intransigence and tyrannical behaviour, which show no sign of abating.

My socialism was nurtured by my father, as I have said, and he must originally have had a bit of a Liverpool accent – totally undetectable after his time as an Oxford undergraduate. He told us that when he got to Oxford as a freshman in the dining hall, he said pass the 'shugger', and we used to send him up about it. They did horrible things to freshers. He bought an upright piano costing £1 for his room, and when he lifted the lid they had put coal in it. Very cruel.

He probably developed his knowledge of socialism in the Oxford Union and he was so thrilled when I was asked to speak there. They asked me because of *The Rag Trade*: the motion was 'The Female of the Species is Deadlier than the Male'. I have to say that my speech was very successful and I have to thank him for that. He knew that I have this habit of leaving everything to the last minute so he came round and gave me some quotations from Dr Johnson and others. I only used ones I might have come across myself. I managed to get a lot of laughs and won the motion. I really enjoyed giving that performance because one used 'But Mr President Sir, I maintain…', which gave one a wonderful sense of power. A couple of years later I was asked to speak at the Union again. That was a good evening too, and the motion wasn't all that dissimilar. I didn't use the same speech, obviously, but I knew then how to put the arguments across, which added to my confidence in debate. During this period I was also invited to speak at the Cambridge Union.[3]

Dad had stood as a Labour candidate on two occasions, the first time when I was a baby. He didn't show off his family as some do

3 'Some Speeches and Letters', pages 232–4.

these days so we weren't involved directly as children. The second time had been in the Eccleshall Division in Sheffield. When I was playing there at the Crucible, which was run at that time by Ann Casson and her husband Douglas Campbell – good old left-wingers both – Dad sent me a copy of the address that he had given at the time because he thought I might be interested. Indeed I was, and showed it to a reporter who was interviewing me. Here is just a tiny extract.

> The Conservative Party has been in power nearly five years, with more than enough support to fulfil its programme. What has it done? And what would the Labour Party do?

He then goes on to elaborate under five headings: Unemployment; Foreign Policy; Education; The Nation's Health; Finance. The journalist printed the full document in the local paper in Sheffield and a couple of nights later a very old, lovely lady came round to see me at the Crucible. The lady had seen the article in the paper and remembered when my father stood. She was a Conservative, and they had been told that a brilliant young barrister was coming up from London, so they had to work harder and wear bigger blue rosettes. It was a solid Conservative constituency but Dad polled more votes for Labour than had ever been polled there in any election until then.

I told Dad I was very proud of him. He is probably having St Vitus' Dance in his grave with what is going on now. He wouldn't have been able to tolerate Blair, that's for sure. I don't think he would have been quite a Bennite, not in the way that I am a Bennite, because I have gone much further to the left than Dad. He would have been very John Smith. He was also pro-Barbara Castle, and absolutely understood her 'In place of Strife': he wrote a very good letter to *The Times* on the subject of wild-cat strikes.

As I said before, I hadn't joined the Labour Party until the Gang of Four formed the SDP. At some Labour meeting I said I'd finally been able to join because 'we've got rid of the rubbish'. That went down very well at the time, but I regret it now because Shirley Williams is a terrific woman. How dare I ever call her rubbish? That fellow William Rodgers was rubbish. David Owen was rubbish – still is. I heard him the other day on television: monstrous creature, and what a narcissist. Why did Shirley Williams ally herself to them? She could have been a wonderful Prime Minister.

In addition to those two fabulous women, Barbara Castle and Shirley Williams, I had a great respect for Mo Mowlam. I have often wondered about Mo maintaining that her brain tumour was benign – I assumed that this was a public front. Then she started taking her wig off and playing a double game. I went to a talk that she gave at the Royal Festival Hall, not long before she died. She had written a book, and the event was to publicise it. That fine woman has never really been given the credit for the Northern Ireland Settlement. Blair moved in and pushed her out of the way when she had so clearly paved the way forwards. A splendid woman and what a loss.

By now I had met Neil and Glenys Kinnock. I first met Neil on the Steering Committee of the Anti Nazi League, and we became very good chums. He was a backbencher at the time but known to be left wing. What we wanted was a real Socialist agenda for the arts, and he was very supportive.

I had been with the Kinnocks – who were and are great theatre people – to see Antony Sher at the Barbican when he did his Shylock. We went to Joe Allen's restaurant afterwards and Neil got a trifle pissed. Tony and I asked what we should be doing about the 'Sharpeville Six'. These were six South African protesters convicted of the murder of the deputy mayor of Sharpeville after a protest march had turned into a riot. The six were arrested in the following months, found guilty of his murder and sentenced to death by hanging.

Neil said, 'You know all those stars in America, you should get them to get on to Reagan and he could influence Botha. Get all those stars and get them to campaign.'

We sort of said, yeah, right.

About ten days later I woke up and thought, days have passed and we've done nothing and something needs to be done. When I get this feeling, the devil gets into me and I just have to do something.

The first person I got onto was Peggy Ashcroft. I admire courage and the person I admired more than anyone was Peggy Ashcroft. She was, as far as I'm concerned, the perfect example of the best of womanhood, of humanity, of theatre. A brilliant woman, a brilliant artist and a great humanitarian and a woman with a great sense of humour: I feel very privileged that she was a friend. Even though she is no longer with us, I cannot cross her out of my old filofax, where hers is the first name. I won't cross her out because she's too precious.

I said to Peggy, 'Look, I had this conversation with Neil Kinnock about the Sharpeville Six and it looks as if they are going to be killed. Are there any American stars that you know that could get onto Reagan?'

Peggy said, 'Gregory Peck?'

'That's a good one for starters.'

She said, 'I wonder if Larry would do something?'

I said that would be fantastic. I asked her if she could write to Thatcher and cable or send a telegram to Reagan and she said, 'Well I can't do Thatcher because they call me the "Red Dame", but I could get onto John Gielgud and we could do Reagan together.'

She got me started. She was going to do all the dames and knights, and Audrey Hepburn, who was not only a big star but also an ambassador for UNICEF. Armed with that success I started phoning. I still have a list of the people I contacted, including Harrison Ford. I am always tentative of contacting people for myself but have courage when it is for someone else. Up until then, Thatcher had refused even to see the wives of the Six.

Julian Glover, who was doing a film with Charlton Heston and Harrison Ford at the time, got Heston to phone Reagan on the grounds that it would be good to show how humanitarian he was.

I spoke to Lee Remick and she sent a telegram as well. Eventually Reagan was inundated with telegrams and faxes from all these stars telling him he had to contact his friend Botha. All this happened in a matter of two weeks.

Then Julian phoned me and asked if I'd heard the news. Apparently Thatcher had agreed to see all the wives at lunchtime the following day, and a week later there was a remission for the men, they weren't going to be killed, but have their sentences commuted. It felt very good being a little cog in a huge wheel.

I played some magnificent women during these years and one of the most wonderful parts I played was Martha in *Who's Afraid of Virginia Woolf?* with Bernard Horsfall as George, Martha's husband. I was one of the first to play Martha twice in one day because most actresses said they couldn't. We opened at Leeds Playhouse and then went on tour. It was when Cameron Mackintosh was starting out as a producer. He wasn't the millionaire that he is now but even so, he was generous and used to come and see us and take us out for a meal after the show.

A million years later, a production of *Who's Afraid of Virginia Woolf?* was playing in London, starring Diana Rigg as Martha. One day my doorbell rang, and a courier was standing there with one of those huge cardboard envelopes. It was from Cameron. When I opened it, I found a playbill from our production, and on the back he had written: 'Dear Mim. Who needs a Dame when I had you? Thought you'd be interested in the prices we charged in those days.' It was fascinating to see: £1, 1 shilling for top price seats in the theatre.

I didn't think of the play as optimistic but I suppose it was, ultimately, because something has been purged by the end of it. I remember I found a great bit of business to do. We'd already been playing for a while and in one of those scenes where I'm screaming at George, I was standing on the settee and I leant across and stuck my hand in the ice bucket and went on talking with my mouthful of ice, which got a huge laugh. I had forgotten that in the very first scene George says, 'I don't know what you do with all that ice, Martha, do you chew it or something?' So I kept it in.

At the time my house in Clapham was being refurbished, so I was in between homes. I had taken essential clothes to my parents, my furniture was in store and I was on tour staying in digs. On the Friday night, prior to the two shows the next day, I woke up in an absolute sweat at about six in the morning. I'd heard in my nightmare a horrendous cough from my father and in my dream I was saying to Mummy, 'Give him his stuff, Mummy, Mummy.'

An hour or so later I heard the phone ring in the digs and I thought that it must be bad news, but it wasn't for me. I didn't want to phone home, I didn't want to hear in case there was some bad news. I managed to get through the two performances and it felt like climbing Everest. After the two shows Bernard drove me back to my parent's place and I crept in and put myself to bed. I woke up a few hours later hearing my mother coming along the corridor and she told me that Dad had had an attack. It was at exactly the time I had had the dream the night before, and I did feel as if I had some kind of psychic connection with my father. He got over it and regained his health quite quickly.

After Liselotte and Martha, I did a stint at the Leicester Haymarket, and each of the parts I played allowed me to explore my abilities to transform. I was Jocasta in *Oedipus* with Brian Blessed – and still have the bruises to show for it – and then played Madame Dubonnet in *The Boyfriend* with Elaine Paige. I rather enjoyed doing *The Boyfriend*. Lovely Crispin Thomas was in it: he was very special, and I worked with him again in *Hay Fever*, which I did the next year with Belinda Lang and David Glover. We used to laugh so much. I am a giggler anyway but I remember the end scene when all the visitors are creeping downstairs to exit, and I said, as Judith Bliss, 'How very rude', which got a round of applause and a bloody good laugh.

Crispin used to laugh with a mouthful of scrambled eggs which went everywhere.

When I was going to do *Hay Fever* and *The Seagull* at the Leicester Haymarket, I thought they were fabulous parts but both were actresses – how the hell was I going to differentiate between the two? Jan Sargent was directing both plays, and I remember asking her. She said, 'For Judith I want you to float like a gazelle through it and I don't want to hear any of those "Mim" vocal tones, whereas Arcadina is more grounded, having had to fight.' The moment she said 'float', the whole timbre of my voice changed and I knew what she meant.

I loved the whole experience of those rehearsals. When we were doing *The Seagull* we did improvisations, and I spent the first few days making up my face and being incredibly narcissistic, thinking how beautiful I was. While I was doing this, my eye would light on Trigorin, sitting there with his fishing rod, and I would notice that the young girl playing Nina was creeping up to him. I gradually felt an insane jealousy which built and built until I got onto the words, which then seemed to come naturally and truthfully. It was a great way to work because it was all there, for real, from the inside. This was similar to the way I had worked with Joan Littlewood. I loved the fact it was going to be a contemporary version, especially because I was still very involved in yoga. In the text it said something like my character 'struts up and down the garden' and instead I did yoga exercises to show how lithe I was, wearing this wonderful pale apricot-coloured, see-through cat suit.

In the first scene Constantin, my son, passed sparklers around the audience. I was sort of representing the National Theatre, very much establishment, and he was very fringe. I sat there watching him with great disdain, thinking, 'How could I have given birth to that?'

Clive Lavagna was the designer for both plays and I remember him saying, 'If only you'd been this shape when we did *The Boyfriend*.' I was horrified with myself for taking my eye off the ball so I went smartly off to the Forest Mere health farm. That was the pattern I had developed by now: I would go to a health farm and starve, live on lemon water or something for a few days and have loads of treatments. I became a queen of health farms and tried them all until they became ludicrously expensive.

Many years before, I was at Forest Mere when John Schlesinger turned up after he had just directed *Billy Liar*. He arrived white, fat, shaking and nervous; as I had already been there two weeks, I was brown, slim and relaxed. At the time I was at the pool and he said, as if he had got the weight of the world on his shoulders, 'I must go into Hazelmere tomorrow and buy myself some swimming trunks.'

A fellow who was in the pool got out and said, 'I'm going into town tomorrow.' Out of his own swimming trunks he took a tape measure and said, 'I'll measure you now but you'll have lost a couple of inches by tomorrow so I'll bring you some smaller ones.'

John laughed so much that he put this scene in one of his movies.

Jan also directed *The Bed Before Yesterday*, which we took on tour after starting at the Leicester Haymarket. Working with my co-star David Stoll was sheer joy. I regard him as the best farceur in the country. They don't make them like that anymore – actors with the incredible comedic style that he has. There is nothing he does not know about playing comedy and farce. His timing is perfection, and it is not surprising to discover that he worked with some of the real greats in comedy such as Tom Walls and Robertson Hare, and that he appeared in other Ben Travers plays prior to our shared experience.

Now then, how is it that with his brilliant track record he is hardly known by today's general public? Or even yesterday's? The answer, quite simply, is *television*. Unless you are appearing regularly on the box (and 'regularly' is the operative word), you are an unknown quantity. It seems that the more you appear either in a soap or a series, the more you are engaged to appear. The same faces reappearing with monotonous regularity – how boring is that? Then, of course, some bright producer casting a stage play thinks it would be a great idea to get Joe (or Joan) Bloggs out of a popular soap and gives them the leading role in the piece to do a national tour, with the intention of a West End transfer. What happens? This brilliant performer can't bloody well be heard beyond the second row of the stalls, doesn't know what to do with their hands or how to project, and certainly has no idea how to give a performance eight times a week. In other words it's a disaster. I have seen some very fine young actors coming out of drama schools, and unless they have 'the look' – the current 'look' – they may not get an agent. The majority of agents nowadays are only interested in young people who will fit into a soap. Fortunately, there is still a minority who see the potential in a young actor and will work hard to build a career path.

However, I always tell students on the point of leaving drama school that even if they haven't an agent or prospect of work, they must go on acting; otherwise everything they've learned in the last three years will be forgotten, and frustration and lack of confidence sets in. So I suggest that they get together with two or three mates with whom they worked well at school, and either improvise something or find a piece that appeals to them, rehearse it and perform it for any audience, for schools, for old people, take it to a fringe theatre…but *keep acting.*

But back to David Stoll, before I started this tirade. While on tour with *The Bed Before Yesterday*, David and I had booked digs in Hull and it had been rather a nasty journey. We'd decided that when we got to Hull we'd unpack and have a little rest and then go out, have a really nice chat and a meal and some *vino*. At the digs in Hull David rang the doorbell, and this woman answered with a fag hanging out of her mouth. David in his charming way said, 'Hello there, I'm David Stoll and this is Ms Karlin and we've got a booking.'

She said, 'Yes, well Ms Karlin you're going to the back room but we had a sailor here last week and he pissed in the bed.'

I went upstairs to find a mattress hanging over the banisters. I had to sleep next to the bed that had been pissed in. It wasn't a joyous week.

We found the Hilton in Hong Kong rather better. We both stayed and played at the Hilton, performing the play as 'dinner theatre' in the hotel dining room. They were very civilised in that they didn't serve whilst we were working – dinner had to be over and tables cleared before we began. Of course they had had enough drinks by then, so the laughs one got at the beginning were as warm as they usually are by the end. It was a real exercise in understanding how important it is to make an audience feel comfortable.

What makes an audience behave in a certain way? Why does an audience have a mass reaction on certain nights? I mean, some nights we come off stage and say, 'God they're ghastly tonight, Christ, terrible.' Another night we'll say, 'Fan-bloody-tastic tonight, they're brilliant.' What makes this mass reaction? I can't understand it, and that's why I've always wanted to start from a level playing-field. For a long time I've had a fantasy to come out front prior to the start of the performance and say:

> We know that a lot of you seeing us tonight have got problems. Some of you may have booked your tickets months ago, since when you're possibly contemplating divorce from the partner for whom you got the other ticket. Others are suffering terrible depression and are possibly contemplating suicide. It's been a ghastly night – some of you have had your hair done and it's got all messed up because of the rain. Others thought that you were going to be late and arrived at the theatre in a state. So we are very conscious that you may not be in the most receptive frame of mind. We, on our side of the curtain, have also got a load of problems; some of us have had people die, some of us have been rather sick, some of us are incredibly nervous. But it's our job to make you feel really, really good. So we have to forget all

our problems and what we have to do is to make you forget all of yours. So let me suggest that before we all start we each take ten deep yoga breaths… Having done that – right – now we can begin.

Well, we didn't have any need of this in Hong Kong; they were warm and receptive.

Sometimes you get a reaction from an audience that's impossible to repeat. A few years before *The Bed Before Yesterday* I had been in a lovely production of the play *Bus Stop*, directed by Vivian Matalon, with Lee Remick, Keir Dullea, Alfred Marks and Jenny Quayle. We were at the Phoenix Theatre, which was famously overrun with mice at the time, and there was a night in the run when one of them got a starring role in the play. I was working behind the counter on the set with Jenny Quayle, and she whispered to me, 'There-is-a-mouse!' I wanted to stand up on the counter with terror! Later on, it practically ran up Lee Remick's fishnet stocking and the audience laughed their heads off. Lee had no idea what was going on. As part of the subplot of the play, a man comes in every so often and flirts with my character, Grace, who runs the café. At one point he says, 'Hiya Grace, I want a sandwich.' I reply, 'Sorry – we're out of cheese.' Well, as you can imagine, on this night the line got a huge laugh, and I was congratulated afterwards for my brilliant ad-lib! I had to confess it was actually in the script.

Bus Stop also gave me the opportunity to meet one of the greats, Stephen Sondheim, who was a good friend of Lee Remick. On opening night, in the interval after the first act, Lee said to me, 'I'm gonna kill him. Stevie Sondheim is in the front row. What a thing to do to me!' When I was introduced to him, I mentally genuflected, and said, 'How wonderful to meet you.'

He smiled and said, 'We have actually met before,' which made me feel terrible.

I looked blank, and he said, 'When you did my number at the *Night of a Hundred Stars*'. This was the strippers' song from *Gypsy*, 'If you're gonna bump it, bump it with a trumpet', which I had sung with Millicent Martin and Barbara Windsor.

He continued, 'When I went back home I was surprised you weren't known in the States'. It was a typically double-edged remark: I took it as a compliment, but he could just have been paying me back for not recognising him!

I was, and am, a great joiner; I'd join anything that interested me. I joined Weight Watchers, because I was so neurotic about the weight going up and down. Bernice Weston was the American woman who brought Weight Watchers over here. The local branch held a meeting every Tuesday morning at a church hall round the corner from me in St John's Wood, so I knew it was happening and thought I must join. I went along and they weighed me and they said, 'Sorry we can't take you, you're too slim.' I was probably nine stone or something, which is why I wanted to join. They said I was under ten stone which was their limit. I thought I can do that easily, started eating and managed to get to ten stone very quickly, went back, and they took me on. I started campaigning for them then, and thought they were great. One had a box of 'number three' vegetables and didn't put on any weight because you could eat yourself silly on these, rather like the earlier diet I had been on with Dr Goller.

When it was the fifth birthday of WW they took the Albert Hall and Bernice asked me to be one of her speakers. At the centre of the Albert Hall they made a huge birthday cake. I climbed up on the cake on this huge rostrum. The audience consisted of people of all shapes and sizes, some who were half their original weight, and some not. I told the audience that I had been a secret biscuit eater. I used to keep biscuits on a very high shelf which involved climbing onto a high-stool to get them down, and would get up at three in the morning, get on the stool, get the biscuit tin down, break about four or five biscuits, tell myself that broken biscuits didn't count and that by some magic I would be slim in the morning. When I told the audience that, they all understood.

I was friendly with Kenneth Williams at this time, with whom I was working in the play *The Undertaking*. Kenneth was very right-wing and, like me, on the Equity Council, so within that context we were enemies.

This was the time when nine of us walked off the stage at the Equity AGM. We wanted to show our disapproval of Marius Goring, who was on the Council and had cost Equity an inordinate amount of unnecessary money by pursuing a high court action against the union and, having lost, taking the case to the Lords on appeal. All this because he wanted to have the principle of a referendum of the entire membership enshrined in our rulebook. (Up until then, a two-thirds majority at an AGM could change a rule, as happened with the TUC.) I was still working in Leicester at the time and the AGM was on the Sunday. I had telephone conversations with our group and I said I'd be back by midnight on the Saturday night. When I got back they came round to my house and we talked about how we were going to deal with it the following day, and helped formulate my speech.

It was a very crafty speech and I didn't indicate until the very end that we were going to resign. We walked off stage and got a huge round of applause. I'll always remember that Corin Redgrave stood up and applauded. Corin up until then had always thought of me as being a 'middle of the road liberal', but suddenly I was one of them.

Kenneth hadn't understood anything I'd said, and he wrote a letter to Maggie Smith which said something like: 'Miriam Karlin said she couldn't be bothered with all of us and so she left with a load of people.'[4]

At that time the membership of Equity went right down from having been very high to perilously low, but we are gradually getting

4 'Some Speeches and Letters', pages 234–5.

our strength back. Sadly we still have the remnants of Thatcher's children who don't know why we need unions. I ask young people in every production I do if they're in the union, and when they ask why, I tell them that if they have an accident, trip over a cable, if an arc lamp bangs on their head and they get concussion, they are not covered by any kind of insurance. I remind them of what happened to Roy Kinnear who died on a film from falling off a horse. Equity fought the case and although it took time, we actually managed to get over half a million for his wife Carmel, who used the money to open the Roy Kinnear Home for children with disabilities.

When Sam Wanamaker was creating the Globe Theatre, I read that he managed to get some money from the cigarette manufacturers Peter Stuyvesant. Then I bumped into him at a party and though I was delighted to see him again, I had given up smoking for the first time and my new-found anti-smoking evangelism took over. I criticised him for taking Peter Stuyvesant's money. He said, 'Occasionally you have to sleep with the devil.' I said I thought that there are times that once you've slept with the devil it's difficult to get out of bed because it's very comfortable.

The only time I consciously slept with the devil, and by God did I regret it (and if this offends anyone by my saying it, I'm sorry, so be it), was when I was asked to do the second lot of *The Rag Trade* in 1976. Having done them all in black and white for the BBC in the early 1960s, this time it was to be ITV/London Weekend in colour. Although my first reaction was that I didn't want to do it again, when I was told by the writers that it was going to be brought up to date and was going to become a multi-racial workshop I agreed, because that's what I'd been campaigning for. However, when we came to it there was one token black actress and she was not overburdened with talent, in fact this particular actress (at this time we still said 'actress' rather than 'actor') used to make what I considered to be racist jokes. I used to say to her each week, 'You can't say that!'

'Why not?'

'Because that's racist, that's why.'

A waste of time. One day a group of young men with dreadlocks came into the canteen, and she said, 'I can't stand these people. In Trinidad we put food out for them in the back yard.'

I was horrified and said, 'Lu, *you're* a bleedin' racist.'

My support for Israel was beginning to change. I continued to do the odd lunches. The organisers of one lunch had invited Topol to be the speaker and thought it would be good to invite me too. After he had spoken at this particular luncheon, I went to the ladies' room. A woman in there said, 'Oh Miriam Karlin, it's so wonderful to meet you, I've been such a fan of yours. I've often wondered why you haven't gone further?'

Her accent was archetypal North West London Jewish. I was a little defensive and said, 'Well, I've worked quite hard and quite a lot.'

'Oh yes, I know, but you should be like Barbra Streisand.'

I said, 'Well I've never actually been overly ambitious.'

I went out and she followed me out of the loo, saying, 'You see some people have the luck. You don't have it, that's what it is, you don't have the luck!'

She probably went home and told her family, 'I saw that Miriam Karlin and I told her, you know, she hadn't had the luck. That's why she hadn't gone very far!'

8

BAD STUFF

In which I had a spine operation from which I thought I'd never recover, and my dependence on pills increased. The National Front pursued me relentlessly, threatening me at my door; my father died; and my mother developed dementia.

I FIND IT HARD now to think back and pinpoint exactly when I began to be aware that I wasn't keeping on top of things.

I was strong-willed, but that didn't continue throughout my life. As I grew older, I became more scared of stuff, scared of being hurt. You can't go through life in this business and not be hurt on a number of occasions. Looking back, I think I built a wall around myself so that I didn't get hurt anymore. That way I protected myself against rejection and disappointment.

Others think I have will-power but I don't, because will-power and ambition go together and my only sort of ambition is to be good once I have a job. My strength comes from weakness, because I am too scared to avoid doing something. This cowardice goes with the double standards which I am always harping on about; I say one thing, am seemingly passionate about something, and then I'll do the opposite.

After all, how can I be a complete socialist, signed up to the NHS and yet be a member of BUPA? How do you marry those two things? It's wrong and I am deeply ashamed. People think I am so brave to have gone through what I have in the last year. What else could I do? I am signed up as a life member of the Voluntary Euthanasia Society, but I am too scared to do it!

As I have said, it was about this time, 1975, that I went 'south of the river' to Clapham. Little did I think when I moved there that within a year my father would die, and I would have to get my mother into a home which would be five minutes' walk from where I was living.

I was very proud of my big new house, but the truth is that I was once again in financial shit, so I sold my beautiful Hamilton Terrace pad and bought the Clapham house, which cost £21,500. (It's now worth over a million.) I think all the moves I've made since then have been because of running out of money. For this last place, I've saved money by buying it on a short, 25-year lease because that reflected my shelf-life. (I suppose I'd better pop off quickly, because the lease is nearly up and I'll be past my sell-by date…)

When I came back from Australia, after I'd done my one-woman show *Liselotte* at the Festival in Adelaide, I didn't give myself time to get over jet lag because the next day I started rehearsing *Bus Stop*. After some days of rehearsal the director Vivian Matalon said to me, 'Welcome back to England, Mim.'

I looked at him and he said, 'You haven't really been with us, have you?' and I realised that I had been on another planet.

Bus Stop finished on a Saturday night. On the Monday morning Dad died. He left it until I had finished the show. My parents had been to the first night, which they always did, and my sister-in-law Hilary who had been staying in Canada with her brother and family got back to England on the Sunday, so it seemed he thought, 'We are all here in one place, now I can die.'

Dad kept saying the morning he died, 'Get Min. I want to see Min.' My mother kept phoning me and I said, 'I'm coming, I'm coming,' but a mini-cab fucked me up and I arrived twenty minutes too late. He was already gone.

I really grieved for the first time in my life.

On the morning of the funeral the undertaker asked my brother and me if we wanted to see him. He was cold and looked so peaceful.

I gave him a kiss, then Michael and I just stood there like two kids bawling our eyes out. I was probably very selfish about the whole thing, because he had left me, and how could he? I wasn't going to have anybody to phone up and get jokes and quotations from now. I felt I wanted to shake him to wake him up.

I was working, so I just had to get on with it. Work had kept me together during the difficult period in *The Diary of Anne Frank*, and it saved me again. Mother was desperate and began to go senile very soon after. We comforted one another for a while – in fact I stayed with her for quite a few nights – but then a kind of role reversal began. I had already had one rehearsal of her dependence when he had the first big heart attack, but now she was older.

They had so complemented one another for the 58 years they were married. They would go away to Bournemouth or Brighton, staying in hotels, dancing together well into their seventies – even after their golden wedding. It must have been like losing half of herself.

I missed my father so much: he had been the main influence on my life. I had had to have Dad's approval and once I had it I could do anything. There have been an awful lot of chaps I have tried to get to take Dad's place since he died, because I always had to have male approval. I still rely on my brother Michael and various people like Philip Hedley and Richard Digby Day, ringing them up saying, 'I am going to send this to the *Independent* or the *Guardian*. What do you think?' Dad had been so special. He was, and still is, irreplaceable.

Throughout my fifties the battle with my health, my weight and my addictions raged, and although I had some wonderful work during the next period of my life, there were many difficult times. I realise in retrospect that much of it was of my own making because of the life I had led, but the doctors that treated me seemed to compound the problem – certainly around the issue of whether to prescribe Valium or not.

For quite a long time, from the mid-1970s, I had back pain and a sciatic pain going down my right leg. I sought opinions and saw loads of doctors. When I had to have a varicose vein operation, I was sent to St Thomas' Hospital. There is a mandatory amount of walking you have to do when you have your veins done and I said to my GP (who was still Patrick Woodcock), 'While I am having the veins done, do you think somebody could look at my back and see why I am having all this pain there and down my leg?'

So an orthopaedic surgeon came in to see me. They gave me an injection with mauve dye (a 'ridiculogram') which showed up a nerve trapped behind a dead disc, and the surgeon said that if he removed the disc, I would be a new woman. I thought that sounded okay, and went along with it.

I was supposed to start rehearsing in Stephen Sondheim's *Company* for Richard Digby Day about two months later, but it was a very painful operation and I was in hospital for two weeks. I phoned my agent Ronnie Waters and said, 'You're going to have to get on to Richard and tell him I can't do it.' I couldn't do anything physical and didn't think I was ever going to walk, let alone work, again.

At the time I was taking about 2mg of Valium a day. I said to the consultant, 'Do you think that it would be a good idea if I came off the Valium whilst I'm in hospital?'

'Very good.'

The next day he came in and said, 'I've been thinking about you, and rather than taking you off Valium, I'd like to increase the dose.'

He put me on 15mg a day of Valium, 15mg of Amitriptyline and 15mg of Nortriptyline. One part of me said this was wrong, but the other part said, goody, goody, it's kosher now.

My lovely friends from across the road came to collect me after the operation. I had asked them, as part of my piss elegant style, to buy some presents for the nurses, so they arrived with all these things which I did up in gift wrapping for everybody. I realised that there were going to be lots of things I couldn't do. For example, there was no way that I could lean over to make my bed (I had had a big bed with blankets and sheets on it). I bought an expensive duvet, which I still use.

I couldn't dress myself properly, either, because I had been put in a steel corset after the operation. I was convalescing at home when my sister-in-law came down from Glasgow and we decided to go to Cyprus for two weeks' holiday – with me still wearing the corset, though I used to take it off during the day to swim and lie on the beach. I was told that I had to be flat or sit upright and was taught how to walk in it. The surgeon had said to me with a grin, 'You'll never do yoga again.' I had wanted to kill him, so I worked really hard at getting fit to prove him wrong. Eventually I got back to being able to move relatively freely.

Well, Richard insisted that despite all this, I do *Company* and sent the musical director round when I returned to teach me my songs, which of course included that wonderful number 'Here's to the Ladies who Lunch'. He saved me from gloom and depression and gave me the will to do the show, and I feel immensely grateful to him because if he had not insisted, I might never have wanted to work again.

Company was my salvation. The designer measured me and I had the most fabulous clothes made which covered the steel corset, and I was even able to do some reasonably high kicks. Gradually the pain subsided, and for about a year I was reasonably pain-free. And then it all came back.

The National Council for Drama Training had started to do its work by this time and as I was on the Equity Council I had wanted to be part of the process of accreditation of drama schools. The work would be interesting and I was going to be able to use my experience in a different way. In order to accredit, we would have to visit all the schools that had applied for accreditation, and we went all over the country here and in Scotland and Wales. We hadn't yet come to any agreement as to a particular standard, but we knew we were looking for excellence and we were going to have to accredit a number of schools by a certain time.

The question I used to ask with monotonous regularity was, 'Why is there no ethnicity here? Why are all the students white?' I never got a straightforward answer from any of the principals. Later on I remember going to the community arts course at Rose Bruford College and for the first time seeing African, Asian and Caribbean people represented. I thought, 'Is this a coincidence?' It wasn't. It was simply that young black and Asian people weren't applying to colleges since they felt that they wouldn't be accepted, whereas they felt that a community arts course would be more receptive to their talents.

We had been to see quite a few schools, and then we went up to Glasgow to the Royal Scottish Academy. The students and tutors were working really hard and there was a huge commitment to the work. I remember coming back on the train and saying to my colleagues that we had now seen a particular standard of excellence to which all the others must attain.

By 1980 we had visited all the drama schools that had applied for accreditation. Then came the day when we were to make the decision on the first six. It was a Sunday and the meeting was held at Equity HQ in Harley Street, starting at about 9.30 in the morning. It went on until about 8 o'clock at night. It was exhausting for all of us: I think I was the only one able to remain upright because of my steel corset. Each time we accredited a school one could almost see blue smoke coming up from Harley Street! All the principals were sitting in another place around the corner, and one by one, as their school was accredited, a runner would go and collect the relevant person and they were told the result.

When it came to the Drama Centre I worried that it was going to be thrown out because there had been some controversy about it. I passed a note to Pat Marmont, an actor-turned-agent, 'If they don't accredit Drama Centre I am going to walk out, how about you?' We both agreed. It got through by one vote. The standard at the Drama Centre had excelled even that of Glasgow, and the school had a director's course, something that the other schools did not have.

Now, of course, drama schools are having to take in more and more students in order to cope financially. In addition to taking in far too many students, the other madness is their forced attachment to universities, so a student comes out with a degree. Who has ever been asked at an audition whether one has a degree? Most important is whether they can act or not.

Things have changed ethnicity-wise, thankfully: nowadays some brilliant black actors have come out of drama schools, particularly RADA. The teaching has changed, though, as the syllabus has had to conform to academic criteria, with a marking system and grades. What I have also discovered is that they are teaching two forms of 'received pronunciation' – one being what I would regard as normal received pronunciation and the other a form of 'estuary English'. (The way people speak has always fascinated me and when I watched the Queen on her 80th birthday programme I noticed how her speech has changed over the years – practically becoming Essex! It's the same with Tony Blair.)

After the operation I began to feel well again and then I did something really foolish. Having been a confirmed non-smoker for sixteen and a half years I was suddenly desperate for nicotine. I went berserk, I had to have nicotine, and I remembered that there was a silver cigarette box which had been given to me by my Australian friend Gordon Chater. I had put it away in my study with seven Disque Bleu cigarettes in it. I went up, found the box, took out a cigarette, yellow with age, couldn't wait to light it, inhaled, and it was bliss!

I started another one, and was soon ringing up chums saying, 'I just smoked a sixteen and a half year old cigarette.' Then I found myself 'accidentally' walking past a cigarette kiosk saying, 'Twenty

Disque Bleu please', and being shocked at the price. When I gave up they had been 4 shillings 7 pence (the equivalent of 24p now).

The guilt of smoking made me smoke more than ever. Then I started to feel terrible, ghastly pains in my legs, pains all over and I didn't know what the hell was the matter with me. I was still taking the Valium, and after extensive investigations in the London Clinic it was unanimously agreed that Valium was actually the cause. The psychiatrist who was one of the team suggested I go to the Charter Clinic for detoxification. I said I was just going into a new play and it was decided that I would phone him when the play was finished, so I obviously delayed going in. Work came first.

The problem with my eyes started at this time too. I went to see a new doctor who had taken over from Patrick Woodcock and she said, 'I've never seen you before but do you always look like that?'

'Like what?'

She said, 'Well, thyroxic – your eyes are bulging.'

She immediately put me on another drug and took some blood. My thyroid turned out to be hyper. So there I was, with hyperactive thyroid and bulging eyes.

I was in a Royal Court production at the Ambassadors, and there was a lot of smoking around me. There were four of us in a tiny dressing room and three of them were smoking like crazy. Actually I was smoking in the play too, but by this time I'd given up again, so it was a herbal cigarette. The smoke was going into my left eye and it got very painful. I had to tape my eyes down at night because they wouldn't close. That resulted in my seeing another specialist, Geoffrey Rose. When I saw him the first time he said, 'I think you and I are going to be seeing rather a lot of each other.' How right he was. Eventually I had to have four operations on my left eye.

I had been asked to do a play in Glasgow, *Lavotchkin 5*, directed by that lovely Russian director Irina Brown, but my eye got so bad that Mr Rose said he wanted to take me into Moorfields. I really wanted to do the play, so he finally agreed, as long as I had radiotherapy at the same time. So I went to Glasgow for the play and got up at six am every day. A car came and took me to Clydebank, to a private hospital (here's my double standards again) where they gave me radiotherapy every morning. Then I'd go back into town and rehearse.

The Anti Nazi League was formed in the late 1970s. This was where I really felt I was carrying on Dad's work, which seemed even more important after his death. He had campaigned actively against Oswald Mosley and his blackshirts and of course started the boycott of German goods during the 1930s.[5]

I was on the steering committee with Neil Kinnock, Peter Hain and Paul Holborough. The focus was the racism of the National Front against black and Asian People, and Jews, of course – Jews always come into it. The National Front were almost the same as the BNP now, except that the BNP is trying to be perceived as respectable. The NF never made any attempt at respectability. When this monster David Irving suddenly reared his disgusting head, I stood outside his house in Mount Street screaming abuse at him. There was a whole group of us doing it. I was really passionate about the fact that this man could actually campaign that there was no such thing as the Holocaust; that it didn't happen, that it was all made up by Jews in order to get sympathy.

I've had bowel problems for some years now, so the last time I saw a real turd was the shit pushed through my letterbox from the National Front, when I lived in Clapham. It was the first time I had to have a burglar alarm fitted and double-glazing on my windows. The Clarks, the lovely couple who had collected me from hospital, became a great support. Tom and Edna were ordinary people but extraordinary in their ordinariness, North-country, and very special.

They were having tea with me in my kitchen and the phone kept ringing. When I answered, it was a man's voice asking for some

5 'Some Speeches and Letters', pages 235–6.

strange name, so I told him he had the wrong number. This happened several times. Then the doorbell went, and I went to answer it. I had a little spy-hole thing and looked through and asked who it was. The chap outside the door said 'Taxi' and mimed signing. I had an account with a taxi firm at the time, but said I hadn't ordered one and started to open the door. He kicked it open and I screamed to Tom and Edna. They immediately came and pushed him out of the door where we saw this strange van painted green without any windows so you couldn't see who was inside. This great big thug of a fellow had obviously been phoning to see if I was in. It was very frightening and I was shaking like a leaf afterwards. The luckiest thing was that the Clarks had been going to go some time earlier and I had persuaded them to have another cup of tea. I was 52 at the time. I poured something stronger after that.

I started to have nightmares at this time, obviously brought on by increasing anxiety. Every profession has nightmares – directors do, I'm sure, about the camera being broken; actors certainly do, about not knowing their lines – but there was one I'll never forget. I was supposed to be playing in a Shaw play, *The Dark Lady of the Sonnets*, and I was sitting in my dressing room, with an Elizabethan ruff round my neck and a vest which only went down to my crotch, when I heard them calling 'Beginners'. I hadn't yet got the script and was trying to form words. I couldn't open my dressing room door because it was locked. I've never been more glad to wake up. The significance of the dream, no knickers – ultimate vulnerability I imagine.

Some years earlier, I had dreamt my own burglary. I had a switch outside my bedroom and if I pressed it the studio lit up. I dreamt that I heard burglars downstairs and that I got out of bed quietly, turned on the switch and it wouldn't come on. I knew the burglars could see me in silhouette and I couldn't see them. I woke up in a sweat. The very next day the cleaning lady said, 'Oh Ms Karlin, you don't have a light bulb in your downstairs loo', and when she said that, it kind of broke my dream. I told her that I'd dreamt that the bulb in the studio had blown. I switched it on and discovered that it had indeed blown.

That evening I came home, changed into my home rags and put my jewellery into a drawer in my dressing table. When I was downstairs on the phone, I thought I heard a slight noise above and thought it was the wind. I assumed the bedroom window was open, so once I finished the phone call I went upstairs to close it – and there, standing on the window ledge, was a man dressed all in black, wearing a balaclava. I slammed the door, screaming obscenities in a would-be male voice, rushed downstairs, turned on the burglar alarm and dialled 999.

'Fire, ambulance or police?' they asked.

'Police!' I screamed.

While I was waiting for a response, I turned off the burglar alarm, which was driving me mad. I breathlessly gave the police my details and said, 'There's a burglar upstairs.'

After I hung up, I stood, shaking, by the front door, constantly looking through the peephole, until the police arrived. We went upstairs. Of course the aforementioned burglar had long since made his getaway, taking with him all my jewellery. He had strewn a load of fake stuff under my bed. Only a few days before, my jeweller in Marylebone High Street had carried out an evaluation of my jewellery, most of which had come from him, and I was to discover a year or so later that not only was he in the nick, but that he was responsible, either personally or through an accomplice, for the burglary.

It was a bad time all round. Mother became a changed personality. When she was still living at home, she would ring me up and tell me something absolutely crazy. She told me that the wardrobe had fallen on top of her, then the grand piano and various other things. It was frightening. There are various stages of dementia, I was told: having always been a reasonably placid woman, she became angry, a totally new persona.

Her anger increased when I moved her into a halfway house in Hendon called Waverley Manor. They weren't really medically equipped and eventually they couldn't keep her because she began to do dreadful things. She would take her teeth out and put them on the table where people were sitting eating. And she did other things too embarrassing to mention.

They told me that they couldn't keep her, so having heard about Nightingale House, I spoke to the director. I'll always remember him saying to me, 'If I can't do something for your mother after all your family has done for the Jewish community, God help us.'

So she went there and her anger decreased: she settled into a state of pure confusion, and then senile contentment. She'd still get irritated with people she thought were stupid. I would see her sitting, with her glasses on, ostensibly reading, and then find that the book was upside-down. That was when she developed the banana phase. I had found banana skins in her handbag so I would take some in for her. She was in the geriatric department and with all these old people all sitting around, having their own chairs – 'This is *my* seat', very proprietorial.

Within a few weeks I was taking more and more bananas. Every Sunday I would go with a huge bag. I would go to my mother first and give her a banana and she would say, 'Oh Min, you're such a darling!'

Then I would hear a voice saying, 'I want a banana, give me a banana', so I'd give whoever said it a banana. And then another woman would say, 'Have you got a banana tree in your garden? You must have a banana tree in your garden' and I'd give her a banana. There was another who could hardly speak and she would say, 'Gi… me anana, gi me anana', and I began to realise that there might be a connection between senile women and the liking of bananas. (Sexual, perhaps?)

I used to have to clean up Ma's handbag every week. I'd find sweet papers and things that didn't belong to her. Then I realised that things belonging to her were in other people's handbags. That was when I joined EXIT (now Dignity in Dying). Even though I joined I couldn't contemplate it for my mother. I had the opportunity, because a doctor from Nightingale House rang me one day and said, 'Did you know your mother was bleeding? She is very difficult, you know, to examine.'

So I said, 'Are you asking for my permission to put her under anaesthetic?'

'Well, yes actually.'

'If you found that there was something malignant, would you feel it your duty to operate?'

'Well, yes.'

I said I would talk to my brother about it, but when I spoke to Michael we agreed we couldn't put her through an operation, so we said no and the opportunity passed. There I am, a member of EXIT and I couldn't do it for my own mother, so how can I expect somebody to do it for me? I have got several friends who have said they would help me, but whether they would when it came to it, I doubt very much. It is a very tough thing to do.

Eventually it came to the point when she was getting that vacant look, a deadness in the eyes, just nothing, it was horrible to see what had become of the mother I had known and loved, who had this wonderful sense of humour and laughed so much. We had been such a giggly family because my father used to have a self-mocking wit and my mother would hold herself laughing rocking to and fro. That is what brought them together. It certainly wasn't my father saying to my mother, 'What is your opinion of the Darwin theory?' She never got over that.

She could still speak several languages, though – extraordinary how the aged brain works with dementia. My neighbours the Clarks went in to see her in the home and told her they were going to Amsterdam for the weekend. Her instant reply was: 'You must go to the Rijksmuseum and see the Rembrandts.' I would speak to her in

Dutch, French, and German, and she would always answer perfectly, but couldn't remember what we had just said.

When I think back, I realise now how incredibly courageous she was. When you consider that she lost her sister and her nephew and niece – both the same age as Michael and me – and then her husband. One whole group of her family all ended in the gas chambers and she never ever carried on about it. When you hear people saying the Holocaust didn't happen, you want to say, 'Do I have to dig up the rotting bones of my mother's family in order to prove that it did?'

9

RECOVERY

In which I worked at the RSC with Trevor Nunn, did Torch Song Trilogy *with Antony Sher, became involved with the Kinnocks, was diagnosed with peripheral neuropathy and started treatment at last.*

I COULD PICK MYSELF UP easily, and I suppose that came from my mother. How could she have gone on, knowing what she knew? Michael was saying recently that Ma had been a more optimistic person than Dad and that we have both inherited Dad's pessimism. My resilience is possibly the best thing I inherited from my mother – that, and the absolute need to laugh.

Because I hadn't married and had children and grandchildren, I had to work to earn a living. I don't think I rejected marriage because I wanted to work, although I can't be sure. Workaholism and a strong work ethic is part and parcel of my family's life. Michael is a workaholic, well into his eighties; and me, I'd feel guilty if I spent the day reading the paper – which my mother would have happily done all the time. Before she got married she had done secretarial work for a couple of years, and was bright enough to have done anything, but in her day it wasn't the done thing to work if you didn't need to.

After *Company* I began to have offers of different kinds of work where I could use my experience to useful purpose, but before that I had to deal with the increasing deterioration of my now ageing body.

One day, when the pain in my legs was almost more than I could bear, I was finally diagnosed with peripheral neuropathy. When I enquired what this meant, the doctor explained it thus: 'If you can imagine an electric wire without its coating, that is the state of the damage to the nerves in your legs.' It results in various sensations, ranging from numbness and pins and needles to excruciating and shooting pains, and to me the pain was as if my legs from the hips to the toes were burning, on edge, with shocks running up them. It was a relief to know what I had, but there was apparently no cure for the damage.

Characteristically I set about finding out researching this condition and joined the Neuropathy Trust. I also wrote to EXIT because I felt I needed to know how to depart if it got more than I could bear.

I became so involved in politics that at one point I was phoned by the Labour Party in Mitcham and Morden and asked if I would consider standing in the forthcoming by-election there. (The incumbent Labour MP, Bruce Douglas-Mann, had joined the newly-formed SDP, and was the only one of the defectors with the decency to resign his seat.) I wasn't even a member of the party at that point. Although I was a staunch Labour supporter, I said, 'No way! I'd never be able to take the whip!'

I felt that there would be times when I wouldn't agree with the party. I thought at the time that the only way you could stand was to be totally loyal and I just couldn't visualise myself doing it. I have to admit, though, that earlier, when I spoke at the Oxford Union, I did feel this sense of power saying, 'Mr President, sir' and could visualise myself saying, 'Mr Speaker', but I never regretted the fact that I didn't stand. I wouldn't have been anything like as good as Glenda Jackson, because she has been an amazing MP. She is such an articulate person and when we were on the Equity Council together I noticed that whenever Glenda spoke people listened. She didn't speak often but when she spoke it was always good sense. Peggy Ashcroft had the same skill.

Despite the pain I was in, I now knew what the diagnosis was and needed to throw myself into work again. While I was doing *The Undertaker*, I was with the director Donald McKechnie in Joe Allen's one night and Trevor Nunn was sitting at a table across from us. I said to Donald, 'I'd love to be in the RSC.'

He said, 'I'll drop a note to Trevor.'

The next thing I knew, my agent phoned me and said would I go along and meet Barry Kyle and John Caird at the Aldwych? So I met them and they gave me two scripts, the Jacobean play *The Witch of Edmonton* and Farquhar's *The Twin-Rivals*. We talked and that was it. They were wonderful parts and I felt pretty good about it. I was also to play Mistress Quickly in *Henry IV* when the RSC opened the Barbican, and *Money* by Bulwer-Lytton, which Bill Alexander was to direct.

I moved to Stratford-upon-Avon and lived in one of those delightful old cottages for the season. However, while I was away my lovely cleaning lady, who lived in the same street as me in London, used to go in regularly to clean and pick up post and do some sorting out. One day she picked up a letter and thought it looked odd and had the very good sense to take it over the road to my friends the Clarks. They held it up to the light and saw five razor blades. If I had opened that letter, it would have taken the tops of my fingers off. The police were then well and truly alerted and at last began to take my phone calls seriously. After that, any time I came back from Stratford and there was another turd or package, I would ring them up and say, 'There is another turd.' They wouldn't actually do anything about it, but at least they knew and took it away.

When I did *The Witch of Edmonton*, the character in a way took me over. Elizabeth Sawyer had only one eye and a hump on her back, and was deformed in other ways. The locals in Edmonton, which in those days was right in the heart of the country, referred to her as a witch – 'Elizabeth Sawyer, she's a witch' – and she was blamed every time the harvest didn't work or a baby died. I remember the director

Barry Kyle saying on the first day of rehearsal: 'You know, for witch, you could read, black, Asian or Jew.'

At the first preview I got beaten up by members of the cast and stupidly didn't have any padding on me. I got bashed really badly and I went back to my little cottage, saying a line from the play to myself: 'I am shunned, I am shunned and hated, I am shunned and hated like a sickness.' I turned on the radio and I listened to the midnight news and heard that the National Front had printed the names of three people from the Anti Nazi League in their filthy rag of a paper – Jonathan Dimbleby, Miriam Karlin and Peter Hain – and had given our addresses. I was in this paranoid state anyway from rehearsal and didn't know which I was more sorry for, Elizabeth Sawyer or me.

The director Barry Kyle phoned me the next morning and said something about coming in for notes and I was horrible to him on the phone. When I went in to the theatre he said to me, 'Look, I can't cope with this ridiculous paranoia. You are bloody marvellous in this part, so I don't know what the fuck you are going on about!'

Actually that was all I wanted to hear and things changed. They got me some more padding and he made sure I wasn't beaten up so badly again. I had been bruised all over, in a terrible state, and then hearing that news at the same time... It had all collided and I couldn't dissociate one from the other. I wanted to be loved. Am I different from anybody else?

While we were performing in Stratford, we started rehearsing *Henry IV Parts One* and *Two* which were to open the Barbican with Trevor Nunn directing. He gave us a talk about it, outlining the wonders of the Barbican and then gave the historical background to the *Henrys*. I am afraid I dropped off, and Gemma Jones said in the lunch break, 'Well, you lasted till the Tudors.' Other elderly actors had preceded me, apparently.

When we finally got to the rehearsals, I wanted to evolve a new accent for Mistress Quickly based on a combination of the dialect spoken at the time of Henry IV and Shakespearean dialect. I had asked my brother to record some Elizabethan speeches, one in fifteenth-century speech and the other in Shakespearean, and thought that I could find an accent which blended the two. When I suggested this to Trevor he wasn't interested and wanted me to do it in cockney. I didn't really like what I was doing because it felt like cheating. I admire Trevor hugely and I liked the way he worked, but I wished that he had listened because I'm sure I could have done something pretty extraordinary.

I was still sporting my fabulous mink coat which I'd now had for fourteen years. It was coming up to Christmas and the snow was deep. I was crossing the High Street in Stratford and twisted my ankle. It had to be strapped up because I had to dance on it and didn't have an understudy. When it came to New Year's Eve I said to the company, 'Let's all go out for a smashing dinner, shall we?' So we went to a Greek restaurant which was highly regarded and for some reason when the waiter said, 'Take your coat, Madam?' I said, 'Yes, take care of it' – having never, ever said that before. So when it came to 2 o'clock in the morning I asked for my coat they brought me a disgusting ginger hearth rug. I said, 'What the hell is this? I gave you a mink!'

'No that is your coat, Madam...'

I made them look again and there were four other manky coats. I was starting to get angry and someone in the company said, 'We'll deal with the police tomorrow. Let's get you home.' So they put their coats around me and I went back to my little cottage. I was wearing a suit because it was cold and I when took my jacket off and opened the wardrobe, I banged the brass knob of the wardrobe against my left tit and because I was pissed I didn't feel the pain.

The next morning, I had a right foot bandaged up and very painful left tit, so I had to go to hospital. I was X-rayed and had actually broken a rib but there is nothing you can do about that, it just had to heal by itself. The restaurant swore blind to the police that they hadn't got the mink, so I got the insurance for it. I must say that within about a year or two I was actually blessing the person who had nicked it because thereafter I would have been spat on if I had worn it anyway, by the anti-fur brigade.

A few years later, Terry Hands directed me in a farce for the RSC which was pretty bad. Terry apparently keeps copies of the notices for it on his wall to remind him he can fail. He is a wonderful director, normally, and I love him for this sense of humility. This was a French farce, not his thing, and it wasn't going well, so Terry had actually said to the cast on opening night, 'When in doubt, shout.' They all seemed to take him at his word, and it was a pretty nightmarish experience.

I was playing a midwife and at first was to play her as rather prim. They had got me an expensive wig made with very neat greyish hair and my clothes were also neat, but I wasn't happy with this interpretation and I suppose it showed. After the first dress rehearsal, I was told, 'Terry can't stand that wig; he wants you in a red wig.' They found something upstairs (the RSC have a fantastic collection of wigs). The red wig didn't really fit the performance I was doing, but it was difficult to change overnight. Just before the preview the next night, the designer said, 'Oh, we think you could do with some bluish eye shadow.'

I thought, 'I see, I'm now playing a different character.' The character was becoming a more slobby character, which now didn't work with my costume. I also decided that I would be a bit of a drinker so I had a flask with me. Everything was changing.

On opening night I was sitting in the dressing room and not on stage for about half an hour. I could hear over the tannoy everybody screaming at one another. It was ghastly, absolutely appalling. I thought, 'I can't stand this.' I went on and at that point I really didn't give a fuck anymore. I had been buggered around so much – the hair, the make up, clothes, the whole lot – so I went on and gave an entirely different performance that nobody had seen and spoke in a proper voice so that I could be heard but sounded a bit like a human being. There was a distance of about a foot between the edge of the table and the edge of the stage and I had to walk in front of the table. I am prone to accidents, I know – so what did I do one night? I was talking and I fell, perchoink, down into the pit. I picked myself up, climbed up and continued talking. The next day there was a bouquet from Terry and a note: 'You are brilliant.'

I replied, 'I know, you want me to do that every night, don't you?'

Since those days, Terry has done some amazing work in Welsh theatre. He has been Artistic Director of Theatr Clwyd for ten years, and, by using local Welsh talent (of which there is plenty), has virtually created a 'National Theatre of Wales'.

My experience with the RSC was an important step in my recovery, as was working with Antony Sher in that super play *Torch Song Trilogy*. That was a joy. Tony and I met at a first night just prior to starting rehearsals and I remember he was lovely to me – he kissed my hand and was very gracious. We became huge friends.

It was wonderful playing Tony Sher's mother. I actually carried it on a little in life, behaving like his mother, criticising him on various occasions when I thought he was playing around too much. We did laugh a great deal. Tony is a terrible giggler – in fact, he has a reputation for being the biggest 'corpser' in the business. I know Nigel Hawthorne once said he would never work with him again because of it. Tony used to swear that it was me that started it; he would say, 'It's your twinkle.' He said he couldn't help corpsing, it was a 'medical problem'.

There was a speech in the play after I had discovered that his character was gay. I was playing an archetypal American Jewish mother and gave him such a bollocking. I had this highly dramatic speech about what his father would have said, but for some reason we couldn't get through it without corpsing. Each time I got to it I fell about. The director, Robert Allan Ackerman, was incredibly tolerant,

but it got to the weekend before the production and I worked myself
up into such a state because I thought, 'How am I ever going to get
through this without laughing?'

I didn't sleep a wink, but during the night I thought, 'I know, I
am going to make this speech and I am going to laugh all the way
through it.' I though I could use the laughter as tragedy and not once
did I ever corpse again. Where did I get that thought from? It is
wonderful how one gets a thought at the eleventh hour. It happened
to me on several occasions – with Auntie Annie and the Bellow Plays
and with Stanley Kubrick about the cats, when I suddenly thought of
hypnosis. Solutions suddenly appear out of nowhere.

After *Torch Song*, I finally went to the Charter clinic to detoxify from
Valium as I had agreed. I went there twice, once for a short time and
the second time for five weeks.

The time I had there was interesting, though not exactly therapeutic. I spent my time studying my fellow inmates and doing impersonations of them. We had group therapy, and there was a rather
pathetic man with a beard and sandals who used to sit in the middle
and wait, and every day there would be a box of tissues handed
round to the one who decided to tell their story. I rather enjoyed it,
because it was like a rehearsal in the theatre, but instead of talking
about a character I was talking about myself. I grabbed this opportunity with both hands. I started talking about my mother's family
and how I felt 'survivor guilt', and how it could have been me if my
mother hadn't married here. Of course the tissues were passed to me
that day because my tears were copious. The story I told had come to
haunt me when I was in *The Diary of Anne Frank* when I thought I
was dying of cancer – which is pretty ironic because here I am now
with that dreaded disease.

Amongst the friends I made there were people who were on drugs
and alcohol, but in the main they were manic-depressives and I
suppose I am inclined to feel that I was that as well. I enjoyed enter-

taining them all and making them laugh, impersonating everyone, which has always been my way of expressing myself, and I suppose of getting control of emotions.

Ma was still alive when I was in the Clinic and I am really embarrassed to say that though I remember so clearly when my father died, I find it hard to remember much about my mother's death. She was in the home and she'd really left me, the Ma I knew, in the last three or four years of her life, and became someone to whom I brought bananas.

I do remember the last time I saw her. The staff in the home obviously knew this would be the last time, but I didn't realise at the time. I had recently worked in Nottingham and some television gardeners had offered to come and re-do my garden in London. They came on that very day and I remember leaving them and going around the corner to Nightingale House to see my mother. I think the staff must have taken her and emptied her, and put her in a wheelchair, which I'd never seen her in before. They wheeled her in alone and she looked white and thinner than I had ever seen her. They had phoned me and said that they thought I should come. She was strange, even more distant: I hadn't realised that she was dying.

She died later that night after I had gone home, and I felt ashamed that I hadn't stayed. I felt a relief for her really because she was not a happy woman. She wasn't herself and she would have hated to have been seen in the way that one saw her, because she had been so full of vitality and fun.

Working with Peter Gill in the play *The Tongue of a Bird* at the Almeida was something else. There is a wonderful simplicity about his productions. To me he exemplifies the best of directors in that he knows how to get the best out of the actors and also knows how to reveal the best of the play. He does not expect the audience to go out singing 'Director!' He has this amazing way of seemingly going off at a tangent and telling us (the cast) a story which one realises later was absolutely relevant to a particular scene. Everything about his productions is truthful, and his attention to detail is incredible. I moved into my present flat on the Friday and started rehearsing on the Monday, surrounded by packing cases. I found a corner, a table and I sat there with the script. My flat stayed like that for quite some time, more or less until we opened.

I was playing a Polish grandmother and some people at the time said I'd cornered that particular market. Most of the Polish grandmothers I played were not necessarily victims, but they had all suffered. The one at the Almeida wasn't full of self-pity, which is something one wants to avoid even if one *is* a victim. The Polish character I played at the Bush Theatre, in the play *Mrs Steinberg and The Biker Boy* by the lovely Michael Wilcox, was a great fighter. It was my 75th birthday during the run of that play, because I remember that at the curtain call of one of the performances, Mike Bradwell, the director of the Bush came on with a huge bouquet of flowers for me.

By this time I'd spent a lifetime protesting for this and that, expressing fury and indignation from platforms, articles and letters, which dated right from the very early days when I first wore my little 'Boycott German Goods' badge.

There hadn't been a specific moment that took me on CND marches to Aldermaston, but I had been often. I did loads of anti-Apartheid protests standing outside South Africa House. When I went there later for Antony Sher's party when he got his knighthood, everyone I was with said it was fantastic actually to be inside the place that we had stood outside for so many years with our placards. I was there again recently when Antony and Greg Doran had their civil partnership, so there has been some progress. Who could have imagined such an event taking place inside South Africa House back during the Apartheid years?

I haven't been able to campaign physically in these later years, which is a bugger. I wasn't able to go on any of the anti Iraq War marches even though I was there with them mentally. In fact, Enyd Williams, a radio director and dear friend, put my name on a piece of paper in her pocket and she phoned me up on a Saturday morning before one march and said, 'I'm marching with you, and for you.'

I remember that when the appalling Poll Tax was introduced at this time, like a great many people, I refused to pay it. I rang the Council on a number of occasions and eventually after a lot of to-ing and fro-ing I wrote this letter:

> With extreme reluctance I enclose my Poll Tax Registration Form, duly filled in by me.
>
> I take great exception to the fact that my name and address will be on display at the Council Offices – I am ex-directory not only because of my telephone but also the address.
>
> I would be grateful if you could let me know what 'more information' you could possibly want as is stated in the accompanying notes.
>
> I trust you will take note of the fact that many of us in this Borough will work very hard to ensure that a government is returned which pledges itself to repealing this monstrously archaic act.

As I did not intend to get sued for non-payment of my poll tax I decided to make it as difficult as possible for them to collect it. I owed something like £110 for the first instalment. I phoned the local post office in Earl's Court Road and asked them if they would be able to give me £110 in very small change (10p and 20p pieces) and then I went along with my shopping trolley containing this load of plastic bags. I had already phoned the *Evening Standard* and told them what I was going to do. They sent a photographer to the Town Hall and I was photographed handing over this load to the poll tax cashier. I apologised to them personally – 'It's not your fault, it's this bloody Government.' Anyway, I wasn't being terribly clever as I did this on a Friday afternoon – too late for that day's edition, and the *Standard* isn't published at the weekend. Still, it made me feel good.

I felt that I was paying the price of appalling health now in return for abusing my body since I first changed shape, and I threw myself into more campaigning and political action. Maybe I was channelling the anger I felt about what I had done to myself into causes? If so, that was good, and although I just went on in my own rather vague way living and doing things as they came up rather than planning my own future, I very often thought more about the future than a lot of my colleagues, certainly as far as Equity was concerned. The last time I was on the Equity Council in 1994, I said in my election statement:

> We have got to think about future technology because we have got to be there in the van, not following in the road after the event.

Equity always seemed to be reacting instead of predicting what might happen and that is why we had feeble contracts, which didn't take into account what was going to happen with video and DVDs. We weren't prepared for them. I have always tried to be aware of the process of change and the need to keep up to date.

The lack of funding for the Arts was a continual concern, and I spoke regularly about the lack of support for children's radio and television. Here is an extract of speech I gave at the TUC.

> I am especially concerned about the part that drama can play in a child's life.
>
> That fine writer Alan Plater said: 'The most precious asset the country can have is a child's imagination.'
>
> And what is happening with children's imaginations? They are out on the streets texting each other in an unintelligible

language or spending so long in front of video games that they think Lara Croft is Britain's greatest actress. We all know that the country is worried sick about violence in schools, violence against teachers, violence against the old and violence against each other. Youthful energy is wondrous – it's exciting – and it only turns to violence if it's channelled in the wrong direction. I know that when it is channelled into creativity, oh what possibilities are opened up. If you have ever watched children's faces during a dramatic performance you will be totally convinced of the importance of Drama.

In a way I am glad that I am not starting out or just early on in my career as things are today, because of this celebrity status stuff and momentary fame. When I started we had to serve an apprenticeship: even before regulated entry, the closed shop meant you had to be an Equity member, and you would have to have had 40 weeks' experience before you could work in the West End. I was responsible for changing 40 weeks to 30 weeks when I was on the Council for the first time in the 1970s. When I started in the business, it was quite easy to chalk up 40 weeks because you would only have to do one long stint in rep, but when repertory companies began closing, one had to do several tours in order to chalk up the 40 weeks. So I got it changed to 30. Then of course the Thatcher government came in and got rid of trade union laws and now there is no apprenticeship of any sort. If you are clever now you learn on the job.

In 1994 a few old chums came round and wanted me to help give them some names for the Equity Council. I gave them some really good ones, including Michael Cashman, and kept ringing him up at Leeds Playhouse where he was working as an actor (he's now an MEP). He finally agreed to stand if I would, so back I went on to the Equity Council. We stood as 'The Representative Conference Group' and our specific priority was to get rid of the AGM in favour of an Annual Representative Council. The AGM had become impossible because of hysterical tirades between factions. We felt that if we could draw representatives from branches, sub-committees and area committees, and each put forward their motions (already democratically voted on by their respective members), the Standing Orders Committee could ensure that the agenda would reflect the members' views. At first we came up against a great deal of opposition from the 'old school', but we got through the first year's ARC with great success and from then on it has been established as the norm.

Back on Equity Council I became very aware of how the Arts Council was operating and how what had once been a great organisation has become a bureaucratic nightmare. I felt more passionately about this than any other thing I had fought for within Equity. I was watching the funding of the arts diminishing, which has continued to this day. I would still make the same assertion, particularly now that the Olympic Games seems to be draining resources from the arts. Years earlier, when the National Lottery was first set up, many of us on the Equity Council were highly suspicious that lottery money would be used in lieu of core funding. The then Arts Minister Virginia Bottomley swore blind that the lottery money was 'the icing on the cake' – in other words, that one would be able to do *additional* work: putting on more productions, using larger casts, and so on. This, of course, never happened.[6]

The Arts are now on a parallel course to the Health Service and Education. Executive Directors are at the helm, who have no real experience of front-line work and little idea of what is really required, and who end up putting money in the wrong place. For instance, a brand new hospital in London, which cost £500 million, is hated by a lot of the staff working there. Recently I had to go down fourteen floors to the basement in a lift that stopped at every floor and then walk along a huge long corridor under glass to get a blood test. No one had thought of people like me, not young and fit, and not yet in a wheelchair. You'd think it wasn't beyond the wit of someone to

6 'Some Speeches and Letters', pages 236–7.

spend money on some seating somewhere. Because of the architecture there are staff in that building who never see the outside – day or night, rain or shine. They haven't a clue how to design a building because they don't consult the people who work there. There is a layer of management now that inhibits the work practitioners do. On one occasion when I was in there I watched aghast as the cleaner on my ward pushed dirt round from one place to another with her mop – the same way as the administrators push paper around, don't you think?

I was in the same hospital – which was then in Gower Street – for my very first operation, not long after the end of the war but prior to the NHS. I had appendicitis, and the night before my operation, the anaesthetist came in to see me, smoking a cigarette, ashtray in hand. He gave me a cursory examination, listening to my chest with his stethoscope. When he left, I called after him, 'I think you've forgotten something.'

He said, 'No, I've got my ashtray.'

I had to point out that he'd left his stethoscope behind.

While I was still at the RSC, I was asked to be on the TV programme *Question Time*. On the panel was Lord Gowrie, who was then Minister for the Arts. A question was asked, specifically aimed at me, about the Anti Nazi League, to which I responded and talked about the growth of the National Front. Lord Gowrie made out that I was paranoid and that the idea of Nazism was crazy, and generally undermined me. A year later when I was on tour in *84 Charing Cross Road* – with the producer David Pugh, who was then 23 years old and working on his first production – I won the Manchester Evening News Award for best performance in a regional theatre. I was asked to go there to be presented with this award by none other than Lord Gowrie. When I accepted it from him, I said something like, 'You and I have met, sir, but under different circumstances.'

After the awards we had our picture taken and I said to his Lordship, 'I think you remember when we met before?'

He looked a bit vague.

'It was on *Question Time* when you made out that I was paranoid about Nazis, and within six weeks of that, Toxteth happened and the Brixton riots.'

He said, 'Oh well that's not my particular subject.'

I thought, bloody hell, not your subject? I mean, either you go on *Question Time* and talk about something or you don't go on the programme.

David Pugh went on to do pretty well for himself, thank you very much. He has produced many hugely successful shows, including *Art*, which ran for ages in the West End, and most recently *Equus* with Daniel Radcliffe. A few months before my eightieth birthday he took me out to Sheekey's and told me that he was booking the private room at the Ivy for my birthday and said I could invite anyone I liked. That was a birthday to remember – fan-bloody-tastic! He organised the birthday just like one of his productions – thinking of everything. Everyone was given a disposable camera, and within four days of the party I had hundreds of prints as a recording of the evening.

I was doing *Rosmersholm* at the Young Vic with Corin Redgrave and Francesca Annis during the Miners' Strike and we agreed to go on the march supporting the miners and meet up there. Corin, Kika Markham and in fact most of the Redgrave family came along, and at the time I was still able to walk reasonably well, if painfully. I got a bus and got as near to Hyde Park Corner as I could and walked. It was bucketing down, I had never seen such rain, and, because I am always so conscious about how one is looking – hair and all of that – I had two or three 'head condoms' with me. (They had been given this name by none other than Neil Kinnock: I had been with the Kinnocks one evening and when I brought the plastic hood thing out Neil said, 'What's that Mim, a head condom?')

Anyway, I finally got to the stage where I didn't care anymore what I looked like. My feet were literally squelching and the rain had come up to my ankles, but I finally reached the place where the march had finished and was told that I was expected to go up on the huge stage that they'd erected. Arthur Scargill was up there, with thousands of people in the crowd. You could see the steam coming off Arthur because he was so wet and under very strong arc lights.

I did know Arthur, and was obviously ambivalent about him, but he was a great speaker, and I have to admire that. He could have been a highly respected figure if he hadn't gone quite so far. Unfortunately it played into Thatcher's hands. This is what has happened all the way along. The unions seemed to be too strong and found people willing to fight against them.

On the stage I made an impassioned speech about what Thatcher was doing to the miners, selling all the mines, which I thought obscene. Francesca Annis had said the day before that everyone should come back to her place. I lost sight of them, so got in a cab at Marble Arch and went home, got out of my wet clothes, put on a face, and arrived at Francesca's. There were radiators full of clothes steaming and drying off and friends were dressed in bits and pieces of clothes grabbed from anywhere. A thoroughly good day was had by all, even though we didn't achieve anything.

I am always amazed by the sheer amount of work Corin and Vanessa Redgrave do for political causes. Corin, for instance, has given at least four one-man shows, each totally different, for ICAF, while Vanessa has worked tirelessly on behalf of the Chechens in their struggle with the Russians. She famously stood bail for the theatre director and actor Akhmed Zakayev when Putin tried to have him extradited.

In addition to directing, my old friend Richard Digby Day is Principal of a drama college for American students: a different group comes over each semester. Richard saw the way my health was continuing to deteriorate, and thought that as accents and dialects are my forte, I should teach a class on them. Never having taught in my life, I was a little scared to begin with, but have since found that I do have a facility for it. With the American students I first of all start off with 'received pronunciation' and get rid of their American. Then I go on to cockney, then Southern Irish, because I don't think they'd be able to cope with Northern Irish. Sometimes I try Scottish and a general North-country accent – that's about as much as one can do in a term.

I really enjoy it. I've taken on private tuition with other students and I've developed my own method. Every accent has its own song and I teach them the song. I don't do phonetic stuff because I don't know about it and even if I did there wouldn't be time. You've either got an ear, or you haven't. It's terribly exciting to find one has enthusiasm for teaching, though sometimes I worry I haven't got any qualifications. Of course I wouldn't be able to teach at any accredited drama school, because the fact that I've got 60 years experience in the theatre doesn't matter a bugger; but if I had a piece of paper that said I had an MA from some crap university or ex-poly, I'd be all right! I have been asked to do masterclasses at some drama schools, though: this is fun, and it is profoundly satisfying to find that I can teach because I like young people so much and they keep me young and forward-looking.

I think they are pretty shocked by me actually, because I do tend to shock. I am careful not to do too much political chat with them because their parents are paying a lot of money and one doesn't want to offend, so I don't do a lot of anti-Republican stuff. I think they know where I stand, though. After the last US election Clinton had been over here speaking at a Labour Party conference. I said to the class:

> That Clinton really is something, he was just over here and I was sitting at home watching him on television and when he finished I actually got up in my own flat, applauded and was ready to give him a blow job.

That group told the rest of the students. Of course, it must seem strange for them to hear a woman in her eighties talking about blow jobs.

Bad language has become the norm with me, I'm afraid, and I do have to be careful, although in theatrical circles swearing is very common and the F-word is all over TV now. I remember when Ken Tynan used the word on TV for the first time it caused a furore, and the country went berserk. It is now so overused that its ubiquity has actually started to offend me!

My relationship with the Labour Party continued during these years. I had developed a friendship with Neil Kinnock a long time previously, even before he was Leader of the Opposition, whereby I would argue with him about the Party, which I accused of not reflecting my socialist views. In fact, I have his reply to a letter of mine, dating from 1987, where he says:

> Who else do you think is going to save the Health Service, introduce preventative medicine, get pensioners a square deal, lift 3.6 million people out of poverty, stop the nuclear obsession, double the aid and development budget, actively oppose Apartheid and the Contras, establish an Arts and Media Ministry to fund 'culture' properly, introduce a Freedom of Information Act, invest in science and technology for peace, generate over a million jobs in two years, build half a million homes, treat women and black people like human beings…and quite a lot more?

He goes on to say:

> The great thing about socialism is that it is not 'utopian'. It is possible, if the fruits of the world are properly used in the interest of the people of the world, to have heaven on earth. But

before that – indeed in order to get that – we've got to stop hell on earth.

He was right, and during the next years as the party struggled to overcome the Thatcher and Major governments, he became an amazing Labour party leader, sincere, passionate and of course a truly committed socialist. He and his wife Glenys have been personal friends of mine for years now, and I campaigned madly on his behalf.

When he did that 'Well all right!' thing at the conference in Sheffield I knew that was not a good thing for him. I was in a state that election night. I was at the Labour party headquarters in Millbank and we all got pissed out of our brains, till about four am when we knew then he had lost.

Newspapers (particularly the *Sun*) were out to get him, and they had done dreadful things. They had reporters hiding in the bushes and in the front garden trying to get dirt on both of them. They even went to the schools that both Glenys and Neil had been to, but they couldn't find anything. Just like burglars who break in and can't find anything, what do they do? They piss all over the furniture, and that's exactly what these newspapers did. That *Sun* headline, in the event he got in – 'Will the last person to leave Britain please turn out the lights?' – was obscene.

It was very, very sad and I felt grief-stricken for my friend. Sheffield had been badly advised and a mistake. I don't think the real Labour people would have voted against him because of that, but the waverers or those who were prejudiced against him would have had their prejudice confirmed. Losing that election was a low moment for me. I wrote him a letter after the election and he wrote the most wonderful reply.

What an amazing woman you are and how lucky we are to know you. Your spirit, your words, your flowers and the immense support that you've given make everything easier. Thank you again and again.

As for scraping through, yes life would have been pretty hellish for us one way and another. But it would have been so much better for all of those poor sods – including the denim-trousered philanthropists of Essex who last Thursday got themselves a government without quality or conscience or mercy.

My old man used to say 'they'll have to learn the hard way.' So they will. And the tragedy is that people who don't need teaching will have to share the lesson.

Anyway, we've got you and so many other fine people as friends. It's worth more than diamonds.

How extraordinary of him to write to me, during what he was going through, because it was an intensely cathartic period for him. I don't think he's got over it yet; actually, I don't think he ever really will.

Glenys is the president of One World Action which was formed in response to the idea of transforming communities in Africa, Asia and Central America rather than donating to governments of countries. The organisation seeks partners in these communities who work together on specific projects and has not only grown as an organisation, but the idea of task driven charity has also developed. I joined with Glenys in the beginning to help bring others on board.

They tend to be from the left and certainly have socialist principals. The very small staff, for example, manage to make 90 per cent of their funds available without the expense of overseas offices and minimal administration.

New Labour hasn't done much to enhance the socialist ideas; in fact they've done their best to ignore them. I suppose they thought that the only way to get back in after that election, was to forsake all the good things, the real foundation of socialism, and appeal to the middle-of-the-road voter. But I believed in equality of opportunity for everybody, a concept which has to have government help. Under Wilson, subsidies gave a hand to many enterprises – and the theatre, like everything else, suddenly blossomed. It has all been thrown out, market forces rule, things are privatised that never should be and everything that had been worked for by people like Attlee and Aneurin Bevan seems to have disappeared.

So I did recover from the bad times and begin again, because I was lucky enough to continue to work in interesting roles and have friends who encouraged me to see how I could use my experience in different ways.

SANS TEETH, SANS FUCKIN' EVERYTHING

In which, having lost my teeth, I got to play in a film without them; having lost my faith in New Labour, God, and the state of Israel I became a Humanist; in which I talked about conscience with my friend Tony Benn and reconnect to Dignity in Dying. In which I had cancer operations, and a knee operation, and came out to the Guardian *as the oldest anorexic in the business.*

TWO OLD MEN ARE SITTING next to each other under a tree and the one turns to the other and says, 'Herbie, I'm 83 years old now and I'm just full of aches and pains. I know you are about the same age, how do you feel?'

Herbie says, 'I feel just like a newborn baby.'

'Really – like a newborn baby?'

Herbie says, 'Yes, yes. No hair, no teeth. And I think I just wet myself.'

Three old guys are out walking. The first one says, 'Windy isn't it?'

The second one says, 'No it's Thursday.'

The third one: 'So am I, let's go for a beer.'

Time has been another obsession for me, and as I have so many of them – work, politics, weight – I see I should have called this book 'some kind of an *obsessional* life'. The tricks that time plays seem unfair to me. When one is a child and someone asks you how old you are, you say, 'five and three quarters', and each of those quarters seems like a decade in my time today. That's because everything that happens when you're young is a new event: it's always the first time, always a new face. Looking back, these times seem to be slow in playback. When you are older, you've been there, done that, and time seems to be in fast-forward, hurtling towards…what?

When I was told that I had cancer and that they would have to take a slice of tongue away, they said it would affect my speech. I went into the most dreadful depression and back onto the anti-depressant Amitriptyline, which I had stopped taking for two or three years. (I am still taking what is regarded as a 'homeopathic' dose.) I thought, 'Et tu, Brute', because I felt that even my good features were beginning to disintegrate. Gradually all the bits of me that were okay were becoming faulty, and I wondered what would become of me if my speech was affected. Talking had been everything to me: I couldn't imagine a life without speech. What on earth would I do? I began to prepare myself for the possibility of losing speech altogether.

I discovered I had the cancer just after I had been called to an interview for a film, *Children of Men*. I had been along to see the casting director simply because I speak German. When I went for the casting they had the video camera on me, which always gets me into a state, and I was asked to say a couple of things like 'My husband is ill and you've got to release us' or something like that in German. When you go for these things, if you don't hear within a few days you assume you haven't got it, so as far as I was concerned it was gone.

In the meantime I was doing a *Miss Marple* for TV and had quite a nice part in that, but I noticed whilst I was filming that I kept biting my tongue in the same place and it got quite painful. I felt it with my finger and there was a lump. I couldn't do anything about it and didn't have time to go to a doctor, but I was worried.

The day after we finished *Miss Marple* I went to my GP. She looked at my tongue and immediately arranged for me to see a consultant.

Two days later I was seeing her on my own, because it just hadn't occurred to me to bring anyone for support. She looked at it and said, 'Well I think it could be cancer but I want you to see the surgeon.'

Anybody who has had that experience knows that it feels like an advancing death sentence. The following Monday I was in hospital having my first slice of tongue taken off. When I woke up I discovered that I'd only had a small section taken away, and my main worry of not being able to talk at all subsided because although I sounded strange, I could speak a little.

Anyway, I was home recovering eight days after the first operation when the phone rang. It was my agent who told me the film-makers wanted me to do the film the very next day. The interview had been about four weeks before and I had forgotten about it, so I didn't know what the hell she was talking about. I told her I'd just had a tongue operation and asked what the film was about.

When she phoned me back she said that she'd told them that I was frail and couldn't go in early and gave me a vague idea about the sort of thing that was going to be required to say in German. Later on a second assistant phoned me and asked if it would be alright if they picked me up at 6.30am. I said, 'Sorry, my agent's already told you that I can't do early.'

'So you don't want to do it?'

I said, 'Exactly, that's what I'm saying', and put the receiver down, hugely relieved.

At 6.50 that night the second assistant phoned back and asked if 8.30am would be all right. Well, I reluctantly agreed and even thought it might be exciting to be filming again.

They sent a car for me at 8.30am, so in order to be ready by that time, knowing that I was going to Winchester, I was terrified to have anything to eat or drink because I thought I'd have to pee on route. (Such are the indignities of age.) Wardrobe had called me the evening before and had explained the character – a rather grand German woman who had lost her wealth. They made me look grubby, dressing me in good clothes that they had 'distressed'.

As I was leaving the make-up trailer, I saw Michael Caine driving away. He and Clive Owen, the stars of the film, had had to work early because I wouldn't. I was amused that there were some advantages to being ancient and frail.

The location was at a disused station and there were huge cages like the ones in Guantánamo Bay. I was introduced to the Spanish director, Alfonso Cuarón, who said, 'I want you to do what you did in the video, it was great', and described gestures I had made. I didn't have a fucking clue. I mean, I'd had a slice of tongue taken away, a few weeks had gone by: how the hell would I know what gesture I'd made?

So I went into the cage, and sat on my horrendously broken-down baggage. Behind me was this bloke who was supposed to be my husband. There were others – my granddaughter and various other relations, plus a few black kids. The objective I had worked out for myself from all these clues was that there was a guard outside the cage and I had to get him to release us because my husband was sick and I didn't want to be stuck here with all these 'black' people. I began to make up horrendous racist stuff in German. I said I'd spoken to the King, because I knew we were talking about 25, 30 years in the future. The film was based on the book by P D James, though I didn't know this at the time as no one had bothered to tell me!

So there I was, trying to figure out what to say with no other German speaker there at all, and there were these other people in the cage who were extras. This was real Ricky Gervais territory. I sat there feeling pretty pathetic working out what I was going to say, mentally translating it into German and suddenly heard this arsehole behind me saying to one of the kids, 'Do you get any holiday pay for this, and what about overtime?' I shut him up pretty forcibly because none of them seemed to understand what I was doing and how an acting performance was created.

I struggled to get it right and the whole thing was finished in a few hours. You do have to watch very carefully, and not fart at any point or sneeze or cough, but I am there, shouting in German.

So I had cancer. I had two slices of tongue taken away by the first surgeon, but because he hadn't taken enough of my tongue away, the cancer remained. After the second operation I happened to meet the wonderful Helena Kennedy and her brilliant husband Iain Hutchison, the best mouth cancer specialist in the country, at Tony Sher's Civil Partnership 'do'. I was determined to go to this despite being pretty weak. After I'd had another unsuccessful operation, Helena persuaded Iain to take me under his aegis, and there followed six weeks of radio- and chemotherapies and the start of this opus.

My speech gradually got better because I work at it, like everything I do, but it's more of a strain because I do have to compensate and be very careful with my S's. I tried to work out ways of doing it: if I keep my teeth together, it almost sounds convincing. Since these three operations and the subsequent long and unpleasant treatment, the cancer hasn't recurred, but during this time, I looked back and realised that my lifestyle had been responsible for my ill-health.

A friend and I went to see a Saturday matinee of David Hare's splendid play *The Permanent Way* at the National, and afterwards, Kika Markham, who had been terrific as Nina Bawden, joined us for tea in the front of house café. Kika brought a whole tray of sandwiches, scones and cakes. The funny thing was that though they never stopped talking about diets, the two of them were stuffing their faces! I ate nothing, just had a cup of tea, and said, 'I don't eat that stuff.'

Kika looked straight at me and said, 'You've got an eating disorder.'

I said, 'Well I've probably had it for over 50 years.'

'You should see a psychotherapist.'

'I've got a psychotherapist – he's lovely.'

'And you've never mentioned this to him?'

'No.'

'Well! Are you in a state of denial!'

I thought about this over the weekend and realised that perhaps she was right. So on Monday I phoned my psychotherapist and said, 'I think I'd better see you. I've been in the closet for over half a century. Not a sex closet. An eating one.'

I was talking about this to my friend and neighbour, and she said, 'Do you mind if I tell my cousin Michele?' The cousin turned out to be Michele Hanson, who writes for the woman's page of the *Guardian*. This is how I 'came out' as the oldest anorexic in the business! Here is an extract from Michele's article.

> Some of the stranger herbal remedies could have been neuro-toxic, and Miriam admits to going on all sorts of crazy diets. She took Preludin, an appetite suppressant available over the counter, until it was banned more than thirty years ago, as well as taking another senna-based laxative – loads of it every evening.

Actually, even though I came out, I didn't think I had a real eating disorder. I still don't. Was I an anorexic? It was a choice I made because it was very easy for me to get fat. But I have been in a state of denial – I suppose that that previous statement reveals that I still am, even though I have admitted it to the world. The only reason I talked is that I actually thought that I might be able to help somebody else who is going through it.

I believe My peripheral neuropathy has been caused by my eating behaviours. None of the top medicos could understand why I should have it, as the majority of people with peripheral neuropathy are either diabetic or get it as part of the AIDS package. Why have I got it? I thought it must be because of all my laxative taking. Despite the fact that I take loads of vitamins, the fact is I flush the whole lot down the loo so all the good things are got rid of as well as the food that could make me fat. I got some letters from people as a result of the article who were going through the same as me who also had peripheral neuropathy and had been on crash diets, so it has to be the reason. Even my own GP admits that it was a possibility.

I did feel relief when I came out, in a way. It looked good on paper. It was like having a bloody good upchuck, an evacuation. The trouble is that when you come out at the age of 80 it is far too late. My eating problems will be with me now until I depart this planet. If you've been doing something for 50 years, you can't change – and what good would it do me now to get fat suddenly and buy roomy clothes? I don't want to be fat. I have total control over what goes into my stomach. It is an ordered disorder. I wouldn't be able to sit down to a plate of potatoes or bread and butter. I haven't bought butter for many years and I don't eat any fats at all. In the days when I was entertaining, which were not so long ago, I bought food for guests which I wouldn't eat myself, even though I loved seeing people enjoying my food.

These habits were all made worse by the swings from eating to dieting that I indulged in over the years. For example, I found that during a time of not eating I went through a period of being addicted to ice cream from a famous American chain. I would find any excuse to wander into a street that had one of these places, go in and eat several. Then I would put on weight and would have a compulsion to take myself to a health farm or starve for a few days.

Other diets I went for included black coffee and apples, grapefruit and hard-boiled eggs. Lately there has been the famous 'Soup Diet'. I slipped from whatever the current diet was so many times and put on weight so easily that I once went to a hypnotherapist. I only had to have two sessions with him and I stopped eating whatever I had been eating – probably biscuits which I still nibble now – so it didn't last long.

I would probably weigh about 20 stone if I hadn't done all the things I did to lose weight. I would be healthier and probably working a lot more because I would be playing all the fat parts!

Now I talk about my condition, and have, of course, become addicted to that in the same way that I was addicted to keeping *schtum*. All I can do is hope I can help younger people who are doing the same as I did, although I know perfectly well if anybody had said to me when I was 30 that by the time you are 80 you will be decrepit, disabled, and you will have cancer, I would have ignored them. Then it was a risk worth taking, and I thought, I wouldn't live to be 80 and wouldn't want to anyhow so it didn't matter. Now I am 80-plus I am horrified at what I have done to myself.

Even if I did eat more, my taste buds have pretty much disintegrated in the last few years. This is not only due to age but also because of an operation on my eye. The procedure is called the Cauldwell Luke Operation, and went through my jaw and right through my cheek and up under the eye. Recently I had a replacement knee operation: although they were very pleased with my recovery, my legs are so bad from the peripheral neuropathy that I have to walk with a stick.

When I was on the Equity Council I had my own chair. There was a chap that I rather disliked on Council and one week he suddenly decided he was going to sit in my chair. I showed my anger and he said, 'What do you mean, it's your chair?'

I said, 'Look I'm just rehearsing for Denville Hall.' That's the actors' rest home, and ironically it was where I went to recover from my knee operation.

I suspect that there will be another operation on my tongue. If Iain does another one he isn't going to be generous to me. He will get rid of it all. They are supposed to leave 5mm gap clear of the tumour all the way round and clearly the first surgeon didn't do that. Iain always does diagrams. He draws tongues and shows exactly where the tumour is and what should be left. The first surgeon took the actual tumour, but the cancer was also in one of the glands. Once when Iain was with me he phoned one or two of his patients and asked them if they would mind talking to someone who was going to have the operation. I talked to a couple of his patients who had had bigger jobs than me done. One of them was a singer and she went back to singing after a huge operation.

In addition to all this I have horrendous bladder and bowel problems, as I mentioned before – my B&B. I often think that contracts should be made out to 'MK Bladder and Bowels'. (Once upon a time B&B stood for something rather different.) It is embarrassing to get to this age and know so little about one's body.

I was having an examination and a urologist was pumping water into me. I eventually said, 'I must let it go, I must let it go!' and he said, 'No, no, not yet, not yet.'

He was looking at the screen and then he said, 'Okay, now you can let it go.'

So I did, and he said, 'Well, finish it.'

I told him that I had, but he showed me that there was a lot still there. He left me with the nurse, who suggested that I pat my stomach – and that's what I have had to do ever since. The patting has now become thump, thump, thump, thump. This is all because I didn't use my bowels and bladder properly most of my life because of my self-inflicted eating disorders. I hope no one is reading this whilst eating! On reflection, I should have sent this to the *Lancet*.

And then there's my teeth. I have spent so much money on my mouth because my mother hated dentists and I inherited her fear of them, so when I was younger I didn't look after my teeth. With smoking my teeth became appalling. When I went to a dentist in Sydney, Joe Rourke, he said, 'What the hell kind of Pommy butcher has been at your mouth? You wanna go to Gavin Ferguson, he's the bloke.'

So I did, and was with Gavin until his death about 20 years ago.
I have been with his successor Clive Debenham ever since. I am
appalled at the amount of money I spent. Once I paid £10,000,
and another time £4,000. I told Clive that I'd bought my place in
Hamilton Terrace for £10,000 and he said, 'Yes, but you can't eat the
walls.' He had a point, and I contented myself with that thought.

Finally the whole top lot had to come out, which may be the reason
I got to play a toothless old woman in *Flashbacks of a Fool*, a film
starring Daniel Craig which I have just done in South Africa. The
script specifically said 'toothless': I'm sure the reason I got the part
is that I'm the only aged female actor who is not so narcissistic that
I don't mind telling the world that I haven't got my own teeth. The
production company sent me to a 'state of the art' place called 'Fangs
FX' to have a set made with two horrible teeth in it. I suppose I've
never been vain when it comes to acting, although in private I'm very
conscious of how I look. On stage, provided the part is good enough,
I don't care what I look like: you are either playing the part or you're
not. A friend of mine who shall remain nameless was playing a
bloody good part, and I said to her, 'You're very good darling, but I
do think your hair is looking too nice.'

'Well I do like to go out to dinner after the show.'

I thought, bloody hell, what kind of narcissism is that?

Speech and the way we talk as humans have been my study all my life
so I am fearful of losing more of my tongue as I think it may augur
the end. Although I am doing this book, I am still 'talking' it rather
than writing as I have a flow of thought that comes from my brain to
my mouth. When I write, it takes longer but is perhaps more beautifully constructed.

There are some aspects of modern speech that infuriate me.
Certain phrases have become overused. For instance, 'No problem'
– I mean, one hasn't said anything that is a problem. 'No probs, no
probs. No problem.' Drives you mad – the only problem is people

saying to me 'no problem'; that is my problem. Then there's 'At the end of the day'. What is that supposed to mean? Or 'At this moment in time'. I remember when I was going all over America promoting *A Clockwork Orange*, the number of interviewers who used to say to me, 'Yeah well Ms Karlin, at this moment in time…', and I would say, 'Excuse me, there's a three-letter word for that. *Now!*' Other annoyances are those endless 'You knows' during interviews, while people pause for thought and 'To be honest with you', when the speaker is being nothing of the sort.

In addition to all these overused phrases is the question of pronunciation: it sometimes makes me physically ill to hear this disgusting 'Estuary' accent. The people upon whom one used to rely were BBC newsreaders, but even these have fallen foul of the dreaded Estuary. (Are they somehow trying to appeal to the young?) Things like 'com*pair*able' and 'laura norder' really get on my nerves, too. Of course, my brother Michael, who is an expert on linguistic changes, is far more tolerant of this than I am!

Language has always been something to play with and I like to think of my voice as an instrument able to be used in many different ways. When I did *The Caretaker*, I managed to evolve a sort of language. The director wanted a lot of noise before I made my entrance, cursing some 'blacks' in the street, and I managed to evolve this speech, which was not a language really, more a vocal noise.

There was another play, Alan Ayckbourn's *How the Other Half Loves*, where I evolved a different language too. My guests have arrived and I pour drinks for them and wait for my husband. During this time I made noises that sounded like posh speech. People thought it funny and a little mad, which summed up the character. As a child I once made up a language called Hölish (pronounced 'Herlish') and made my parents sit an exam in it. Language and the use of sound to communicate has been a lifetime interest.

People say I have a distinctive voice and I suppose I have but you never really hear or see yourself as others do, do you? Cab drivers still think of me as working class. They say, 'I come from the same place as you'; I say, 'Where is that?' and they say 'The East End.'

In one way being identified as working class affected me adversely because it took a while for casting people to realise that I wasn't. It was simply *The Rag Trade* and *Fings Ain't Wot They Used T'Be* that were cockney. They led to more cockney things on film too, which became a bit irritating. Still, I am grateful for being known for something, anything – because, when one thinks of it, the majority of the world go to their grave anonymously.

I've never been mobbed but it's nice that people care enough to come to the stage door and ask for an autograph, and I 'play the game'. I don't believe in being uncivil to an audience, it's a short-sighted policy. When I first started there used to be gallery 'first nighters' who were an audience to be feared. If they didn't like you, did they let you know! There were actors they loathed and they would go purposely in order to boo on the first night. Thankfully they were usually lovely to me. They were a group of very ordinary people who used to queue for the gallery and as we don't have that tradition anymore, they disappeared. The ones I knew were mainly 'getting on'. Sophie was the leader, a great big woman, with huge tits. She was also Jewish and thought of me as 'a nice Jewish actress'.

Things have changed over the 63 years I have been acting. When I began to do films in the 1940s, which these days suddenly appear at three o'clock in the morning on telly, I would think nothing of being up at five and walking a couple of miles from the station to the studio. Filming is different now because of the hours you work. There was a time, long before the unions became the target for the right wing, when they were pretty strong. Sometimes they went too far – for instance, when they stopped on the dot of ten to six – but if you were in the middle of a scene, the director would get hold of the shop steward and say, 'Can we finish this?' The shop steward would go into a corner and say, 'Shall we call the half on this one, boys?' and usually we would have another half hour. Now, nobody thinks anything of going on working, so that you could be doing a fourteen or fifteen-hour day. As for the poor crew, make-up girls sometimes go to bed at about two o'clock in the morning and have to be up again at half past four. It's all to do with money. I don't think there is any way we will ever go back to better days and I don't want to accuse all producers of flagrantly flouting working hours. There are some who are very thoughtful and caring – and, due to Equity, we do now get overtime.

In some areas progress has been made. I can actually see the results of work I did on the Equity Council in the changes that have happened over the past 25 years. When I first went on to the Afro-Asian committee, I called myself 'the token white Jewish woman'. At that time, there was one black newscaster, Trevor McDonald, but there were absolutely no black or Asian actors in leading roles. They played servants or menial, small roles. As for a love scene between a black and white person, it was not to be contemplated. Although a lot of members carried on about equality, it has to be said that sadly they did very little to help themselves. Equity had organised a conference and I discovered that writers had not been invited to attend with the directors and producers. I spent a whole weekend in desperation begging writers to come to the conference in order to persuade them to state at the start of their scripts that quite a lot of parts could be played by Asian or black actors. We eventually managed to get a lot of writers to sign up to the idea.

When it came to commercials, you never saw a black or Asian face playing anything other than a background artist. Nowadays it can be all black. I didn't go along with quotas, although it was considered out of frustration. Then we realised that to be employed simply because one is making up a quota is not good for one's ego. It was a difficult decision because in America they did have quotas and they got to where we are much earlier. Having said that, there is still an inordinate amount of prejudice and homophobia in America. There are certain actors who will be in closets until their dying day because they just wouldn't get the work if they came out. During the Clause 28 campaign, Tony Sher phoned me up and said, 'Some of us gay actors are writing a letter to the *Guardian*. Do you know any lesbian actors?'

'Pam St Clement.'

He said, 'Yes we've got her.'

I gave him another name. He replied, 'No, no, she won't. She won't sign. She is making a name for herself in the States and she doesn't want it known.'

I was astonished because this actress is someone who comes into a room and says, 'Are there any homosexuals here, because I am one!'

There is a story about a splendid actor who, although not a lesbian had a very deep voice. Despite being married and becoming a Catholic, she was having an affair. She thought she ought to go and confess but she didn't want to go to a church near where they lived, so she went to some place far away where she wasn't known. She went into the confessional and told the priest what she'd done. When she finished the priest said, 'And tell me my son, how long have you been a homosexual?'

Despite all that has happened to the Labour Party, I still care passionately about politics. A long time ago, I went to speak for Tony Benn when he first stood for Chesterfield. He was very anti this whole celebrity thing which had somehow insidiously crept into the political scene, probably from the US, bringing out people who are known from the media, not for their political beliefs, suddenly brought out to stand on a platform with a politician.

Tony Benn clearly knew of my track record as far as Labour was concerned and had asked for me specifically. When I arrived he said, 'Do you remember when we first met in 1957 in a house in Hampstead?'

We had both been invited to speak at a luncheon, an *Any Questions* type thing, at a pro-Israel Zionist event. This was only nine years after Israel was created so I was still very passionate about my Zionism. Whether it was his amazing memory or whether he had looked me up in his diaries, it impressed me hugely that he'd remembered me from so many years earlier.

He always responds to letters. At a Labour Party conference a year ago he fell ill and was taken to hospital. I was really concerned. When he got out of hospital I sent him a card. He immediately responded and said how lovely it was to hear from me. He's an extraordinary man and the greatest Prime Minister we never had. I admire him because he has remained true to the ideals of socialism and there are very few that can say that. I am sure Tony Benn isn't a member of BUPA like me!

It would have been wondrous to have an egalitarian society which lasted. We were beginning to see the preliminaries of one during Harold Wilson's first reign when Benn was part of the Cabinet. We had a very left-wing Cabinet for a short time, with Tony Benn, Michael Foot, and Barbara Castle – three real goodies. Unfortunately it didn't last very long, possibly because Harold Wilson was a pragmatist. However, something he refused to do was to go into Vietnam; I am sure he would have refused to go into Iraq and he would not have stood 'shoulder to shoulder' with Bush. Why should we have a special relationship? All right, so they came in and helped us out in the war, but it took them a hell of a time to do that.

As far as Labour is concerned, I am still Labour, still passionately Labour: it's Labour that is not Labour anymore. I was horrified that I had to vote against them in 1997, when all my friends, with very few exceptions, voted Labour and thought Blair was the greatest thing. In '97 I was about to do a play at the Tron Theatre in Glasgow and so I asked for a postal vote. As usual when in Glasgow, I was staying with my brother and sister-in-law Hilary. I had decided with a friend of mine, Imogen Claire – who lived, as I did, in the Royal Borough of Kensington and Chelsea – that we would tactically vote Lib Dem. One had to get rid of the Tories. We decided that the Tory member at the time, Sir Nicholas Scott, was a dreadful man. We thought there might be a lot of disenchanted Tories in the borough who couldn't bring themselves to vote Labour and might vote Lib Dem, and there might be a lot of people like me not enchanted by Blair who would vote that way too. The Lib Dem manifesto was far more left-wing than New Labour's.

Well, I was talking to Imogen on the phone and said, 'Listen, I've got my postal vote papers in front of me and if I vote whilst I'm talking to you, perhaps you can anaesthetise me from this terrible moment – the first time in my life that I will not be voting Labour.'

I had a copy of the *Guardian* on the table and my ballot paper underneath it. I knew that the Lib Dem man began with a W and was at the bottom of the page. We were chatting on and Imogen said, 'Have you done it yet?'

'No, but I'm going to do it right now.'

I picked up the pen and put the cross, then pulled out the ballot paper and screamed. 'Oh shit, oh fuck!'

She said, 'What's the matter?'

'I've only voted Rainbow Party!'

She told me to phone the Town Hall first thing in the morning and ask them for a duplicate, so first thing in the morning I left a message saying that somehow my ballot paper had got damaged, giving them all my details plus my brother's address and telephone number. When I came back from rehearsal that evening my sister-in-law Hilary told me that I had had a phone call from Kensington Town Hall, saying that I should return everything that they sent me in an envelope marked 'urgent'. So I looked at my paper and there it was, clean as anything with the Rainbow Party marked. I thought, I can't send them this. So I tore off that bit, but it still looked very clean. So I went to the fridge, got some yoghurt and threw some all over it. It went all bubbly, so I put tissue on it. I put a covering note with it saying that inadvertently some yoghurt had got spilt on it, and please would they send me a duplicate. This they did. So that's how I came to vote Lib Dem for the first time in my life and that broke the spell.

I had no problem at all after that, especially when I saw what Blair was doing, and that my disenchantment had been well based. I had no problem voting Lib Dem the second time around either.

I know that there have been some improvements in the NHS. New Labour have clearly poured more money in, but where has it gone? More bureaucrats, and billions on administration. Teachers, too, are going berserk with the amount of paper-pushing that they have to do instead of teaching, which was their whole *raison d'être*. Exactly the same has happened to the Arts. I've got figures showing what has been spent by the Arts Council on administration and consultants who don't get out of bed for less than £800–£1,000 per day. How much is actually reaching the creative side of things? Artistic Directors (now an endangered species), who have been engaged as creative people, are being turned into administrators, begging for funds, writing letters and filling in forms. The amount of form-filling has spread to every area of life. Most people of my age already find form-filling pretty daunting, and those in power seem to have made it more and more difficult.

For me the most dreadful part of the Blair government is that he brought us into the Iraq war. That is something for which I could never forgive him. At the time 9/11 happened I was speaking at the TUC conference and had just finished my speech. Blair was going to be speaking next and they had just voted on a motion about the lack of black and Asian people behind the camera, which I had been seconding. I said to my colleague Andrew Ray (sadly no longer with us), 'I'm just going to get myself a cup of black coffee, I don't want to fall asleep again when Blair is talking.' The last time I had dozed off and somebody had poked me, because a camera could have caught me.

I came back from my coffee, literally five minutes later, during which time Blair had been and gone, they'd heard about the Twin Towers and the conference had then finished. I will never forget Blair saying to Bush, 'We are shoulder to shoulder with you.' When I heard that I shuddered. It has turned out to be an absolute tragedy and I wonder how either Blair or Bush can sleep at night. They both have so much blood on their hands.

When I voted that way all my friends were shocked, but I have disliked Blair since the moment he was elected leader of the party. I remember saying to Neil Kinnock, 'Tell me about this fellow Blair. I don't really trust him.'

He said, 'Oh, don't worry Mim, Tony is a great socialist!'

'What, a socialist?'

'Of course he's a socialist. Don't you worry about Tony, he's great.'

Well, Neil is saying other things about him now. He has been incredibly loyal over the years, but he eventually came out over education and very openly criticised Blair. Glenys has been much more openly critical.

However, I have high hopes of Gordon Brown, and have let him know it! Here is part of the letter I sent him in August 2007.

> Dear Prime Minister,
>
> My instinctive mistrust of your predecessor from the moment he was elected Leader of the Party was proven to be absolutely right. This resulted in me having to do something deeply painful.
>
> Having voted and campaigned for Labour for over half a century, at the age of seventy-two (ten years ago), I tore up my party card.

With your accession I have regained my belief and confidence in Labour and will very happily rejoin the party. I do like my Prime Minister to have some gravitas as I see enough smiling actors in my professional life!

Long may you continue to show strength, courage and integrity.

As of September 2007, I am indeed a Labour Party member again!

I am irritated because I can't work so much now. I make a semblance of being busy but I can't go to as many meetings and take part in things in the same way.

I'm not a great political analyst. I wouldn't be able to write a book on socialism, I only know what I feel to be right, or rather left. It's an emotional response based on instinct. I wasn't that enthusiastic about Gorbachev or *Perestroika*, and when the wall came down I thought that underneath there were going to be some nasty worms waiting to creep out. And indeed, what has happened is that suddenly a country which had ideals – admittedly ones which were questionable – became like the worst of America. Now there are the 'oligarchs', these ludicrous billionaires – it is becoming frightening. McDonalds is there too, a symbol of decadence. So I did not rejoice when the wall came down with such speed.

It took me longer than my brother to realise that even contemplating the existence of God was quite ridiculous. Michael realised it about 60 or 70 years ago; it took me until about 15 years ago. When I realised it, I decided that I was a 'born-again atheist'. Then I decided that I was a 'fundamentalist atheist'. Claire Rayner got to hear about this, and wrote to me: 'I've heard about you and your atheism. I think it's about time you joined us, the Humanists.' She sent me some literature about the British Humanist Association and I joined.

As I've said before, I'm an inveterate joiner. In addition to the Humanists, Weight Watchers and the Peripheral Neuropathy Trust, I've also joined the ME Association, and the list goes on. It is probably part and parcel of living on my own. Mind you, I couldn't bear to have a partner who didn't agree with me politically, that would be horrendous, so perhaps it's a good thing that I don't share my life. I don't know how anybody could possibly put up with me in my present state, having my own ritualistic way of living, and if anybody came along now and tried to change that, I would kick them out right away. It is not something that I regret anymore. There was possibly a time when I did.

Being a Humanist means to me that I have a certain spirituality and a good moral sense, but the spirituality is held in beauty and music rather than God. Music is a great solace to me and listening to music helps me to get things into perspective. The composers I regard as mine, my property, are all Baroque: I feel a personal relationship with Bach, Handel, Vivaldi, Telemann, Albinoni, Corelli and so many others. On Good Friday, I go to St John's in Smith Square to hear Bach's *St John Passion*. I have decreed that one of the pieces of music to be played at my cremation will be the penultimate chorale of the work, 'Ruht wohl', which means 'Rest well' – quite apposite.

Something extraordinary happened the last time I went two years ago. Suddenly, right towards the end, a woman in the front row had a heart attack or some sort of seizure. Staff came along the aisle with a wheelchair and, incredibly, James Gilchrist, who was singing the Evangelist, came down from the rostrum and attended to her. I had noticed in the programme that he had trained as a medical student in Dublin and it was wonderful that he was able to use his medical skills, perhaps even to save her life. They wheeled her out and he went back and continued to sing. If one was a believer…!

Even though it can restore me to peaceful thoughts – and I can say with every bit of sincerity that I want the arts to be accessible to people – my double standards still kick in. Harrods uses an aria from

Handel's *Rinaldo* to advertise their sales and I should be delighted that they use a beautiful piece of music but I admit it, I am an elitist. Great for a socialist!

The other things of beauty I have surrounded myself with are my paintings. Unfortunately I've had to sell a lot because I have had to downsize my dwelling. They are mainly Australian, because I found it easier to find art there: one could spend the time looking round the galleries, and I got to know some Australian painters quite well. I have two paintings by Sir Russell Drysdale, which he painted specifically for me, and two by David Boyd, who comes from an amazing artistic family, and a sculpture by his brother Guy. Clifton Pugh became quite a chum and I bought two of his paintings. He also did an amazing caricature of me, plus three British political leaders: Harold Wilson, Jeremy Thorpe and Edward Heath.

I've never been quite sure why I buy art, but I treasure my paintings, all originals. I suppose my need to be surrounded by beautiful things also brings me serenity. I think they have been in place of children, in a way. I have said that I don't think I wanted children, but I do have relationships with a lot of young people. Posterity is the thing you think about if you don't have a child. Plants are all I have to leave to posterity, and there are plants all over the world that are still growing and some trees as well. I don't just mean my grandfather's trees in Israel: I've given olive trees to people that are, I'm told, still growing. I had a fabulous magnolia plant in my garden in Hamilton Terrace, and I recently bumped into the woman who bought my house and she told me the magnolia tree had blossomed twice that year. I wanted to kill her, because my doctor Patrick Woodcock had given it to me as a moving-in present, when it was a tiny thing in a pot. I wished I hadn't met her again, I was so jealous!

Gardens and plants have always featured in my life and I have a wonderful florist, with whom I have had an account since the early 1960s. Every time friends have birthdays, weddings or various big occasions I send orchids or other plants, sometimes all over the world. When a friend of mine who had moved to Kuala Lumpur had their wedding anniversary, I was able to send them plants. They have since sent me a photograph of the plants to show how huge they have grown.

My disillusionment with Israel has been very gradual over the years – or at any rate my admitting to it has been. The big turning point for me was in 1995, when Yitzhak Rabin was murdered by an Ultra-Orthodox Jew. What happened to Rabin actually was a cathartic experience for me, and a lot of others, and I began to be disillusioned not only with Israel but with Judaism also. I had already become a little disenchanted with Israel prior to Rabin becoming PM, but when he had said what he was going to do with the West Bank – turn the settlers off the land and give it back to the Palestinians – I thought this is great, we're finally going to have an Israel that everyone can believe in.

Because of the change in my attitude to Israel over the years I have kept my head down and not spoken of my feelings publicly. More recently – well, a few years ago – I very stupidly accepted an invitation to speak at a Women's Zionist luncheon, something I used to do regularly. I thought the only honest thing I could do was tell them about my background, and about my grandfather. So during that talk I gave them a whole history of my relationship with Israel. I must have talked for about three quarters of an hour and finished up by saying, because I couldn't stop myself, 'Seeing what has happened in the intervening years and particularly where we are now, I just thank God that my darling Grandpa Herman Aronowitz isn't alive today to see what has happened to his dream smashed to smithereens.'

There was total silence. Then a couple of claps and a few more joined in and then, my God, they gave me a hard time. I stood up for myself but swore I wouldn't do it again.

I think there has been a collective nervous breakdown amongst the Jewish community in this country, though not so much in America.

American Jews still retain an extraordinary loyalty, but here I think the majority of Jews are very angry about the actions of the Israeli government. You only have to look at the list of people who have joined not only the Peace Now Movement but also Jews for Justice for Palestinians. I am a trustee of the Shalom-Salaam Trust, and recently Nick Hytner wrote to us to say that a mobile theatre has been set up in Palestine under their auspices. Another group I belong to is called Neve Shalom Wahat-al Salam ('Oasis of peace'), which supports a village outside Jerusalem where Israeli and Palestinian children go to school and live together. They are all bilingual. If only it could grow and become the norm all over the country...

I wish that our Government was more robust in denouncing some of Israel's actions. Tony Blair refused to call for a halt to the bombardment of Lebanon in 2006, when two Israeli soldiers were kidnapped. It was awful for the kidnapped soldiers, but do we have to have a war about it? As I wrote in a letter in the *Independent*:

> Now with the totally disproportionate Israeli bombardment of Lebanon, there will be countless Lebanese, hitherto unsympathetic to Hizbollah, who will be queuing to join them. What will have been achieved by this terrifying cycle of killing? Simply more and more generations growing up with hatred in their hearts.

I'm very aware of the rockets that Hizbollah fire into Israel and I am truly sad that Israel has had to go through this, but the extent of their retaliation helps not one jot. It's easy to say 'turn the other cheek', but if they had just given back the West Bank and Gaza I don't think that 9/11 would have happened, or that any of the horrors that we're going through today would have developed in such a way. It all seems to stem from the lack of magnanimity after the Six Day War.

The tragedy is that each generation since Israel was created has grown up with more and more hatred. That's happening on both sides now. You do get occasional beacons of wonderment – someone like Daniel Barenboim, an idealist who has brought his idea to reality. He is an another iconic figure for me. I went to a concert at the Royal Albert Hall where the 'East West Divan Orchestra', which he set up, was playing – all these young Israelis, Palestinians and young people from many Arab countries playing music together. He spoke brilliantly and also conducted a piece of Wagner, which of course isn't allowed in Israel. I'm not a Wagner fan but you can't disallow a composer simply because Hitler liked him.

There are wonderful Israeli writers like Amos Oz and David Grossman who are both members of Peace Now. There hasn't been an outpouring of migration because people are still hoping that the right-wing government will be changed. They have a form of proportional representation which makes that very difficult. It is the same system that Italy has, and governments in both parliaments last for a short time because they have to form coalitions with enemies.

The Ultra-Orthodox have a lot of power there, even though they are a minority. When there was a war on, these Orthodox people would not allow emergency vehicles to go through their district on the Sabbath, can you believe that? Extraordinarily, some of the Ultra-Orthodox don't even believe in the State of Israel because they believe that only the arrival of 'The Messiah' would legitimise Israel's existence. A year or so ago some Ultra-Orthodox from Stamford Hill, who have the same beliefs as the Ultra-Orthodox in Israel, were demonstrating against Israel. They are a small minority but nevertheless, it is pretty weird to have those kind of people in the government.

There was a time when I campaigned to get Soviet Jews out of Russia and into Israel in the 1970s. I remember sitting with Janet Suzman outside the Russian Embassy with placards. There was one, Nathan Sharanski, whom we helped get out of Russia – and what is he now? He in the Knesset as part of the Ultra-Orthodox movement. Thank you very much. I worked to get *you* out of Russia? He's a real right-wing shit and would be totally against giving back anything to the Palestinians. They are building more and more and more settlements illegally, and someone has to stop them.

I suppose I am often angry about 'Jewish' issues. I certainly spend a lot of time writing to the newspapers!

Intelligent people who still believe in a god I find very hard to understand, especially converts. I heard a wonderful story about Graham Greene who was a famous convert to Catholicism and was granted audience with the Pope – an old one, one of the Piuses. The Pope was very ancient and frail, but Greene was granted audience. The Papal Secretaries had heard how Greene tended to run on, and said, 'We give him six minutes and that's it.' They explained to Greene that he only had six minutes, because the Pope was rather poorly. Greene understood completely. They ushered him in, closed the doors and sat outside. Six minutes went by; they looked at their watches and said, 'We'll give him another six minutes and then we'll chuck him out.' Another six minutes went by and that was his lot, so they opened the doors and they heard the Pope saying: 'But you see Mr Greene, I *am* a Catholic...'

As for the extremes of religion where the beliefs dominate civil life, I had thought that this was a thing of the past, but it seems that there has been a revival. I'd like all fundamentalists from every religion to be sent off to an island. They are monstrous.

There are degrees of orthodoxy. When I look back, my upbringing was pretty Orthodox – but compared to the Ultra-Orthodox, we wouldn't be recognised as Jews. I think I got the best of Judaism as a child, in that I was brought up with a conscience. The basic tenets and mores of Judaism are the same as in all religions: you learn to lead a decent life and don't go out and harm your neighbour. What happens then is that you discover that there are kids who beat up people and get pleasure out of it and you wonder where their parents were. Were they born without a conscience?

I find that I am constantly asking this question, wondering whether it is nurture rather than nature. I asked Tony Benn this when I went to one of his talks at the Shaw Theatre. First he talked, then people asked questions and he said, 'This is where it becomes interesting, because I really learn stuff from you.'

I waited practically until the end and said, 'Tony, you talked earlier about your conscience and I am pretty obsessional about mine because I don't know, was I born with it or did I get it from my parents?'

He said, 'I don't think I know the answer to that. All I know is that I suffer a great deal of guilt.'

I agreed and said that everything makes me guilty. I suppose if one has got a conscience it goes together with guilt. Catholic friends of mine say they feel exactly the same thing. Jewish women in particular suffer guilt. Is it because one is brought up to be so very good?

I think I've made rather a mess of the relationship thing. I always wanted the unobtainable and once I'd got someone easily, I didn't really want them. Actually there were three chaps that I really loved.

Living at home as late as I did, I couldn't really show my parents what I was feeling, because I couldn't tell them I'd had affairs or been to bed with anybody.

When I was first 'de-virginated' – deflowered – there was no way that I could tell Mother, because of my upbringing. That's why I had to have abortions, however horrendous, because I thought that if my parents had known, it would have killed them. My brother and I talked recently about how we felt about our parents. It is quite ridiculous that we have to reach our eighties before we can talk really openly with one another: my brother is going to be 87, I am now 82 and only now are we discussing intimate subjects. If one or us had gone years ago, we would never have had these conversations. My father was on a pedestal as far as I was concerned, and my mother was on a pedestal for my brother. Michael had a bad time with Dad, which I found hard to comprehend, but he was being forced to stick to so many Jewish rituals which are only applicable to the males. The son gets it worse than the daughter. Michael thought it was a load of bollocks, but he wasn't brave enough to rebel. He would never have kicked up a fuss or made a row. He would have just gone out for a while and walked off his rage.

If I had rebelled, I wouldn't have had two abortions and maybe I'd have great-grandchildren now. One of the reasons that I sometimes remember my mother with anger is remembering a phone conversation with her when I was well past my child-bearing days. She told me that my much younger first cousin Ann Elizabeth had come to see her, and had brought her 'beautiful little baby'. Knowing my mother, I said I didn't know that Ann Elizabeth was married. My mother then quite calmly told me that she wasn't married, but that she had a lovely baby. When I realised the implication of what she had said, I wanted to scream at her and tell her that I went through two horrendous abortions because of her – and here she was, actually saying to me that she didn't care about wedlock. It really hurt and I never quite forgave her.

It has been rather worrying looking back, because I am horrified how much I have forgotten. I have realised mistakes I have made and performances that could have been a lot better. Mind you, I always thought that, however long one runs in a show. I remember when I'd done a whole year in *Fiddler* I thought of all sorts of things that I could have done better – why didn't I do such and such? That's what I'm thinking now, that everything I've done in my life was just not good enough. I should be able to look back on my life with far more pride than I am doing. In a way I am a bit ashamed of that. I don't know exactly where the shame comes from, I just feel I haven't fulfilled all the promise that I had, or indeed the talent with which I was born. I think I have been a good enough friend to people but I don't think I was a good enough daughter. In my teens I was in competition with

Michael, because he was much more diligent than me and that was approved of by my family – hugely approved of. They saw us as two totally different children: one was diligent and the other was funny. As far as they were concerned it was all right to be funny. As far as I am concerned, though, it wasn't all right. I have always regretted not being good enough to even contemplate going to university.

This regret on my part has, of course, taken nothing away from the huge pride I have in my brother's achievements. After winning a scholarship in Classics at Balliol College, Oxford, he took up Middle English, and the study of the English language became his life's work. In 2006, Glasgow University, where Michael was Professor of English Language between 1959 and 1990, gave him an honorary doctorate. The ceremony described him as:

> One of the most distinguished linguists of his generation. His publications are still amongst the most cited in the subject, and his international standing is immense.

So many of my friends have gone; I've practically got a season ticket to St Paul's in Covent Garden and Golders Green Crematorium. I didn't expect to be here this long but because I get on very well with young people I don't feel lonely. I remember John Gielgud saying that he felt all his friends were gone and he was the only one left.

My friends now tend to be in their fifties and sixties, and I've got friends who are in their twenties whom I regard as real chums, students who I've worked with and so on. We go to the theatre together. My ability to get on with younger generations is because I loathe talking about things that are past, which is why I am having difficulty delving deep into the memory glands to try and remember stuff that happened years ago. Actually, I am far more interested in what is happening today and tomorrow. That is my interest – always has been. I decided to come off the Equity Council when I did because I wanted to see younger people involved in their Union. I urge them to get interested, go to meetings and get themselves on the council. The average age of councillors at the moment is about 60. How can you expect young actors to be interested in the union when their council look like a lot of old fogeys? How can older people know the way the young feel, or understand their interests and worries? They often go on about what happened 25 or 30 years ago. When I was on the Council there was a very well-meaning chap, who 30 or 40 years previously had been a BBC floor manager. Whenever we talked about the BBC on Council he would always start saying, 'Well of course one used to...' and I remember having to stop him: 'Just a minute, we are now in a different technology, we can't talk about that.' It used to drive me mad, but I'm afraid it happens a lot with people of my age.

As for the modern world, I am a bit of a Luddite as far as technology goes. I don't have a computer – I think I will go to my ashes without ever owning one. I have a mobile but accessing messages is a difficulty. I get irritated walking down the street, or even being in a cab when the driver has to pull up because some child is crossing the road talking on their mobile. Children will eventually be born with mobiles stuck to their ears. Mobiles do seem to encourage a sense of disengagement.

One exception to my anti-technological tendencies is my fax machine, which I bought as soon as they became affordable. When it arrived, I had no idea what to do with it. Lovely Peter, who then worked for me, said he would set it up for me and had – I thought – reasonable technical knowledge to do so. He worked away for hours, and finally said, 'Right, it's working.'

I said, 'Oh, I'll fax my agent.'

I wrote a note saying 'I hope you get this. This is from my new fax machine. Love Mim.' Peter had to show me where to put the sheet and how to phone the fax number. When I got the fax noise, I said, 'What do I do?' and he pressed the start button.

As we sat there, my sheet of paper came out of the bottom of the machine. We looked at each other aghast and said, 'Oh God, it's come back!'

I phoned my agent and said, 'I sent you a fax, but it came back.'

My agent, falling about laughing, asked me, 'Where do you think it had gone?'

I hadn't the faintest clue – it was a total mystery. Since then, of course, I have used the fax machine constantly and grown to love it. However, what with e-mail, the poor thing is now practically obsolete, and there are very few people to whom I can still send a fax. Another reason to hate technology!

I get angry about junk mail. With everyone knowing that I campaign for things, I am inundated with appeals. The trouble is I am a sucker, and once I open something that is obviously an appeal I feel totally duty bound to give money. I know that some people are very sensible and have about four or five charities to which they donate regularly, but I find children's charities very difficult to ignore. There are specific charities with which I am involved myself, the International Committee for Artists' Freedom, the International Performers' Aid Trust, One World Action, Amnesty International, Liberty and CND. I agree with the Socialist argument that if everyone stopped supporting charities the government would have to do something; I get angry when I know so much is being spent on administration yet again, and I am getting sick to death of being sent pens and sticky labels as some sort of bribe. I don't know the answer. When you get something like the tsunami, a flood, an earthquake, you just have to delve into your pocket.

When I was at RADA we still had something that is frowned upon now: the gold medal and silver medal. The gold medallist of my lot was Patricia Lawrence. I didn't see her for a good few years after we left RADA and then we bumped into one another by the lift in

Harrods and we fell round each other's necks. I said, 'Darling, how wonderful to see you. I heard you married someone called "Prick."'

'No darling, Poke.'

Indeed, she had married a lovely man, Greville Poke, who was on a lot of theatre boards including the Royal Court. He was wealthy and incredibly philanthropic and they were the most generous couple I've ever known, and each time I was involved in campaigns and needed money for this or that, there would always be a very generous cheque within days. I remember phoning Patricia and saying, 'Thank you, you're wonderful, I won't bother you again.' And she said, 'Darling, if we've got it, we believe in spreading it about, why not.' If only more people thought like that.

My recent experience in South Africa on *Flashbacks of a Fool* changed my whole perspective, at least for a while. I was actually conscious of the fact that I was feeling happy, as I did when I was a child, incredibly happy. I didn't think it was possible to know that one was happy in the moment, as I was all the time that I was in Cape Town. I came back a very happy person because it felt as if I had been given a wonderful present – a sort of bonus on my life, which could so easily have ended the previous year. It is probably my swan-song, but what an amazing swan-song to have.

The irony is that over the years I was asked many times to act in South Africa and I would say, 'I will not come while you have Apartheid.' I had thought, when I sat, crying at home, and watched Mandela coming out of jail, hoping that no one was going to take a pot-shot at him: 'Isn't it sad I shall never be able to go to South Africa?' And now I've been!

Cape Town is the most wonderful city, so beautiful, and I stayed in the best hotel, the Mount Nelson. I could see Robben Island from Table Mountain. My driver organised a wheelchair, so we went up in the cable car and he wheeled me around the entire mountain. I saw every single view, and it happened to be the most beautiful day. On top of Table Mountain was the nearest one could get to being in a spiritual space.

The director/writer of the film, Baillie Walsh, and all the cast and crew, were very special people. The production built three houses on the beach, including 'my' house, and the house which Daniel Craig's character lived in when he was a little boy. At the wrap party, I said to one of the producers that I supposed the houses would be demolished, and she said, 'No, we got them rebuilt properly and moved them to a place so that people who are homeless could live in them.'

A production company with compassion. Everything about it was extraordinary. (They gave me a lovely 82nd birthday party, too!)

I don't think I'll last much longer. I have to say that the contemplation of my own death only frightens me if I think it's going to be painful and if I can't control how I go. The idea of not being here only frightens me in terms of my vanity: I hope that I die looking good with my teeth in and that people won't say awful things about me. I hope that the obituaries will be nice. Perhaps what I am writing now is my own; that's what it feels like, some sort of a life story.

I don't want another 20 years in pain, and it's not a lot of fun getting up to pee four times a night sitting on the loo, banging my stomach, and it's probably going to get worse. I can't contemplate very much more of it. I want to say that's enough, thank you, been there, done that, got all the T-shirts, let's now finish it in a dignified fashion. I don't want to die throwing up everywhere; I would just like to die nice and quietly. If only I hadn't given that damn 'Do It Yourself' book to somebody who never gave it back...

I'm a telephone-aholic, a landline-aholic. I love conversations and talking on the phone, but it's probably because I have always lived alone. I'd miss gossip, not being here. I'd miss going to wonderful concerts listening to beautiful music. I don't believe any longer in heaven; I don't think I am going to hear beautiful harps in a mystic place. I think this is all there is. I'd miss music and my friends. I've got some wonderful, wonderful friends that I've had for a very long time, and of course I'd miss my brother, my sister-in-law and my niece Vivien. I can't really say 'I'd miss' because I'd be dead, so I wouldn't know how to; but if one could, those are the things I'd miss.

If I could have only one wish for the world it would be that a new Mandela, a young Mandela, would suddenly appear somewhere and he or she would change the world and make the world realise what a bleeding fuck-up they've made.

I mean here I am, with a belief in euthanasia, and yet I despise the world for quite intentionally committing suicide – because that seems to me what it's trying to do. If I had great-grandchildren, I would fear for their future.

SOME SPEECHES AND LETTERS

Note: the pages in the text which refer to these speeches are given in square brackets at the end of each speech.

Oxford Union Debate – 'Vive la différence'

(1968)

Madam President,

When you first did me the honour of inviting me to speak at this meeting, you asked me to oppose the motion. I had to decline – for one very good reason. Four years ago (when you, Madam President, were but a schoolgirl and I myself barely out of my gym tunic) – four years ago I stood on this very floor and spoke in favour of the motion 'The Female of the Species is Deadlier than the Male'. Needless to say, that motion was carried, as I confidently predict this one will be tonight.

When I spoke then I spoke my convictions. Not possessing the unlimited capacity of members of Her Majesty's Government to change their convictions as it suits them, I asked you to allow me to speak in favour. You were kind enough to appreciate my position, and that is why I am here tonight.

My object on this occasion, Madam President, is not to add fuel to the ever-raging battle of the sexes. This ground is being well and truly covered by many more militantly-minded ladies, better equipped and far more willing to do this than myself – particularly in this, the fiftieth anniversary year of our emancipation. No, I am here to convince you that 'La Différence', like sex, is here to stay. [...]

That there are fundamental differences between man and woman of a biological kind, no one can deny. Whether they make woman superior or inferior to man is a moot point, and requires no graphic elaboration on my part. But they certainly make woman unequal. So much for our bodies; now for our minds. I maintain, Madam President, that mentally woman is superior – I exclude myself, Madam President (I am an exception). However, she *is* mentally superior, and for this, man has only himself to blame. For centuries, men kept women in legal and economic subjugation, and during the whole of this period, what was woman doing? She was quietly and unostentatiously developing another of nature's gifts – her intuition – to perfection, so that when at last she was able to beat down some of the barriers of law and economics, she had an additional weapon in her armoury. So much so, that as Kipling wrote 'A woman's guess is much more accurate than a man's certainty'. Mark you, I am not necessarily advocating the attitude of the woman who said to her husband, 'My mind's made up – don't confuse me with the facts.'

Woman is able to use her reason quite as well as man. Long ago, the wise Socrates foresaw this when he said, 'Once made equal to man, woman becomes superior.' Centuries later, Dr Johnson, who obviously feared this superiority, wrote, 'Nature has given women so much power that the law has very wisely given them little.' So – woman is now able to beat man at his own game, thanks to her intuition. Once she has made up her mind, she has more confidence and determination to act than man. It is man, not woman, who waffles. I was told that when the long economic discussions were going on recently, Harold Wilson was asked by a friend to tell him in confidence whether the cabinet was united on the next step. He said: 'Half the Cabinet and I are for devaluation, and half the Cabinet and I are against it.' (My apologies to John Bird.)

And the Opposition to this motion – what can they say? 'Mort à la différence' or 'La différence au diable'? Do they envisage a completely sexless world? A world inhabited by eunuchs, amoebas and transvestites? (Admittedly an easy solution to the population problem.) Or do they foresee some unsatisfactory compound of man and woman after the fashion, say, of a centaur or a mermaid, half woman and half fish, of whom a sailor once complained: 'Not enough woman to make it interesting, and not enough fish to make a meal'. Have they a pipe-dream of a world in which one turns on one's radio to hear an announcement like this: 'And here we are, ladies and gentlemen, at the Albert Hall, to watch this fifteen-round contest for the world heavyweight championship, and the contestants are just coming into the ring now...here is Muhammad Ali, better known as Cassius Clay, holder of the title...and from the other corner, the challenger...Linda Cartwright...both weighed in at...'

Perhaps they visualise our being able to change our bodies and our sex according to our whims. For instance today, as I start to put on my false eyelashes, and step into my mini-skirt, I decide to shave instead and get into my Cecil Gee gear. Are they asking Mother Nature herself to place her seal on the modern tendency to eradicate all visible differences between the sexes? The other day I was sitting in a crowded tube and couldn't help noticing a very strange girl in a wild flowered suit, beads, bells, hair everywhere. I turned to the person sitting next to me and said, 'Gawd – just look at that. Now she really has gone too far, don't you think?'

The person turned to me and said, 'Do you mind, that's my son.' 'Oh,' I said, 'terribly sorry, I didn't realise you were his father.' 'Would you mind – I'm his mother.'

After all, Madam President, what does this motion say – 'Vive la différence'? All that it says is there is a difference between the sexes, and long live that difference. That, I suggest, is a simple and self-evident truth – a plain statement of facts. May I submit, with all respect to the opposition, that they are guilty (or certainly will be) of a fundamental confusion of thought. They identify equality as such with equality of opportunity. I am all for the latter, the former – equality as such, I maintain that that was, is, and always will be an impossibility.

Let me conclude with a couplet I found in a long lost manuscript, which I think can only be attributed to that great Scottish poet William McGonagall:

'Know ye therefore, ma' male & female friends,
In this world of ours, each one lives on sufferance;
But wha'e'er the future may hold in store,
For the Lord's sake, *Vive la différence!*' [148]

Speech given to Equity Meeting

(1976)

Mr Chairman – fellow members – I am speaking on behalf of the minority group on the Council – Firstly, let me say that I find it amazing that the Council actually has the gall to put this motion at all.

Because of the unavoidably complicated nature of Rules and their wording, the manner in which they were posed made them in the main totally incomprehensible, even to the most trained of our Union-minded members. You yourself, Mr President, well versed in these matters, on first being presented with the proposed rule-changes said: 'I don't understand a word of this – Marius, please explain.' Fascinating that the one question which *was* understandable, the one on subscription, was the only one which was lost to the Council.

The Rule Book, my friends, is *SACROSANCT*. Everything else in the Union changes – is ephemeral – the Council – the organisers – politics – the membership – we all die and new blood comes in, but the Rule Book *must remain constant*.

On these grounds alone this motion must be defeated – But, Mr Chairman, despite legal advice taken by the previous Council, this 'Act for Equity' Council went ahead, wasted thousands of pounds on futile legal action; then, without waiting for the result of the appeal, went ahead with their referenda (again at incredible cost), now proven to be completely invalid *as referenda*.

One would have imagined that after such a history of irresponsible behaviour this Act for Equity majority on the Council would, in all conscience, have resigned. When asked to do so by Graham Hamilton at the Council meeting last Tuesday, Marius Goring said, 'You are highly impertinent.'

Since they have failed to resign, some of my colleagues on the Council who have opposed this ludicrous, ill-advised action from its inception, regretfully feel that we can no longer serve on this Council, and we hope that by our action we will bring home to you the depth of our feeling, the importance we attach to this issue, and we hope to set an example that other Councillors will follow. Therefore, we, the following nine Councillors, formally resign as from now:

Roger Begley   Donald Groves
Graham Hamilton   Paul Janssen
Miriam Karlin   Louis Mahoney
Vivian Matalon   Kathleen Michael
Anton Rogers

BUT WE'LL BE BACK! [160]

Speech on behalf of the Anti Nazi League

(1978)

So it isn't very hard to explain why I'm in the Anti Nazi League. At first I really believed, as a lot of people do, there was a possibility right at the outset, provided they were given no publicity, that the National Front would just go away. But that's like living in Cloud-cuckoo-land.

There's this phrase I keep hearing everywhere – 'It's good to bring it out into the open.' I don't believe that for one minute. I think probably the majority of people have prejudices of all kinds deep down. The only people who don't are babies and children, because you're not born with prejudice, it's given to you later.

The way I look at it, it's like a dustbin where you know there are maggots. It's better to keep the lid firmly down. It's better that people know it's not acceptable for them to make racialist remarks, that they won't be tolerated.

'Bringing it all out into the open,' really means making racism respectable.

Enoch Powell started the process off in 1968 when he made his speech about the rivers of blood. Here is this politician of tremendous status with a brilliant classically-trained mind, saying it's okay, it's fine to be a racist.

And the media have fed the fire: always looking for confrontations; inviting these Nazis to come and debate with churchmen and liberals, so they look like decent people. I myself, and my colleagues in the Anti Nazi League, will not sit down to debate with a Nazi. They asked me to go onto Thames Television to debate with [Martin] Webster. I will not do it. Why should the media give these Nazis so much space and time to spread their poison?

The television companies like confrontation, it makes good television. The danger is it comes right into people's homes. [171]

The Arts Council: A Case for Abolition

(1996)

ARMS LENGTH

The arms length principle has historically been regarded by Equity as a good thing. It was believed to be a safeguard in the event of a government seen to be unfriendly towards the arts. I now question this policy in today's climate. Why? Because it is draining away the funds (funds hard fought for by the Culture Secretary), which should have been channelled into creativity instead of lining the pockets of the bureaucrats in Great Peter Street.

Last year an additional £30 million was given to the arts, so why are we clamouring for more? It should have been enough – why was it not?

In 1997/98 the total bill for staff salaries, agency staff, professional fees and external assessment across the arts funding system was nearly £28.5 million. The promise of saving '£2 million per year for frontline arts activity' hardly seems radical or generous. Also £7 million was held back this year, £9 million is to be held back next year and £11 million for the following year. What for? 'Innovative ideas'.

And who are going to decide which are the innovative ideas? Not the creative artists or directors. Oh no! It will be, once again, the suits.

TODAY'S PICTURE

Last year the arts actually received £218,781,000. Out of this, £56 million went to the National Companies.

Despite the increase in subsidy mentioned above, so many of our regional theatres continue to be in a state of terminal decline. There are schemes galore which on the surface look as if they could alleviate the situation, but to enter such a scheme can cost a theatre an incalculable amount of time, money and energy, not necessarily resulting in a favourable response.

The so-called restructuring of the Arts Council may have resulted in some staff cuts. However, there has been a vast increase in salary of some of the remaining staff. The great devolution to the regions has simply involved more staff being recruited regionally. [190]

IPAT *Mission Statement*

(1999)

The International Performers' Aid Trust has been established by leading members of the acting profession in Britain in order to provide support and relief of poverty to colleagues who are in emergency situations overseas. Its decisions are made on professional and humanitarian principles, without political bias. Wherever performers' or stage-workers' freedom to exercise their art is at risk – whether the threat is from natural disaster or from persecution or repression, prison or torture – the Trust will endeavour to supply such aid and encouragement as is appropriate, both for the preservation of life and health and the nurturing of the imaginative faculty which is at the heart of drama. [147]

Appeal on behalf of ICAF *and* ARC

(2002)

I am proud to have been a member of the International Committee for Artists' Freedom since its inception in 1978. Its purpose to campaign against the persecution of performers worldwide – wherever they face oppression, are caught up in wars, suffer censorship, imprisonment, torture or even death. Those who face imprisonment for speaking their minds, or struggle to entertain children in a city totally wrecked and destroyed by war, as in Sarajevo. We also provide aid in emergency situations – the earthquake in Colombia, the floods in Bangladesh.

For over 20 years the Committee achieved this by donating money, lobbying MPs, sending delegations to embassies, writing letters to foreign governments, and by asking Equity members to sign petitions or send postcards on behalf of those imprisoned or tortured. Each case is assessed individually, impartially and *apolitically*. None of our work could be accomplished without the constant support of Equity members, the Variety and General Branches and the Committees. You have consistently raised funds for the Committee's work, and we thank you. Recently ICAF has been able to celebrate two successes and it is these I want to share with you.

First – for years we campaigned for the release of two Burmese comedians, U Pa Pa Lay and U Lu Zaw, known as 'The Moustache Brothers'. In Burma they are as famous as Morecambe and Wise. They were arrested in 1996 for performances satirising the government co-operatives as thieves and singing comic songs poking fun at the Generals. With no legal representation they were tried and sentenced to seven years on a charge of 'spreading false news'. They were sent to a labour camp, starved and forced to work with iron bars across their legs. As well as our own campaigning, ICAF collaborated with Amnesty International on their 2001 comedy event entitled 'We Know Where You Live', compèred by Eddie Izzard who had chosen the two comedians as a mascot for the evening. At the same time, Equity circulated 40,000 postcards calling on the Burmese authorities to release them. Soon after, we were delighted to hear that the comedians had been released two years before their sentence expired. This was hugely encouraging to ICAF, but although they are free, they are not allowed to perform in public. However, they are making and selling puppets. ICAF, Amnesty and the Burma Action Group continue to explore ways of helping them to survive their freedom.

Success number two was the release of Ngawang Cheophel, a Tibetan musicologist, sentenced in 1996 by the Chinese authorities to 18 years imprisonment on 'spying' charges. When Ngawang was two years old his mother, Sonam Dekyi, carried him across the mountain passes into India to escape from the terrible Chinese oppression of Tibet. He grew up in a Tibetan refugee camp in Southern India and from a very early age showed great musical talent, and later won a prestigious Fulbright Scholarship to a college in Vermont, USA. On completion of his studies he returned to India, determined to go into Tibet to film the last remnants of Tibetan culture, song and dance, and got permission from the Chinese to do so in the summer of 1995. Shortly after arriving he disappeared. His mother reported him missing, and news emerged that he had been detained two months after entering Tibet. Chinese guards surrounded him as he was filming in the market place. He was held in a detention centre without charge, without trial, for 14 months. Then it was announced officially on Chinese radio that he had been sentenced to 18 years for espionage and 'counter-revolutionary activities'. No evidence was ever found to substantiate this accusation. He was sent to a terrible prison in a remote corner of Tibet. Reports filtered through that he had been tortured. His mother, now suffering from TB, began a desperate campaign to be allowed to visit her son. The Free Tibet Campaign organised her visit to London to talk about her case, during which ICAF held a reception for her at Guild House. It was a memorable occasion. The extraordinary dignity of that frail, courageous woman we all found to be incredibly moving. After five years of continuous campaigning, she was finally allowed to visit. She was allowed two one-hour visits under close surveillance by at least five officials. When Ngawang entered the room Sonam Dekyi did not recognise her son – 'he was skin and bone'. They stood separated by two layers of wire netting, not allowed to touch, and were told their meeting would be curtailed if they did not stop crying. His health was declining rapidly. ICAF members, along with Amnesty and the Free Tibet Campaign, redoubled their protests and postcard campaign on Ngawang's behalf. In January of this year [2002], prior to George Bush's visit to Beijing, surprise, surprise, Ngawang was released on medical parole and flown to America. The extraordinary number of letters and postcards received by the Chinese authorities, more than for any other prisoner of conscience, was certainly a major factor in the decision to release him. [...]

Currently ICAF is helping actors in Kenya; Chechen artists living in Grozny, and those in exile in Georgia. We are giving a grant to Al Kasabah Theatre in the West Bank town of Ramallah, in dire straits as a result of the Middle East conflict. In Argentina – where there is terrible economic turmoil following the collapse of their currency – we have sent help to the Argentine Actors' House of Theatre in Buenos Aires. This house provides residence and care for 45 elderly professional actors. It faces closure, with dreadful consequences for the frail old actors who live there – it's the Argentinian Denville Hall, if you like.

One cannot speak of the ICAF without acknowledging and giving huge thanks to the very special Diane Fisk who works tirelessly with total commitment on our behalf. Also huge thanks to Michael Branwell who gives so much of himself, his time and his energy to our cause. I must also give huge thanks to Corin Redgrave for giving the most amazing performance of Oscar Wilde's *De Profundis* on behalf of ICAF. We are very grateful. So please – just before tearing out to lunch – decide to forgo one round of drinks, and put its equivalent in one of our buckets strategically placed by the doors. Thank you. [147]

Some Letters

THE COST OF POST

(1997)

Remember Consignia [the renaming of Royal Mail]? How much did that little exercise cost? Then, of course, there was the sudden realisation that perhaps it was not such a brilliant idea after all, and it would be terrific to revert back to Royal Mail. How much did that cost? If the cost of those two abortive exercises had been distributed among the postal workers, we would now all be opening our mail.

KILLING OFF THE TECHNOLOGICALLY ILLITERATE?

(2003)

In 1939 as a 14-year-old school kid I had a gas mask – we all had gas masks – and I knew exactly how to deport myself in an emergency such as an air raid. Now in 2003, as a 77-year-old, I gather from the Home Office that were we to be attacked by any chemical or biological, we would have to 'log on' to some website in order to find out how to cope. Am I being paranoid, or is there a government conspiracy to get rid of all of us senile technological illiterates? We are, admittedly, a drain on the economy with our state pensions and increased use of the NHS, whereas the young will know how to keep themselves alive and won't expect a pension.

NO HOLOCAUST DAY

(2005)

Sir: As one whose mother lost many of her close relatives in the gas chambers, I suppose I am meant to feel gratitude that 27 January is deemed Holocaust Day. Not a bit of it, I feel sickened.

If this government insists on pushing through that most unjust Asylum Bill, surely this will cancel out any possible *raison d'être* for a Holocaust Day and it will be seen to be a banal and hypocritical exercise.

So we will have 'No smoking Day', 'No Car Day 'and 'Holocaust Day'. The most horrendous chapter of our history will be reduced to 'a tale full of sound and fury, signifying nothing'.

THE BBC'S FAKERY

(July 2007)

While I agree with Mark Ravenhill ('When the BBC was caught faking, it was only following in New Labour's footsteps') he does not address the root cause. Remember Thatcher? She it was who was adamant that a third of BBC programmes must be made by independent producers. Prior to that the BBC (and ITV) had proper training programmes which meant all producers and directors understood that truth and morals were essential in broadcasting.

Index

242